SPEECH COMMUNICATION

MADE SIMPLE

Third Edition

Paulette Dale, Ph.D. • **James C. Wolf, M.A.**

Miami-Dade College

PEARSON
Longman

Speech Communication Made Simple
Third Edition

Copyright © 2006, 2000, 1998 by Pearson Education, Inc.
All rights reserved.
No part of this publication may be reproduced,
stored in a retrieval system, or transmitted
in any form or by any means, electronic, mechanical,
photocopying, recording, or otherwise,
without the prior permission of the publisher.

Pearson Education, 10 Bank Street, White Plains, NY 10606

Staff credits: The people who made up the *Speech Communication Made Simple* team—
representing editorial, production, design, marketing, and manufacturing services—are
Rhea Banker, Karen Davy, Dave Dickey, Mike Kemper, Laura LeDréan, Amy McCormick,
Shana McGuire, and Pat Wosczyk.
Text Composition: Laserwords Private Limited
Illustrations: Roger Penwill, Don Martinetti, Laserwords Private Limited
Text font: 10/13 New Aster
Photo credits: Page 19, © Joel W. Rogers/Corbis; p. 25, © Archivo Iconografico,
S.A./Corbis; p. 30, left, © Larry Williams/Corbis; p. 30, middle; © Steve Prezant/ Corbis;
p. 30, right, © Iconica/Getty Images; p. 67, © David Spindel/ SuperStock; p. 72, © Itsuo
Inouye/APWide World Photos; p. 92, © BananaStock/ SuperStock; p. 93, top, © Stockbyte
Platinum/ Getty Images; p. 93, middle; © Royalty-Free/ Corbis; p. 93, © Royalty-Free/
Corbis; p. 97, left, © Gianni Dagli Orti/ Corbis; p. 97, right, © Beth A. Keiser/ Corbis; p. 130,
© Ariel Skelley/ Corbis; p. 138, © Eleanor Bentall/ Corbis; p. 197, © Photonica/ Getty
Images; pp. 242–243, © James C. Wolf.

Library of Congress Cataloging-in-Publication Data

Dale, Paulette.
  Speech communication made simple / Paulette Dale, James C.
Wolf.-- 3rd ed.
  p. cm.
  Rev. ed. of : Speech Communication Made Simple.
White Plains, NY : Addison Wesley Longman, c2000.
  Includes bibliographical references and index.
  ISBN 0-13-195544-6 (alk. paper)
  1. Public speaking--Problems, exercises, etc. 2. Oral
communication--Problems, exercises, etc. 3. English
language--Textbooks for foreign speakers. I. Wolf,
James C., 1946- II. Dale, Paulette. Speech
Communication Made Simple. III. Title.

  PN4129.15.D33 2006
  808.5'1--dc22

2005037055

Printed in the United States of America
17 18 19 20-V092-15 14

CONTENTS

For more than sixty collective years, the authors have been teaching speech communication classes composed of students from a wide variety of cultures. Many of their students are international students who have learned English as a second language. Most of the available texts that deal with speech communication and public speaking are written for American students and, thus, do not meet the particular speech communication needs of students with such eclectic backgrounds. Their teachers are not interested in discussing complicated communication theory and fancy terminology, such as "communication dyads," "message channels," or "transmitters." They want practical material that is relevant to the backgrounds and experiences of their students—information that their students can apply in their everyday lives.

Speech Communication Made Simple is designed to meet the needs of speech communication students and their teachers around the world. It helps students to:

- develop confidence when speaking before a group

- improve their use of eye contact, posture, gestures, and voice

- orally present information, ideas, and opinions in a coherent and organized fashion

- learn the basics of informative and persuasive speaking

- listen critically and objectively

- lead and participate in group discussions

- improve their understanding of interpersonal and intercultural communication

- learn the basics of Internet research including evaluating websites and citing sources

- learn to use audio and visual aids to enhance presentations and keep listeners interested

A glance at the table of contents reveals specific chapter titles and their contents.

Chapter 1: Developing Self-Confidence is designed to help students overcome their fears and succeed at public speaking.

Chapter 2: Delivering Your Message is full of activities to help students improve their use of eye contact, posture, gestures, and voice so that they speak more effectively.

Chapter 3: Putting Your Speech Together teaches students how to organize and outline their information for their speeches.

Chapter 4: Speaking to Inform gives step-by-step procedures for preparing a speech that presents new information in a comprehensible and memorable way.

Chapter 5: Using Dynamic Visual Aids gives general guidelines for the effective use of audio and visual aids including PowerPoint to enhance presentations.

Chapter 6: Using the Internet teaches students how to conduct Internet research, evaluate website quality, and cite Internet sources in a presentation.

Chapter 7: Speaking to Persuade gives step-by-step procedures for preparing a speech that persuades others to change their beliefs, opinions, or behaviors.

Chapter 8: Listening includes both suggestions and exercises to improve listening skills.

Chapter 9: Participating in Group Discussions teaches students how to lead as well as how to participate in a problem-solving group discussion.

Chapter 10: Understanding Interpersonal Communication helps students avoid misunderstandings while enabling them to interact more effectively.

Chapter 11: Understanding Intercultural Communication helps students understand and appreciate the diverse beliefs and customs of people from different backgrounds in order to communicate across cultures more effectively.

Chapter 12: Thinking on Your Feet teaches students to organize their ideas quickly in order to give meaningful impromptu speeches.

Chapter 13: Using Idioms and Proverbs helps students improve their ability to both understand and use idiomatic expressions and proverbs.

Chapter 14: Speaking for Special Purposes contains a variety of fun and educational speech communication activities that challenge students to draw on the skills learned in previous chapters.

Teachers know that a learning-by-doing approach is the best way to learn any skill. For this reason, in addition to guiding students through the principles of speech communication, *Speech Communication Made Simple* provides a variety of exercises, activities, and assignments. Traditional exercises (such as multiple-choice exercises), innovative activities (such as communicative discussions), and extensive assignments (such as actual presentations) help students improve their communication skills in different contexts. Evaluation forms in Appendix I suggest evaluation criteria for each presentation. In addition, tips at the end of each chapter help students improve their pronunciation and intonation.

Appendix II follows the book chapter-by-chapter and provides end-of-chapter quizzes, transcripts for the listening exercises, and answer keys for the various activities and exercises throughout the book.

The authors' experience with thousands of students from around the world has shown that the key to lifelong feelings of confidence lies in the ability to communicate well. Developing clear and direct communication skills can lead to positive results when dealing with others, success at school and in business, and an enjoyable, rewarding life. *Speech Communication Made Simple* will enable students to become confident, effective communicators.

ACKNOWLEDGMENTS

The authors wish to express their sincerest gratitude and indebtedness to the many people who assisted in developing this book:

Professor Kathleen Watson of Florida International University for writing the extremely insightful chapter on understanding intercultural communication

Professor Ellen Karsh of Florida International University for her constructive suggestions

Professor Marie Knepper of Miami-Dade College and our other colleagues who recommended valuable improvements

Our editors Karen Davy, Amy McCormick, Laura LeDréan, and Mike Kemper who were extremely helpful, understanding, and patient, and helped transform the manuscript into this wonderful third edition

The anonymous reviewers who read the material and provided valuable feedback and suggestions for improvements

Our students, for encouraging us and for giving us many practical suggestions to help us better meet their needs

Our families and friends for their support and encouragement throughout the project

Whether you are from Miami or New York, New Delhi or Tokyo, Taiwan or Mexico City, you will find the study of speech communication to be one of the most exciting, challenging, and positive learning experiences you may ever have.

The study of speech communication, or rhetoric as it was called by the ancient Greeks, will engage you in one of the oldest academic subjects known. By studying speech communication, you are participating in an area that has been considered essential to the functioning of a democratic state and to the growth of the individual within society for over two thousand years. The study of speech communication will help you improve your knowledge, self-confidence, understanding of human nature, listening skills, critical-thinking skills, organization of thoughts, use of posture and voice, and ability to give and accept constructive criticism.

Throughout your life, you will give many types of speeches. You will need to be able to organize your thoughts logically in order to persuade others to your way of thinking. Success in many careers, such as those in administration, government, public relations, personnel, politics, education, sales, and private industry, depends on good speech communication skills. As you can see, the study of speech communication will be applicable throughout your lifetime.

The more effort you put into the study of speech communication, the more you will benefit. Though you may be nervous about the idea of standing before an audience and making a speech, your fears will fade as you progress through this book. By the time you have finished, you will be proud of the progress you have made.

You will have many chances to speak. Some of your speaking assignments will not be graded. These assignments will give you confidence and help you to improve future speeches. Your teacher will help you learn how to select topics, make them interesting to your audience, get over problem spots, and improve your speech communication skills.

Daniel Webster, a famous American orator, once said,

If all my talents and powers were to be taken from me by some inscrutable Providence, and I had my choice of keeping but one, I would unhesitatingly ask to be allowed to keep the Power of Speaking, for through it, I would quickly recover all the rest.

Let's begin!

CHAPTER 1

Developing Self-Confidence

It is the beginning of the semester, and this speech class has just begun. It is natural to be nervous about speaking in front of people you've never met before. Relax—your classmates will soon become new friends and will no longer seem like strangers.

This chapter is full of helpful suggestions for presentations. Believe it or not, you are already prepared to deliver many excellent speeches. Talking about yourself, your experiences, your opinions, and your concerns or fears is one of the best ways to do this.

PRESENTATION ANXIETY

Does the thought of making a presentation in front of a group of people make you nervous? Does it make your heart race? Do you feel nauseated or sick to your stomach? Do your muscles tense? Do you begin to sweat? Do you want to run away and hide?

If you answered "yes" to any or all of these questions, you are in the majority. Researchers consistently report that most people fear public speaking even more than death or flying!

Feeling nervous at the thought of public speaking is perfectly normal. You respond the same way you would to any stressful situation. Your body produces extra adrenaline. This is what makes your heart pound faster and your hands shake. This extra adrenaline also makes your knees feel weak and tenses your muscles.

The good news is that you can learn to control your nervousness and make it work in your favor.

HOW TO CONTROL PRESENTATION ANXIETY

Talk Yourself Out of Negative Thoughts

The first step toward controlling your nervousness is to identify its causes. After you've analyzed your fears, you can do something about them.

Step 1: Identify Your Fears

1. Think of five reasons you have presentation anxiety. Use some of the following reasons if they apply, or come up with five of your own personal fears. (Your teacher will decide whether to ask you to do this in class or to assign it as homework.)

   - I'll forget what I want to say.
   - I'm afraid no one will be interested in my topic.
   - The audience is too large.
   - I don't know anyone in the audience.
   - I don't speak well in public.
   - Everyone will see how nervous I am.
   - I might not be prepared enough.
   - Listeners won't understand me.
   - My English isn't very good.
   - The audience won't like me; they will reject me.

2. Rank the reasons from 1 to 5, 1 being the reason that causes you the most anxiety. Write them in the following chart.

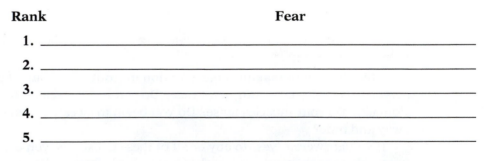

Rank	Fear
1.	_____
2.	_____
3.	_____
4.	_____
5.	_____

Step 2: Replace Your Fears with Positive Thoughts

Substitute at least two positive beliefs for each fear you identified. Use the form on the next page to record your positive thoughts.

Example

Fear	**Positive Beliefs**
The audience is too large.	The size of the group doesn't matter. People are listening one at a time.
Everyone will see how nervous I am.	Nervousness is normal. Everyone feels the same way. Besides, I know I don't look as nervous as I feel.

1. _____   _____

2. _____   _____

3. _____   _____

4. _____   _____

5. _____   _____

Step 3: Share Your Strategies

In small groups, discuss your fears.

1. Share the positive thoughts you substituted for each negative one with your group members.
2. Then, meeting as a class, compare strategies. Check your strategies with the suggestions on page 264 in Appendix II.

Take Advantage of Small Occasions to Speak Up

In addition to identifying your fears, you can use several other strategies to reduce presentation anxiety. For instance, you can "speak up" in fun or nonthreatening situations. Try one or more of the following:

- Make yourself give the toast at a birthday party.
- Give the order in a restaurant.
- Ask a question when you are an audience member during another person's speech.

Plan and Prepare

Preparation is one of the best antidotes for presentation anxiety. With proper preparation, you will feel confident that you know your subject matter and have just the right amount of information for the allotted time.

Use Audio and Visual Aids

Audio and visual aids create a lot of interest. They will make you feel less self-conscious as the audience will focus some of their attention on your visuals.

Practice!

Rehearse your speech in front of family or friends. Ask them for feedback. This will help you to feel more comfortable when you face your "real" audience.

Breathe Deeply and Slowly

Breathing exercises are one of society's oldest techniques for relieving stress. When we exhale, we release carbon dioxide. This increases the oxygen in our brains, which helps us to relax. So, take a deep breath. Hold it. Let it out slowly. Do it over and over until you feel calmer. For additional work on breathing, see Learn to Breathe Deeply and Slowly on page 264 in Appendix II.

Remember: Nervousness is normal. Talk yourself out of negative thoughts. Your listeners want you to succeed! When you are the listener, be sure to help the speaker to feel more comfortable.

Suggestions for Listeners

Give the Speaker Positive Reinforcement

Show speakers you are interested in them and in what they are saying. Give them encouragement. Look at the speakers, smile reassuringly, and nod your head from time to time while they are talking. This will help give them confidence and put them at ease.

Ask Questions After the Speech

If a speaker invites questions from the audience after the speech, participate! Asking questions of presenters after a speech compliments them. It shows speakers that you are interested in their topics and would like to know more. It is very discouraging when a presenter asks, "Does anyone have any questions?" and no one responds.

SPEECH 1: SELF-INTRODUCTION

You will overcome your speech fears more quickly if you have an opportunity to speak about a very familiar topic—yourself. For this reason, all the speeches in this chapter focus on you as an individual. Depending on your background and culture, you might be a bit reluctant to express your opinions and to describe personal experiences or your feelings to the class. However, sharing your experiences and feelings is highly appropriate in the United States and will help make your speech interesting and relevant to your listeners. It is also a wonderful way to get to know your classmates.

Your first assignment is to give a speech about yourself. Because the goal is to be very natural and spontaneous as you speak, instead of writing your speech beforehand, you will choose one of the following three methods to prepare and present your speech:

- Picture Story
- The Old Bag Speech[1]
- Speech Preparation Worksheet

METHOD A: PICTURE STORY

Try to think of your speech as if it were a photo album. As your eyes move from picture to picture, recall different events in your life. Pictures make it possible for you to talk comfortably and naturally in front of a group of people. By using simple pictures as your speaking "notes," you will be able to remember what you want to say. You will be able to talk through your speech with your audience in a relaxed manner, needing only an occasional glance at your pictures to trigger your memory.

Assignment: Give a "Picture Story" speech.

1. Prepare a 3- to 4-minute autobiographical speech. Your speech should include information about your:
   - Background (early childhood)
   - Family
   - Present involvements (work, school)
   - Hobbies and special interests
   - Future goals and dreams

2. Prepare five sets of pictures, one set for each of the five areas you talk about. Use a different picture for each piece of information you want to share with your audience.
   a. Where will you find the pictures? Use any combination of the following:
      - Draw your own pictures. (Don't worry if you are not an artist. Simple stick figures or sketches are fine as long as they represent what you want to say about yourself.)
      - Use computer clip art (cartoons or pictures). Choose clip art that reminds you of what you want to say. Be sure to enlarge the clip art so that your audience can see it easily, should you decide to share your pictures with them.
      - Use photographs from your photo albums at home.
      - Cut out pictures from magazines or newspapers.
   b. Each of your five sets of pictures should be on heavyweight paper, at least 8.5" by 11". (Construction paper works well.)

3. Your teacher may use the evaluation form on page 247 of Appendix I. Look it over so you know exactly how you will be evaluated.

---

[1]The authors gratefully acknowledge the idea for the Old Bag Speech, which was presented by a speaker at a National Communication Association conference, and would appreciate being contacted by anyone who knows that person's name so that he or she can be properly credited.

Example

Pedro would like to mention that he came to the United States two years ago and lived in New York for one year before moving to Miami. He could draw:

He could also select the following clip art:

Example

Stefan is planning to talk about his hobbies, which include listening to music, reading books, sailing, and fishing. He could draw:

He could also select the following clip art:

Example

Noriko wants to to say that she is studying photography and hopes to be a famous underwater photographer someday. She could draw:

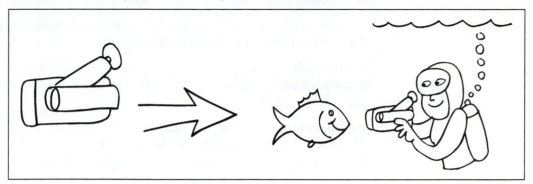

She could also select the following clip art:

METHOD B: THE OLD BAG SPEECH

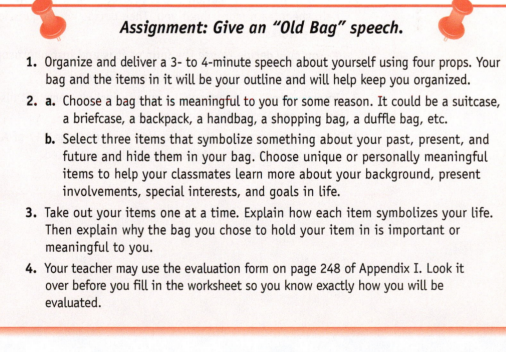

Assignment: Give an "Old Bag" speech.

1. Organize and deliver a 3- to 4-minute speech about yourself using four props. Your bag and the items in it will be your outline and will help keep you organized.

2. **a.** Choose a bag that is meaningful to you for some reason. It could be a suitcase, a briefcase, a backpack, a handbag, a shopping bag, a duffle bag, etc.

   b. Select three items that symbolize something about your past, present, and future and hide them in your bag. Choose unique or personally meaningful items to help your classmates learn more about your background, present involvements, special interests, and goals in life.

3. Take out your items one at a time. Explain how each item symbolizes your life. Then explain why the bag you chose to hold your item in is important or meaningful to you.

4. Your teacher may use the evaluation form on page 248 of Appendix I. Look it over before you fill in the worksheet so you know exactly how you will be evaluated.

Examples

Items symbolizing the past: a piece of the Berlin Wall from when communism was abolished in East Germany; a beautiful white first-communion dress.

Items symbolizing the present: a waitress's uniform; a rattle representing the birth of a child; an insulin syringe representing living with diabetes.

Items symbolizing the future: a bottle of prescription medicine (she is majoring in pharmacy); an IRS tax return (he wants to be an accountant); a stethoscope (she wants to study medicine).

Bag: an old, beat-up, mildewed suitcase that had carried a student's belongings to Miami when he escaped from Cuba on a raft; a plastic Minnie Mouse purse that her grandmother bought on her first trip to Disney World.

METHOD C: SPEECH PREPARATION WORKSHEET

You can use a worksheet with questions and answers to help you organize your thoughts. Use the Speech Preparation Worksheet on page 9 as your guide. When you are delivering your speech, a quick look at the Worksheet will remind you of what to say about yourself. Fill in the blanks with key words or phrases.

Assignment: Give a speech of self-introduction using a worksheet.

1. Prepare and deliver a 3- to 4-minute speech about yourself using a Speech Preparation Worksheet such as the one on page 9.

2. Try to think of information about yourself that will interest your classmates and help them learn more about you. Then decide which questions you should have on the Worksheet.
   - You may decide to use the form as it is and just photocopy it, or
   - You may choose to change some of the questions.

3. In answering the questions, be sure to include some details that will make your speech come alive for your listeners.

4. Your teacher may use the evaluation form on page 247 of Appendix I. Look it over so you know exactly how you will be evaluated.

SELF-INTRODUCTION SPEECH PREPARATION WORKSHEET

What is your name?[1]
Where are you from?
How long have you been in this country?
Why did you come to this country?
How many brothers or sisters do you have?[2]
Who do you live with?
What are you studying here?[3]
What do you like to do in your free time?
What hobbies or special interests do you have?
What are your future plans and goals?
How do you think you will benefit from taking this course?

AFTER THE SPEECH

After each speech, your teacher will encourage your classmates to ask you questions about what you said. Or your teacher may ask you to elaborate on specific pieces of information.

Examples

- Akiko, you mentioned that one of your hobbies is origami. Please explain what that is.
- Roberto, how old were you when you began your stamp collecting hobby? How did you become interested in this hobby?

---

[1]Be sure to say your name clearly. If it is unusual, spell it for the class.
[2]Give names and ages.
[3]Describe the other classes you are taking.

1. After all the speeches of self-introduction have been delivered, your teacher will check how well you listened to each other by asking the class questions based on the information your classmates shared. For example:
   - Where is Luisa from?
   - Who rides horses?
   - What is Omar majoring in?

2. Your teacher might decide to give you a short "listening quiz" of five to ten general questions based on your classmates' speeches. This will encourage you to pay full attention and listen carefully!

SPEECH 2: A PERSONAL EXPERIENCE

Everybody has had experiences that are unforgettable in some way. These experiences make wonderful speech topics. When you give a speech describing a personal experience, your challenge is to make the audience relive the experience with you. If you had a happy experience, you should make your listeners feel happy. If you had a sad experience, you should make them feel sad. If you had a scary experience, they should feel afraid. If you had a funny experience, they should laugh. Make your audience feel the way you felt.

You can talk about an experience that was:

dangerous	exciting	happy	surprising
educational	frightening	interesting	uncomfortable
embarrassing	funny	sad	unique

Your goal is to speak naturally and to maintain eye contact with your listeners. As with your first speech, you cannot write it down and read it. However, you can write down your main ideas and present your speech from notes.

Two different personal experience speech assignments are described. One is for an experience you have had as an adult. The other is for an experience you had as a child. Your assignment is to give a speech describing a personal experience. Whether you do Assignment A, Assignment B, or both, your task is to make the audience relive the experience with you.

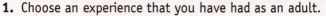

Assignment A: Give a speech about an experience you have had as an adult.

1. Choose an experience that you have had as an adult.
2. Using the Personal Experience Speech Preparation Worksheet on page 15, prepare notes for a speech about this experience. Be sure to include some interesting details that will help your audience relive this experience with you.
3. See below for an example of a speech and page 12 for an example of a completed Speech Preparation Worksheet.
4. Your teacher may use the form on page 249 of Appendix I to evaluate your speech. Look it over so you know exactly how you will be evaluated.
5. Give a 3- to 4-minute speech about your experience.

Example: *Francisco's Speech*

INTRODUCTION

Do you think it's possible to have an experience that is dangerous, happy, sad, uncomfortable, and very scary at the same time? I had one, and I'll remember it for the rest of my life.

BODY

I escaped from Cuba three years ago at the age of eighteen with my fifteen-year-old brother José. My father wanted us to live in a free country, get a good education, and have many opportunities. In Cuba, there was no hope for a good future. My father put José and me on a raft at a nearby beach in the middle of the night.

He told us that a city called Key West in the United States was only about ninety miles north of Cuba.

Our trip from Havana to Key West took three days. We were all alone without food or water. Sharks were swimming all around us. I thought we were going to starve, drown, or be eaten by the sharks.

I tried to comfort my brother José by telling him how much better our lives would be when we finally got to Miami. I made myself feel better by thinking that we would go to heaven and meet my parents there one day. By some miracle, the U.S. Coast Guard rescued us several miles from Key West. Relatives of ours in Miami were notified by the immigration authorities. Our aunt and uncle picked us up in Key West and we went to live with them in Miami. After two years, we saw our parents again. They finally escaped from Cuba also. That was a very happy day for me.

CONCLUSION

Now that you know my experience, I think you can understand why it was scary, sad, dangerous, uncomfortable, and finally, happy all at the same time. I didn't know it then, but it was also the most important personal experience of my life. It was important because without that experience, I wouldn't be here today in a free and wonderful country talking to all of you. Thank you.

Example: *Francisco's Speech Preparation Worksheet*

PERSONAL EXPERIENCE SPEECH PREPARATION WORKSHEET

What type of experience was it?	dangerous, scary, uncomfortable
Where were you?	beach in Cuba, middle of the night
When were you there?	3 years ago, 18 years old
Who was with you?	brother José – 15 years old
What were you doing?	father put us on raft
Why were you there?	escaping to freedom
How were you feeling?	alone, scared, uncomfortable
Why did you feel that way?	no food or water, afraid of starving, sharks
What was your goal?	arrive in Key West, freedom, opportunities
How did you react?	comforted my brother and thought about a better life ahead
How did the story end?	U.S. Coast Guard rescued us
Why will you never forget this experience?	I'm here today!

Assignment B: Give a speech about an experience you had as a child.

1. Think of an experience you had as a child. The experience can be good, bad, interesting, or funny. Possible topics include:

The Time I Got Lost	The Day I Played Hooky
My Most Memorable Birthday	The Day I Ran Away from Home
My First Bicycle	An Important Lesson I Learned
A Terrible Lie I Told	My First Pet
My First Day at School	My First Childhood Sweetheart

2. Using the Personal Experience Speech Preparation Worksheet on page 15, prepare notes for a speech about this experience. Be sure to include all the information that will help your audience relive this experience with you.

3. Your teacher may use the form on page 249 of Appendix I to evaluate your speech. Look it over so you know exactly how you will be evaluated.

4. Give a 3- to 4-minute speech about your experience.

Example: *Leila's Speech*

In my hands, I have a jar of honey.

(Leila showed her
visual aid here.)

If you look closely, you can see part of the honey beehive in the jar. You are probably wondering why I brought a jar of honey to show you today. Every time I see honey, it reminds me of a "stinging" experience I had when I was in the sixth grade.

BODY

As a child I grew up on a farm not far from Kuala Lumpur, Malaysia. One warm summer day, my friend and I were walking home from school. We happened to see a beehive in a tree.

(Leila showed
another visual aid here.)

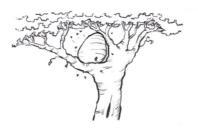

We had just studied in school about bee colonies and how bees make honey. This was my big chance to show off to my mother and father what I had learned in school.

It looked easy! I found a stick about two meters long. I handed it to my friend and told her to sneak up to the tree and hit the hive with the stick. I said I would wait until the bees came out and then I could grab the hive and run away with it.

I soon learned a very important lesson. I learned that things don't always work out the way you plan them. My friend pushed the hive down from the tree and then ran at full speed up a nearby hill. The bees did not go after her. However, they were all over me instantly. They stung my arms; they flew down my blouse and stung me. They flew up my skirt and stung me; they got in my hair and stung me. My parents took me to the hospital. I had to stay there for two days until my fever was gone.

CONCLUSION

That was the first and last beehive I have ever touched. If anyone here has ever been stung by a bee, you are probably as afraid of bees as I am. I have never touched a beehive again and never will. I'm sure you can see how this jar of honey I brought to show you reminds me of a very "stinging" experience!

WRITE LEILA'S NOTES

What do you think the speaking notes that Leila used to make her speech looked like? Using her speech as a guide, complete the Personal Experience Speech Preparation Worksheet below. (Answers can be found on page 265 of Appendix II.)

LEILA'S EXPERIENCE SPEECH PREPARATION WORKSHEET

What type of experience was it?	painful, unpleasant, scary
Where were you?	
When were you there?	
Who was with you?	
What were you doing?	
Why were you there?	
How were you feeling?	
Why did you feel that way?	
What was your goal?	
How did you react?	
How did the story end?	
Why will you never forget this experience?	

Use the following worksheet to prepare your notes for your personal experience speech.

PERSONAL EXPERIENCE SPEECH PREPARATION WORKSHEET	
What type of experience was it?	
Where were you?	
When were you there?	
Who was with you?	
What were you doing?	
Why were you there?	
How were you feeling?	
Why did you feel that way?	
What was your goal?	
How did you react?	
How did the story end?	
Why will you never forget this experience?	

SPEECH 3: A MEANINGFUL OBJECT

Is there an object that has special meaning for you? It can be a painting, picture, piece of clothing or jewelry, or anything else. How would you describe it? Why does it have special meaning for you? The object you choose and how you describe it can give unique information about you.

Your assignment is to bring a meaningful object to class and give a speech about it. Be sure to include both objective information and subjective information about your "treasure."

- Objective information is not influenced by your own feelings. It includes observable or factual information.
- Subjective information is influenced by your feelings or personal opinions rather than facts.

This time, instead of presenting your speech to the whole class, you will work in a small group.

Assignment: Give a speech about a meaningful object.

1. Choose an object that has special meaning for you.

2. Using the Meaningful Object Speech Preparation Worksheet on page 18, prepare notes for a speech about this object. Be sure to include all the information that will help your audience understand why the object is meaningful to you.

3. Your teacher may use the form on page 250 of Appendix I to evaluate your speech. Look it over so you know exactly how you will be evaluated.

4. Meet in small groups. Each student in the group will give a 3- to 4-minute speech and then listen to the stories of the other members.

5. After all groups are finished, your teacher will ask you the following questions. Share your answers with the entire class.

   a. How did you feel speaking to your group? Were you nervous? Relaxed?

   b. Did you look directly at your group members as you were speaking?

   c. Were your group members good listeners? Did they make you feel comfortable or uncomfortable? How? What did they do that you liked or disliked?

   d. Will you feel differently when you are asked to stand in front of the entire class to tell your story? Why?

Example: *Henry's Speech*

INTRODUCTION

In my hand I have an object in which spirits live. They float through bluish-green stone and live forever. Would you like to see the object in which spirits live? I'll now show it to you.

BODY

This is a turquoise gemstone. It is from the southwestern United States. My father gave this to me for my sixth birthday. We were living in our hogan on the Navajo reservation. The stone is over 170 years old. It's an oval shape the size of a nickel and weighs about two ounces.

This turquoise stone was first polished by my great-grandfather when he was a young man in the summer of 1831. I want you to know that turquoise is a mineral of aluminum and copper; when it is polished, it becomes a brilliant bluish-green gemstone. This turquoise has a very special meaning for me because it represents the Navajo way of life. For the Navajo, all things of our earth contain the spirits of all the life forms that have touched them. When I look at this stone, its spirits help my mind to see scenes from the past: my grandfather's mud hogan, the cedarwood fires, our struggle for survival, the desert in the summer, desert flowers and cactus, the human spirit of the Navajo. All these things belong to me in the memory of this stone.

I wanted to share this turquoise stone with all of you because we all need to realize that man must work with nature to change life for the better. I think you now understand why this magnificent object has special meaning for me. In this gemstone, many wonderful memories and spirits from the past live again.

Example: *Henry's Speech Preparation Worksheet*

MEANINGFUL OBJECT SPEECH PREPARATION WORKSHEET

OBJECTIVE INFORMATION

What is it?	turquoise gemstone
How old is it?	over 170 years old
Where is it from?	southwestern U.S.
When did you get it?	when I was 6 years old
How did you get it?	gift from my father
Why did you get it?	birthday present
What size is it?	about the size of a nickel
What shape is it?	oval
How much does it weigh?	2 ounces
What is it made of?	mineral of aluminum and copper
What features does it have?	smooth, brilliant bluish-green color

SUBJECTIVE INFORMATION

Why does it have special meaning for you?	represents Navajo way of life, contains spirits of life forms
Why do you feel strongly about it?	reminds me of my ancestors' past
Why do you want to share it with the class?	We all need to realize that man must work with nature to change life for the better.

Use the following worksheet to prepare notes for your meaningful object speech.

MEANINGFUL OBJECT SPEECH PRESENTATION WORKSHEET

OBJECTIVE INFORMATION	
What is it?	
How old is it?	
Where is it from?	
When did you get it?	
How did you get it?	
Why did you get it?	
What size is it?	
What shape is it?	
How much does it weigh?	
What is it made of?	
What features does it have?	
SUBJECTIVE INFORMATION	
Why does it have special meaning for you?	
Why do you feel strongly about it?	
Why do you want to share it with the class?	

SPEECH 4: A SPECIFIC FEAR

Everybody is afraid of something. Anyone who says "I'm not afraid of anything" is probably not telling the truth. Being able to talk about something you are afraid of and to share your feelings with the class is a good way to gain confidence when speaking before an audience. Also, you might be surprised to learn that others are afraid of the same thing as you! For example, many people are afraid of:

flying in planes	the dark
public speaking	going to a new country
meeting new people	interviewing for a job
snakes	large dogs
taking tests	going to the hospital

Your assignment is to give a speech describing a fear. Your teacher will decide whether to ask you to present this to the class or to meet in small groups.

Assignment: Give a speech about a specific fear.

1. Choose a specific fear that you have.
2. Using the Specific Fear Speech Preparation Worksheet on page 20, prepare notes for a speech about this fear. Be sure to include all the information that will help your audience understand your fear and the reasons for it.
3. Your teacher may use the form on page 249 of Appendix I to evaluate your speech. Look it over so you know exactly how you will be evaluated.
4. Give a 3- to 4-minute speech about your fear.

Example: *Humberto's Speech*

INTRODUCTION

The earth was far below us. The weather was very bad. I looked at the instrument panel of the plane and saw a red warning light flashing. The pilot was very nervous. At that moment, the engine of the plane became silent!

BODY

This happened to me last year when I was flying from Cancún to Cozumel in Yucatán, Mexico. I will explain exactly what happened so you can understand why I now have a great fear of flying in small planes.

(Humberto showed a picture of a small plane.)

Right after we took off from the airport in Cancún, the weather turned very bad. There was a lot of thunder and lightning. It was raining very hard. It was impossible for the pilot to see out the windows of the plane. I was the only person in the plane with the pilot. After being in the air for fifteen minutes, the plane started to shake and make strange noises. All of a sudden, the engine just stopped.

When red warning lights started flashing, I became very afraid. I began to tremble and was soaked with sweat. I remember thinking that my life was about to end. I thought about how young I was and how I didn't want to die. All of a sudden, the engine started to work again. The pilot turned to me, smiled, and said, *"¡No te preocupes!"* (That means "Don't worry!")

My mother and father do not want me to fly in small planes ever again. They say I should fly on the big airlines or take a boat. I promised myself, from now on, I will do what they tell me!

CONCLUSION

I don't think I will ever fly in a small plane again. I get upset every time I think about it. I know that I will never be able to overcome this fear.

Use the following worksheet to prepare notes for your specific fear speech.

SPECIFIC FEAR SPEECH PREPARATION WORKSHEET	
What is the nature of the fear?	
When did the fear develop?	
Where did it develop?	
Why did it develop?	
How do you react when faced with this fear?	
How do your friends and family react to your fear?	
What have you done to try to overcome this fear?	

SPEECH 5: A PERSONAL OPINION SPEECH

A personal opinion speech expresses the speaker's attitude and feelings about a topic. The feelings could be positive, such as enthusiasm or excitement, or negative, such as anger or worry. The topic could be an issue, a policy, a situation, an attitude, or a behavior. Topics that people feel strongly about include:

cruelty to animals	learning a second language
child abuse	punishing criminals
world peace	children
their city	dishonesty
their school	rudeness

- In the introduction of a personal opinion speech, the speaker makes a clear statement.
- In the body, the speaker explains the reasons for this opinion and gives at least one example.
- In the conclusion, the speaker restates the opinion and offers ideas.

Note that in personal opinion speeches, it is especially effective for speakers to use emotion so that the audience can empathize with their feelings.

Assignment: Give a personal opinion speech.

1. Choose a topic that you feel strongly about.

2. Using the Personal Opinion Speech Preparation Worksheet on page 22, prepare notes for a speech about this opinion. Be sure to include all the information that will help your audience understand your opinion and the reasons for it.

3. Your teacher may use the form on page 251 of Appendix I to evaluate your speech. Look it over so you know exactly how you will be evaluated.

4. Give a 3- to 4-minute speech about your point of view.

Example: *Indira's Speech*

INTRODUCTION

The other day I heard an American student say, "All foreign students are the same! They can't understand me and I can't understand them." This comment bothered me. In my opinion, American students should give other people a chance and not assume all students from other countries are alike.

BODY

I believe that all people are unique. We all look different; we like different foods; some of us are shy and some are brave; and we all have different good and bad qualities. I say that just because we don't speak perfect English yet, all foreign students are not the same. I may be from another country, but I understand what Americans say, and every day I'm learning to speak English much better. People should not jump to conclusions about other people. We all must learn to be patient and give each person a chance.

CONCLUSION

Foreign students cannot be lumped together and called the same. American students are not all the same either. We are all different and we all have our own problems to face and solve. We must learn to be more patient with one another and realize that no one is perfect. That's my opinion.

Example: *Indira's Speech Preparation Worksheet*

PERSONAL OPINION SPEECH PREPARATION WORKSHEET

What is the nature of your opinion?	Americans should not assume all foreign students are alike.
When did you develop this opinion?	just the other day
How did you develop this opinion?	overheard an American say "All foreign students are the same"
Why do you feel the way you do?	people are different, they should not be lumped together
How do you feel about those who disagree with you?	bothered, annoyed, angry
What examples support your opinion?	we all look different; we have different personalities; we like different foods; we speak different languages
What advice do you have for others?	be more patient with each other; respect differences between people

Use the following worksheet to prepare notes for your personal opinion speech.

PERSONAL OPINION SPEECH PREPARATION WORKSHEET

What is the nature of your opinion?	
When did you develop this opinion?	
How did you develop this opinion?	
Why do you feel the way you do?	
How do you feel about those who disagree with you?	
What examples support your opinion?	
What advice do you have for others?	

EXERCISE 1

Read the following expressions aloud. Be sure to stress the content words, not the function words.

1. in a **moment**
2. to **tell** the **truth**
3. **Silence** is **golden**.
4. **Honesty** is the **best policy**.
5. A **penny saved** is a **penny earned**.
6. as **good** as **gold**
7. as **light** as a **feather**
8. It's **now** or **never**.
9. **luck** of the **draw**
10. as **dry** as a **bone**

Speakers sometimes stress certain words in a sentence to call attention to them. This can change the meaning, or focus, of the sentence.

Example

He is my speech teacher. (This emphasizes *who* the teacher is.)
He is **my** speech teacher. (This emphasizes that it is the *speaker's* teacher.)
He is my **speech** teacher. (This emphasizes *what kind of* teacher he is.)

EXERCISE 2

Read the following sentences aloud. Be sure to stress the boldfaced words.

1. Mary is Anne's **friend**. She **isn't** her cousin.
2. John is **married** to Anne. They aren't **engaged**.
3. They **own** a small home. They don't **rent**.
4. They live in Washington, **D.C.**, not Washington **State**.
5. Anne will open a **pet** store, not a **toy** store.

Practice reading the following dialogue aloud with a classmate. Be sure to stress the boldfaced words.

JOHN: Anne, who was on the **phone**?

ANNE: My old friend **Mary**.

JOHN: Mary **Jones**?

ANNE: No, Mary **Hall**.

JOHN: I don't know Mary **Hall**. Where is she **from**?

ANNE: She's from **Washington**.

JOHN: Washington, the **state**, or Washington, the **city**?

ANNE: Washington, **D.C.**, our nation's **capital**.

JOHN: Is that where she **lives**?

ANNE: Yes, she still lives in the white **house**.

JOHN: The **White** House? With the **president**?

ANNE: No, silly. The white **house** on **First** Street.

JOHN: What did she **want**?

ANNE: She wants to **come** here.

JOHN: Come **here**? **When**?

ANNE: In a **week**. She's bringing her black **bird**, her **collie**, her **snakes**, her . . .

JOHN: **Stop**! She's bringing a **zoo** to our house?

ANNE: No, John. She's opening a **pet** store here in **town**.

CHAPTER 2

Delivering Your Message

William Shakespeare wrote that all speakers give two speeches at the same time: the one that is heard and the one that is seen.

Believe it or not, most people are frequently more influenced by what they see than by what they hear.

A professor at UCLA found that only 7 percent of our credibility with listeners comes from the actual words we speak, while 93 percent of it comes from our vocal qualities and visual characteristics. The presidential debates between John F. Kennedy and Richard Nixon in 1960 are an excellent example of how facial expressions, gestures, eye contact, and posture can either hurt or help speakers. These debates were the first ever to be televised. The people who heard them on the radio said that Nixon won the debates. However, the people who watched them on TV insisted that Kennedy won. Kennedy's body language made a more powerful impression on the viewers than anything the candidates were actually saying.

What is *body language*? Body language means posture, eye contact, facial expressions, and gestures. Your body language, as well as your speech patterns, reflects how you feel about yourself. It also affects how others react to you. It can help you convey an aura of confidence, or it can make you appear uncertain before you even open your mouth.

People will pay attention to you and your words if you look them in the eye, improve your posture and use of gestures, and use decisive-sounding speech patterns. This chapter will introduce you to techniques for delivering your message in both formal and informal speaking.

POSTURE TALKS

Your posture tells how you feel about yourself. It can say, "I'm timid and afraid of my own shadow. Don't listen to me; just ignore me." On the other hand, your posture can send the message, "Listen to me. I know what I'm talking about." Looking down and not facing people directly gives the impression that you're ashamed or embarrassed. Cocking your head to the side, rounding your shoulders, dropping your chin, clutching your arms across your shoulders, wrapping your arms around your body, or clasping your hands tightly in front of you can also make you appear insecure or defeated.

Observe the body language of the following individuals. Who looks the most confident?

If you said Cheryl, you're right. What is it about Cheryl's posture that causes her to project courage and confidence?

Diane   **Carl**   **Cheryl**   **Simon**

When giving a speech, here are five ways you can radiate confidence and strength of character even before you open your mouth:

- Keep your spine straight and rotate your shoulders back.
- Keep your head erect.
- Keep your hands at your sides with your fingers open or slightly curled.
- Keep both feet flat on the floor and slightly apart.
- If you are using a lectern, be careful not to bend over it or lean on it. Instead, stand naturally erect and gently rest your hands on the sides of the lectern.

Here are three ways you can project confidence when sitting and listening:

- Sit straight while leaning forward slightly to show interest in the speaker.
- Rest your hands lightly in your lap or on the arms of your chair.
- Keep your legs together with your feet flat on the floor or crossed at the ankles.

Improving your posture isn't difficult. It's as simple as doing what your mother probably used to tell you all the time: "Stand up straight," "Stop slouching," or "Sit up in your chair!" The old trick of walking around your house with a book on your head still works wonders.

Remember: Your speech starts before you even say one word. Your audience takes notice of you before you begin to speak. They watch you as you walk to the front of the room. They form an impression about your level of confidence, your ability, and your credibility during your short trip to the podium.

Manolo Martín-Vásquez, a famous Spanish matador, said, "The most important lesson in courage is physical, not mental. From the age of twelve, I was taught to walk in a way that produces courage. The mental part comes later." If you want to appear confident when you walk up to the podium, walk the walk of the matador.

ACTIVITY

BUILD YOUR CONFIDENCE

1. Come to class prepared with a favorite saying, proverb, or piece of advice your grandmother always told you! (e.g., "Do unto others as you would have them do unto you." "Life is like a box of chocolates; you never know what you are going to get." "Don't put off for tomorrow what you can do today.")

2. Practice the "walk of the matador."
   a. Walk to the front of the classroom with your head up, your spine straight, and your shoulders back.
   b. Spend a few moments standing at the lectern looking directly at your audience.
   c. Say "Good morning" or "Good afternoon." Deliver your quote or saying. When you finish, look at the audience and smile while they clap. Wait until the applause dies down.
   d. Walk back to your seat with your head up, your spine straight, and your shoulders back.

LOOK THEM IN THE EYE

Eye contact customs vary from culture to culture. In some Eastern cultures, women are expected to lower their eyes in communication situations. In other cultures, it is a sign of respect to lower one's eyes when speaking to older people.

In Japan, audiences look down in order to show respect for a speaker. The speaker may acknowledge the audience's humility by looking down as well. Japanese schoolchildren are taught to look at their teacher's neck. As adults, they show respect by lowering their eyes when speaking to a superior. On the other hand, American children are taught just the opposite. Their parents and teachers often tell them, "Look at me when I'm speaking."

In some Latin American and African cultures, prolonged eye contact from a person of lower status is considered disrespectful. In Brazil, for example, the less powerful person generally glances away from the more important individual.

In the United States, making eye contact with your listeners is absolutely essential for becoming an effective communicator.

Good eye contact:

- shows that you are open and honest (looking away conveys insincerity/embarrassment)
- is more effective than the words you say
- encourages listeners to pay attention to you, to respond to you, and to respect you
- indicates that you have confidence in yourself and what you are saying
- allows you to "read" your listeners' faces to get feedback on how they like your speech
- allows you to see your listeners' feedback (their nods, gestures, and smiles let you know that they understand and are interested in what you're saying)

If the thought of maintaining eye contact with one or more people seems disconcerting, remember that effective eye contact does not mean staring at a person. It means shifting your focus to and from a person's eyes.

ACTIVITY

LOOK YOUR PARTNER IN THE EYE

With a conversation partner, take turns talking about any topic for 2–3 minutes. For example, you can talk about your weekend, your summer vacation, or a new pet.

1. Focus on your partner's left eye for four seconds.
2. Shift your focus to your partner's right eye for four seconds.
3. Look at your partner's entire face for four seconds.
4. Glance at your partner's nose for four seconds, chin for four seconds, and forehead for four seconds.
5. Repeat steps 1–4.

ACTIVITY ## WALK THE WALK OF THE MATADOR

Practice walking confidently to the front of the room and looking at your audience as you speak about any topic.

1. Walk the walk of the matador to the front of the room.
2. Greet your audience.
3. Speak about your topic for 2–3 minutes. As you speak, move your eyes from one section of the audience to another. Look at one person for 4–5 seconds, then another person for 4–5 seconds.
4. Thank your audience.

ACTIVITY ## TALK ABOUT IT

In small groups, discuss the questions below. When you have finished, share your ideas with the class.

1. As a child, what were you taught about eye contact?
2. How did you feel when participating in Look Your Partner in the Eye as the speaker? As the listener?
3. How did you feel when participating in Walk the Walk of the Matador as the speaker? As the listener?
4. What were your listeners' reactions to your conscious efforts to maintain eye contact with them?

FACIAL EXPRESSIONS AND GESTURES

Facial expressions and gestures also vary greatly in different cultures. In some societies, speakers limit facial expressions and inhibit gestures. In others, gestures are used frequently.

For example, in Japan, speakers rarely vary facial expressions or gestures. Brazilian and French speakers use gestures with greater frequency than North Americans, and Italian speakers tend to gesture more than other cultural groups.

During a business presentation in Japan, a speaker who smiles or chuckles might convey confusion or embarrassment to his or her listeners. On the other hand, an American speaker might purposely laugh to express irony or humor.

Speakers in the United States use a variety of gestures and facial expressions to help maintain listeners' interest in their message and to appear relaxed and in control.

FACIAL EXPRESSIONS

If you smile before you speak, you give your listeners the impression that you are confident and looking forward to speaking. Don't fake a big politician-type smile! A small, natural smile will be fine. A smile is a good way to establish rapport with your audience and to help put both you and your audience at ease. Other facial expressions can be used to convey different emotions. Try to change your facial expressions during your speech to convey the emotions that you feel.

ACTIVITY

PRACTICE DIFFERENT FACIAL EXPRESSIONS

Experiment with the following facial expressions at home while looking at yourself in a full-length mirror. This practice will help you become aware of how you appear to others when you talk to them.

a. Look happy.	**i.** Look unhappy.
b. Look worried.	**j.** Look neutral.
c. Wrinkle your eyebrows.	**k.** Look surprised.
d. Look interested.	**l.** Look excited.
e. Squint your eyes.	**m.** Look fearful.
f. Bite your lip.	**n.** Look frustrated.
g. Lick your lips.	**o.** Look doubtful.
h. Look angry.	

MOVEMENT

Listeners find it extremely distracting to watch speakers nervously twirl strands of hair with their fingers; fiddle with earrings, necklaces, or other items of jewelry; or constantly push slipping eyeglasses up on their noses. If you have long hair, tie it back during your presentation so you won't be tempted to play with it or to fling it away from your face. Try to keep jewelry to a minimum, and if you wear glasses, make sure they fit properly.

While speaking, don't hide your hands in your pockets and jingle your keys or loose change. Keep your hands at your sides. On the other hand, don't stand "frozen" in one place for your entire speech. If you're nervous, take a few steps to your right or left while speaking. This will help you to relax and move naturally.

GESTURES

Important points in your speech can be emphasized by using gestures—hand and arm movements. Here are some examples:

Size: Show the width or height of an object by using your hands.

Enthusiasm for an idea: Punch the air with your fist to show your enthusiasm for a new policy.

Symbolic action: Wave your hand in greeting to show how you felt when you saw a long-lost friend.

Location: Point your index finger to show a specific location on a map or use your hand in a sweeping motion to show a wider area.

ACTIVITY

EXPLORE BODY LANGUAGE

Experiment with the following body language at home while looking at yourself in a full-length mirror. This practice will help you become aware of how you appear to others when you talk to them.

   a. Cover your mouth with your hand while speaking.

   b. Sway back and forth on your feet.

   c. Cross your arms in front of you.

   d. Wrap your arms around your body.

   e. Tilt your head.

   f. Twirl a strand of hair around your finger.

   g. Play with a button or an item of jewelry.

   h. Nod your head excessively while speaking.

   i. Cross your legs.

   j. Look down at your feet.

COMMUNICATE THROUGH BODY LANGUAGE

The following are different messages that can be expressed through body language without speaking. This activity will help you lose your inhibitions about using nonverbal gestures.

"I don't know."	"Great job."	"You're crazy."
"Wait a moment."	"Absolutely not."	"See you later."
"Go away."	"You're right."	"I'm full."
"Stop!"	"I'm starving."	"It's getting late."
"Don't do that."	"Take it easy."	"Come here."
"That's OK."	"You're late."	"That's enough."

1. Your teacher will call you to the front of the room. Select any message from the box on page 31. Don't tell the rest of the class which one you chose.

2. Express the message using nonverbal gestures. The messages may be expressed through different gestures in different cultures. Use the gestures that you feel most comfortable with based on your culture and experience. Your teacher will tell you if the gesture you used is the one most English speakers use.

3. Call on a classmate to guess which message you demonstrated.

DIFFERENT MODES OF SPEECH DELIVERY

Four different methods for presenting a speech are described below. In which of them does the speaker use eye contact and body language to make a strong connection with the audience? Which method do you think is the most desirable? Why?

1. The Manuscript Delivery

- Speech is written out word for word on sheets of paper.
- The language is usually intended to be read rather than listened to.
- Speaker reads speech word for word with little or no eye contact with the audience.
- Audience generally loses interest.

2. The Memorized Delivery

- Speaker writes out a speech (or parts of a speech) and memorizes it word for word.
- Memorized speeches can be effective if the lines are presented the way a good actor would deliver them; however, more often they sound mechanical and stiff.
- Speakers who rely on memory for their entire speech run the risk of forgetting their lines.
- It is more practical to memorize short segments of a speech (the introduction, any brief quotes, and the concluding remarks).

3. The Impromptu Delivery

- Speakers are generally taken by surprise, have only a few minutes to prepare, and must gather their thoughts quickly.
- Speakers do not usually have notes prepared in advance.
- Delivery is typically spontaneous and conversational.
- Speech may seem disorganized, but it can also be very effective.

4. The Extemporaneous Delivery

- Speech is carefully planned, organized, and practiced.
- Speaker uses an outline which includes main points, key words, phrases, and quotes.
- Speaker maintains eye contact with the audience.
- Speaker uses voice expressively, delivering content in a dynamic, conversational way.

Effective Speeches

Now that you have had some experience giving speeches, listening to them, and reading about different modes of delivery, what do you see as the elements of effective extemporaneous speeches? What are the most important skills you need to learn in order to be an effective speaker?

ACTIVITY

THINK ABOUT WHAT MAKES AN EFFECTIVE SPEECH

Meet in small groups.

1. **Make a list of**

    a. the criteria you think are important,

    b. the skills you need to learn.

2. **Share these with the class.**

3. **At the end, your teacher may contribute to the list.**

(Possible answers can be found on page 268 of Appendix II.)

EFFECTIVE USE OF NOTES

When talking extemporaneously, speakers depend on good notes that allow them to maintain their connection with the audience through continuous eye contact as well as use of a conversational, natural style of speech. In Chapter 1 you practiced giving extemporaneous speeches using three different approaches, all of which served the same function as notes. They helped you remember your main ideas, and, in the case of the Speech Preparation Worksheet, they also allowed you to add some details. A more traditional approach is to use note cards, in which you write your main points and brief notes on index cards.

The following guidelines will help you to use note cards effectively:

1. Buy a packet of large index cards (4" × 6" or 5" × 7") at any stationery or office supply store. One card slides easily behind the other when you are finished with it. Do not use regular paper; it is not as heavy as index cards and makes fluttering sounds. This can be very distracting to your listeners.

2. Write only key words or short phrases on the cards to help you remember your main ideas.

3. Use one card for your introduction, one for your preview, one for each main point, one for each transition, one for the summary, and one for the conclusion. If your supporting points are brief, you might put two supporting points on one card. Be sure not to put too much information on each card.

4. Write your notes in dark ink or type them using a very large font size. Double or triple space your notes. It is important for your notes to be very visible and clear so that you can read them easily and not lose your place.

5. Write on only one side of each card. This makes the cards easy to handle. You can gracefully and unobtrusively slide one behind the other while you are speaking without distracting the audience.

6. <u>Underline</u>, WRITE IN CAPITAL LETTERS, **boldface**, or use a larger font.

7. Practice your speech several times using the note cards in order to become familiar with them. You should become so familiar with the information on your cards that you only need to look at them briefly to trigger your memory about what you want to say.

8. Number each card so you don't lose your place. If you accidentally drop them, you will be able to put them in their correct order quickly.

SAMPLE NOTE CARDS FOR A SPEECH ABOUT IDENTITY THEFT

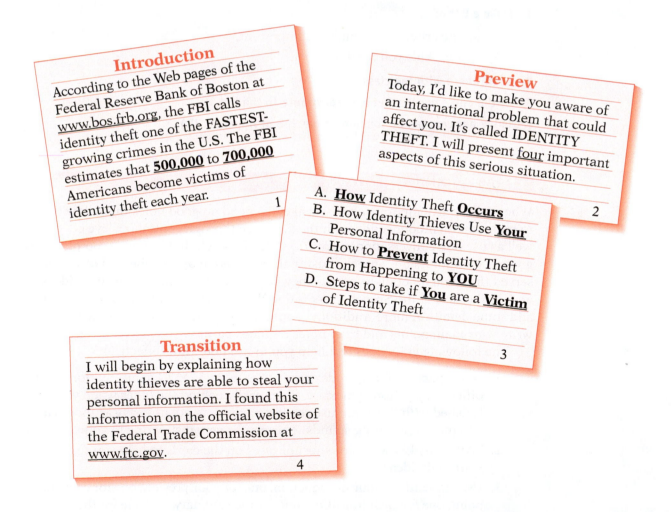

Introduction
According to the Web pages of the Federal Reserve Bank of Boston at <u>www.bos.frb.org</u>, the FBI calls identity theft one of the FASTEST-growing crimes in the U.S. The FBI estimates that **500,000** to **700,000** Americans become victims of identity theft each year.

1

Preview
Today, I'd like to make you aware of an international problem that could affect you. It's called IDENTITY THEFT. I will present <u>four</u> important aspects of this serious situation.

2

A. **<u>How</u>** Identity Theft **<u>Occurs</u>**
B. How Identity Thieves Use **<u>Your</u>** Personal Information
C. How to **<u>Prevent</u>** Identity Theft from Happening to **YOU**
D. Steps to take if **<u>You</u>** are a **<u>Victim</u>** of Identity Theft

3

Transition
I will begin by explaining how identity thieves are able to steal your personal information. I found this information on the official website of the Federal Trade Commission at <u>www.ftc.gov</u>.

4

ARE YOU ASKING ME OR TELLING ME?

This is a declarative sentence? The way some people speak, it may as well be!

Your voice has a natural upward inflection when you ask a question such as, "Would you like coffee?" If you use the upward inflection too much, you'll sound unsure of yourself and your listeners won't take you seriously. You'll sound like you're asking a question rather than making a statement. This is exactly what happened to Sally.

Sally was twenty-eight years old and a new math teacher at a large junior high school. She had discipline problems with her students and was not as effective a teacher as she knew she could be. At lunch one day, she discussed her problem with Judd, the speech teacher. After observing her teach a lesson, Judd diagnosed the problem. Her classes frequently ignored her instructions because she always sounded like she was asking rather than telling her students to do assignments. "Do the exercises on page thirty-five for homework?" "Study your formulas for the quiz Tuesday?"

Judd helped Sally get rid of her "up talk." Once she learned to drop the pitch of her voice at the end of sentences, her students began to take her seriously. They realized that she meant what she said.

People won't listen to you if your voice turns every sentence into a question. Why should they? Using an upward inflection at the end of your statements tells your listeners that you don't know what you're talking about. After all, how much faith would you have in a doctor who says, "Your wrist isn't sprained? It's broken? I need to operate?"

In written form, punctuation marks tell us whether a sentence is a question or a statement.

Example: *It's raining?*
It's raining.

In speaking, rising intonation generally signals a question and falling intonation generally signals a statement.

ACTIVITY

THINK ABOUT YOUR INTONATION

Practice saying the following pairs of sentences aloud. Use falling intonation for the sentences that end with exclamation marks. Use rising intonation for those that end with question marks. Notice how falling intonation makes you sound certain, while rising intonation makes you sound doubtful.

1. **a.** We need a better cafeteria!

   b. We need a better cafeteria?

2. **a.** I'm going to get an A in this class!

   b. I'm going to get an A in this class?

3. **a.** I deserve a raise!

   b. I deserve a raise?

4. **a.** I'm a good student!

   b. I'm a good student?

5. **a.** I worked hard on the project!

   b. I worked hard on the project?

6. **a.** Susana is my best friend!

   b. Susana is my best friend?

7. **a.** Rafael doesn't like pizza!

   b. Rafael doesn't like pizza?

8. **a.** We saw Avi's new car!

   b. We saw Avi's new car?

DISCARD THOSE DISCLAIMERS AND APOLOGIES

Too many speakers use disclaimers or apologies for their comments before they even begin their speeches. Disclaimers are remarks that weaken or diminish the impact of what the speaker is about to say. Likewise, when the speaker apologizes for a speech beforehand, he or she makes an admission that it is less than perfect before the members of the audience have the chance to judge the speech for themselves. They can kill good ideas before they're even born.

In some cultures, beginning a presentation with an apology is a sign of humility. Japanese speakers, for example, frequently begin with an apology before expressing their ideas. They tend to portray themselves, their products, their companies, and their accomplishments as being humble and barely significant.

In the United States, speakers who use disclaimers and apologies when they speak sound unsure of themselves. Don't begin your speech by saying, "I'm sorry I didn't have more time to prepare," or "I'm not an expert on this topic." Comments like these reduce your credibility and diminish the value of your opinions and feelings. Avoid these types of remarks. Deliver your message without either first apologizing or first disclaiming your words.

SILENCE IS GOLDEN

Expressions and noises such as "You know?" "You know what I mean?" "Um!" "Er!" "Uh!" are called "vocal fillers." They distract from the speaker's message and signal that he or she is uneasy. They cause the speaker to appear even more nervous than he or she really is.

Assertive, confident speakers know the importance of deliberate silences when they speak. Speakers who use well-placed pauses and avoid vocal fillers are regarded as being more confident and knowledgeable than speakers who don't. For some reason, many people are uneasy with silence and feel that every second needs to be filled with sound. However, silence can be golden. You can use a moment of silence to think about what you want to say next or to recollect your ideas if you temporarily forget what you want to say. Silences or pauses between your comments also give your listeners time to consider what you've just said.

In *Speak With Power and Grace*, speech expert Linda D. Swink writes, "I firmly believe the first two words in the English language are, 'Well, ah!' Watch any TV news program or game show when the reporter or host asks a question. You'll notice the person responding will begin by saying, 'Well, ah.' And the ahs don't stop there; they are peppered throughout our speech unknowingly. Filler words are distracting, annoying, and unprofessional."

Don't fill every pause with unnecessary vocal fillers. Learn to feel comfortable with silences between your thoughts and ideas.

ACTIVITY

LISTEN TO YOURSELF IN CONVERSATION

Practice tape-recording and listening to your conversations.

1. Tape-record yourself while having conversations in as many situations as possible outside of class.
2. Listen to the recordings.
3. Analyze how you sound. Become aware of any distracting vocal habits (e.g., up talk, disclaimers, or vocal fillers).
4. Be prepared to discuss your observations in class.

ACTIVITY

PRACTICE GIVING A SPEECH

Practice giving an impromptu (unprepared) speech in front of the class.

1. Go to the front of the class.
2. You will be assigned a simple topic, such as one of the following:

   apples   pens   chairs   rocks   trees
   dogs   bicycles   rain   eyes   teeth
3. Without preparing, speak about the topic for sixty seconds. Concentrate on speaking fluently and avoiding pauses, hesitations, and other vocal fillers. Don't worry about organization.

ACTIVITY

LISTEN TO YOURSELF GIVING A SPEECH

At home, practice tape-recording and listening to yourself giving a short speech.

1. Choose a topic from the preceding activity or think of your own topic.
2. Tape-record yourself while speaking fluently about the topic for at least sixty seconds.
3. Listen to the recording.
4. Analyze how you sound. Become aware of any distracting vocal habits (e.g., up talk, disclaimers, or vocal fillers).

WRITE FOR THE EAR

The speech delivery style of Europeans and Asians tends to be very formal. Speakers of these cultures often read oral presentations from carefully written manuscripts.

On the other hand, American speakers are generally more informal relative to speakers in other cultures. American audiences prefer a natural, spontaneous delivery that conveys a lively sense of communication. They don't relate well to speakers who read from a manuscript. If you use an outline of your ideas instead of a prepared text, your speech will not only sound more natural, but you will also be able to establish better rapport with your listeners and keep their attention. For specific information about how to organize and outline your speech, see Chapter 3: Putting Your Speech Together. In addition, example speech outlines are presented throughout this book.

The language and style you use when making an oral presentation should not be the same as the language and style you use when writing. Well-written information that is meant to be read does not work as well when it is heard. It is therefore important for you to adapt written texts or outlines for presentations. For example, I once heard a speaker say, "Several examples of what is described above are listed below." I wanted to scream, "Above what? Above your head? Listed where? Below what? Below your feet? I'm not reading your information! I'm listening to it!" It would have been much more effective for the speaker to say, "I will now give you several examples of what I just described."

Good speakers are much more informal when speaking than when writing. They also use their own words and develop their own speaking styles. Whenever possible, they use short words. Listeners appreciate it when speakers use simple, everyday words in a presentation. One advantage is that it is much easier for speakers to pronounce short words correctly. Another is that long and sophisticated vocabulary choices make listening more difficult. For example, which would you rather hear?

The facilitation of a listener's comprehension of information can be better accomplished by the speaker's utilization of succinct words.

or

Listeners understand information more easily when a speaker uses short words.

Good speakers use short sentences. If you can say a sentence in one breath, it's probably a good length. Try to keep your spoken sentences under fifteen words, and never use fifteen words when ten will do. Unnecessary words detract from your message. Long sentences are difficult for listeners to follow and hard for speakers to say.

| ACTIVITY |

PRACTICE YOUR EDITING SKILLS

The following sentences are loaded with unnecessary words. Rewrite them using simpler language and as few words as possible. (Answers can be found on page 268 of Appendix II.)

Example

The rights for distribution of the book in thirty countries had been sold by him as well as the rights for distribution in twelve different languages.

He sold rights to distribute the book in thirty countries and twelve different languages.

1. It is unfortunate that the number of students enrolled at the college this year has been reduced.

   _____

   _____

2. It was our travel agent who recommended that we go through the process of changing our plans and visit Spain in addition to the rest of our travel itinerary.

   _____

   _____

3. There is a tendency for teenagers and their mothers and fathers to be in conflict about their curfews.

   _____

   _____

4. It is my understanding that students and faculty members are not in agreement about the scheduling of final exams.

   _____

   _____

5. At this point in time, my initial trip to Europe is fondly remembered by me.

   _____

   _____

PRACTICE MAKES PERFECT

Now that you know the basic principles of effective delivery, the next step is to practice your speech. The following tips will help you rehearse effectively:

- Begin practicing several days before your presentation.
- Choose a location to practice that is private, quiet, and free from distractions (e.g., an empty classroom or your bedroom).
- Allow yourself enough time to rehearse your speech from start to finish.
- Practice your speech in front of a full-length mirror. Monitor your eye contact and body language.
- Tape-record or videotape yourself while practicing. When you listen to the recording, check for errors in content and delivery. Write down any corrections and work on improving your speech the next time you practice.
- Practice your speech in front of a few friends or family members. Pretend that you are actually delivering your speech in front of your classmates. Ask your "audience" to comment on various aspects of your delivery.

Intonation refers to the use of melody and the rise and fall of the voice when speaking. It can determine grammatical meaning as well as the speaker's attitude. Correct use of intonation will convey your message effectively and help you sound like a native English speaker.

Intonation should **fall** (↘) at the end of declarative statements or information questions.

Examples

I like school. ↘
She is kind. ↘
Where is it? ↘
Why should I do it? ↘

Intonation should **rise** (↗) on the last stressed syllable of statements expressing doubt or *yes/no* questions.

Examples

I got an A? ↗
You ate twenty-five hot dogs? ↗
Will he stay? ↗
Did it rain? ↗

EXERCISE 1

Read each of the following statements twice. First use falling intonation, and then use rising intonation. Notice how the falling intonation makes you sound certain, while rising intonation makes you sound uncertain.

Stated with Certainty ↘	Stated with Doubt ↗
1. You ran fifty-five miles.	You ran fifty-five miles?
2. He drank eight gallons of wine.	He drank eight gallons of wine?
3. She lifted 500 pounds.	She lifted 500 pounds?
4. They have twenty children.	They have twenty children?

EXERCISE 2

With a partner, practice reading the following *yes/no* questions and responses aloud. Be sure your intonation rises at the end of each question and falls at the end of each response.

Questions ↗	Responses ↘
1. Can you see?	Yes, I can.
2. Are we leaving?	No, we're staying.
3. May I help you?	Yes, please do.
4. Is Sue your sister?	No, she's my friend.
5. Did he arrive?	Yes, he's here now.

Read the following statements and questions aloud. Next to each sentence, draw an upward arrow if rising intonation is used and a downward arrow if falling intonation is used.

Example

Can you sing? ____↗

1. I feel fine. _____
2. When's your birthday? _____
3. Did you see my friend? _____
4. Why did Tom leave? _____
5. We like to travel. _____

CHAPTER 3

Putting Your Speech Together

"Where do I begin?" is a question students often ask when faced with the task of writing a speech. This chapter will help you organize and outline your thoughts and your information so that you can deliver your speech logically and clearly.

Every speech needs a topic and a purpose. Before you can begin gathering and organizing information for your speech, select a topic and clearly define your purpose. For example, your purpose might be to inform people about an unfamiliar topic or to persuade them to change their opinion about an issue. Chapters 4 and 7 will help you to choose a topic and define your specific purpose.

PREPARING THE SPEECH

Every speech has three parts: the introduction, the body, and the conclusion. Which part of a speech do you think you prepare first? Write the numbers 1, 2, and 3 to indicate which part of your speech you should prepare first, second, and third.

_____ Introduction
_____ Body
_____ Conclusion

The correct answers may surprise you. They are 3, 1, 2. First, you should write the body of your speech. Then, you should write the conclusion. Finally, you should write the introduction.

Step 1: Prepare the Body

The body of a speech contains three or four sections related to the topic. It includes an outline of the major ideas, and it also has information that supports and clarifies those ideas.

To prepare the body, first list subtopics that you might include in your speech. Write them as you think of them. Some ideas will be important, and some will not. At this time, just concentrate on writing all the ideas you can think of that relate to the topic and purpose of your speech.

Example A: Speech entitled "Having a Happy Marriage"

- Choose the best honeymoon vacation.
- Discuss important financial matters together.
- Be courteous to each other.
- Learn to compromise.
- Bring up your children well.
- Respect your spouse's property.
- Buy a nice home together.

Example B: Speech entitled "Applying for a Job"

- Choose an appropriate wardrobe.
- Behave appropriately during the personal interview.
- Write a résumé.
- Find the desired position.
- Schedule appointments.
- Get a flexible work schedule.
- Learn new skills.

Second, narrow your list of subtopics. Review your list and select the three or four subtopics that will best develop your speech in the time allowed. These subtopics will become the main headings of your speech.

Example A: "Having a Happy Marriage"

- ~~Choose the best honeymoon vacation.~~
- Discuss important financial matters together.
- Be courteous to each other.
- Learn to compromise.
- ~~Bring up your children well.~~
- Respect your spouse's property.
- ~~Buy a nice home together.~~

Example B: "Applying for a Job"

- ~~Choose an appropriate wardrobe.~~
- Behave appropriately during the personal interview.
- Write a résumé.
- Find the desired position.
- Schedule appointments.
- ~~Get a flexible work schedule.~~
- ~~Learn new skills.~~

Third, order your subtopics logically so that one leads naturally into the next one.

Example A: "Having a Happy Marriage"

    I. Respect your spouse's property.

   II. Be courteous to each other.

  III. Discuss important financial matters together.

  IV. Learn to compromise.

Example B: "Applying for a Job"

    I. Find the desired position.

   II. Write a résumé.

  III. Schedule appointments.

  IV. Behave appropriately during the personal interview.

(Detailed explanations about different ways to organize your speech are presented in Chapter 4: Speaking to Inform.)

Fourth, develop your subtopics with factual information, logical proof, and visual aids. If your subtopics are supported and well organized, your sections will be interesting and your listeners will better understand and remember your speech.

The sections entitled "Gathering Information" in Chapters 4 and 7 give specific information about how to develop your subtopics by using your own knowledge, your own experience, concrete examples, quotes from experts, visual aids, and information from books, newspapers, magazines, and the Internet. The section entitled "Outlining Your Speech" on pages 47–48 of this chapter shows how to organize and outline this information.

Step 2: Prepare the Conclusion

The conclusion includes:

- a summary of the main points
- final remarks to end the speech gracefully

A good summary:

- briefly reviews your purpose
- repeats or restates the main ideas

Memorable concluding remarks:

- are delivered after the summary of main points
- leave your audience thinking about what you've said

Example: "Having a Happy Marriage"

   I. Now you know four factors that are important in order to have a happy marriage.

     A. Respect your spouse's property.

     B. Be courteous to each other.

     C. Discuss important financial matters together.

     D. Learn to compromise.

  II. So be sure to follow these four guidelines for a long and happy marriage. And please don't forget to invite me to your fiftieth wedding anniversary!

(The sections entitled "Prepare a Summary" and "Prepare Memorable Concluding Remarks" in Chapter 4 provide many examples of ways to effectively conclude speeches.)

Step 3: Prepare the Introduction

Your introduction should have:

- an attention-getting opener (or "hook")
- a preview of the body

A good introduction:

- captures the listeners' attention immediately
- makes them interested in the rest of the speech
- alerts them to what they can expect to hear in the presentation
- helps them to follow the information easily

Powerful ways to begin your speech include:

- telling a brief story
- asking a question to arouse curiosity
- shocking your audience with a startling quote or fact

After you have delivered your introduction, tell your listeners the main points of your speech by briefly previewing its main sections.

Example A: "Applying for a Job"

   I. What I'm about to tell you could change your life. If you listen carefully to what I have to say, you'll be able to land the job of your dreams.

  II. I'm going to discuss four important aspects to consider when applying for a job.

     A. Find the desired position.

     B. Write a successful résumé.

     C. Schedule appointments.

     D. Behave appropriately during the personal interview.

Example B: "Electronic Espionage in Business and Industry"

    I. In my hand I have the prototype of a new computer-enhanced electronic microphone that is so sensitive it can pick up the sound of a fly walking across a pane of glass a block away. Sounds incredible, right? But it's true!

    II. My presentation will cover three aspects of electronic espionage in business and industry.

        A. Different types of devices used in electronic espionage

        B. Ethical implications of using electronic espionage

        C. Advantages of using such technology in business and industry

(The sections entitled "Prepare a Preview" and "Prepare an Attention-Getting Opener" in Chapter 4 provide additional information about preparing introductions.)

OUTLINES

With a good outline, you'll never have to worry about forgetting what you want to say. Outlines:

- make it easy for you to deliver your speech,
- assure you that you have organized your ideas,
- help you remember all your information.

Even when you're not giving a speech, an outline can make your life easier. For example, if you have several errands to do after class, you could organize them as follows:

Example

    I. Post office

    II. Grocery store

    III. Gas station

    IV. Bank

When one item doesn't depend on another, any random order of organization is fine. However, suppose your car's gas gauge reads "empty" and you don't have any money to pay for gas. You would have to change your organizational pattern. Your new outline would look like this:

Example

    I. Bank

    II. Gas station

    III. Post office

    IV. Grocery store

You may have a lot on your mind. As a result, you may forget what you want to do at each of the places you need to go to. No problem! Add specific details to each point of your outline:

Example

    I. Bank
        A. Cash check from Uncle Mario
        B. Deposit paycheck into savings account
        C. Pay fine for bouncing check
    II. Gas station
        A. Fill up tank
        B. Check water in battery
        C. Check oil level
        D. Put air in tires

As you can see, the key to outlining is to identify subtopics and add specific details. With such an outline, you will never arrive home having forgotten something you had to do. Do this for your speeches and you will never again have the worry, "What if I forget what I was going to say?"

OUTLINING YOUR SPEECH

Now that you have gathered enough information to prepare the introduction, body, and conclusion of your speech, you are ready to reorganize it and outline it. A good outline meets four basic requirements:

- Each supporting point relates to the main point.
- Each supporting point contains only one idea.
- Supporting points are not repeated or restated.
- Each supporting parallel point has an equal level of importance.

Each Supporting Point Relates to the Main Point

Which supporting idea in the example below does not belong? Why not?

    I. Alcoholism is an international problem.
        A. Russia has a high alcoholism rate.
        B. France has the highest alcoholism rate in Europe.
        C. Alcoholics have more car accidents than nondrinkers.
        D. Japan has a severe juvenile alcoholism problem.

The answer is C. Although it is an interesting fact, it is not directly related to the main point—I. Alcoholism is an international problem.

Each Supporting Point Contains Only One Idea

What is wrong with the example below?

    I. Small cars are better than large cars.
        A. They are less expensive and easier to park.
        B. They get better gas mileage.

Point A contains two separate ideas. The information should be outlined as follows:

    I. Small cars are better than large cars.
        A. They are less expensive.
        B. They are easier to park.
        C. They get better gas mileage.

Supporting Points Are Not Repeated or Restated

What is wrong with the example below?

    I. Students dislike the school cafeteria.
        A. There is very little to choose from.
        B. The food is too expensive.
        C. The menu is extremely limited.

Points A and C repeat the same idea. The example below contains three supporting points that express different ideas.

    I. Students dislike the school cafeteria.
        A. There is very little to choose from.
        B. The food is too expensive.
        C. The eating utensils are always dirty.

Each Supporting Parallel Point Has an Equal Level of Importance

What is wrong with the example below?

    I. Sales in South America have fallen drastically.
        A. Colombia
        B. Lima
        C. Ecuador

Points A and C are countries. Point B is a city. The points should be all cities or all countries. The information should be outlined as follows:

    I. Sales in South America have fallen drastically.
        A. Colombia
        B. Peru
        C. Ecuador

RECOGNIZE WHAT MAKES A GOOD OUTLINE

Choose the best description of each of the outlines by labeling them as follows:

    a. incorrect: Each supporting point does not relate to the main point.

    b. incorrect: Each supporting point does not contain only one idea.

    c. incorrect: Supporting points are repeated or restated.

    d. incorrect: Each supporting parallel point does not have an equal level of importance.

    ✓ correct

(Answers can be found on page 271 of Appendix II.)

Example

      b   **I.** Polyester is better than cotton.
- **A.** It is less expensive and easier to wash.
- **B.** It lasts longer.
- **C.** It requires less ironing.
    (A. contains more than one idea.)

1. _____ **I.** Tourists buy many products in the United States.
- **A.** They buy camera equipment.
- **B.** They buy toasters.
- **C.** They purchase kitchen appliances.
- **D.** They purchase designer clothing.

2. _____ **I.** There are many advantages to freeze-drying.
- **A.** Foods keep their nutritional value almost indefinitely.
- **B.** Freeze-dried foods don't require refrigeration.
- **C.** It's a relatively new technology.
- **D.** Freeze-dried foods maintain their flavor longer than regular frozen foods.

3. _____ **I.** There are many good ways to invest your money.
- **A.** Stocks
- **B.** Mutual funds
- **C.** Real estate
- **D.** Corporate bonds

4. _____ **I.** The bank offers a variety of accounts.
- **A.** Certificates of deposit
- **B.** Checking and money-market savings accounts
- **C.** Retirement accounts

5. _____ **I.** Attending college is very expensive.
- **A.** Tuition fees are quite high.
- **B.** It costs a fortune to go to college today.
- **C.** Textbooks are extremely expensive.

6. _____ **I.** Juvenile delinquency is a nationwide problem.
   - **A.** The Northeast
   - **B.** New York
   - **C.** The Southwest
   - **D.** The Midwest

7. _____ **I.** Cats make wonderful pets.
   - **A.** They are easy to care for.
   - **B.** They were worshipped in ancient Egypt.
   - **C.** Cats provide excellent companionship.

8. _____ **I.** Reasons for students' parking problems on campus
   - **A.** There are too many students with cars.
   - **B.** Many outsiders illegally park in the lots.
   - **C.** Students could take the bus to campus.

9. _____ **I.** Gambling takes many forms.
   - **A.** Casino gambling
   - **B.** Horse racing
   - **C.** Lotteries

10. _____ **I.** Ways to fight inflation
   - **A.** Buy things on sale.
   - **B.** Comparison-shop for the best prices.
   - **C.** The annual inflation rate is approximately five percent.

EXERCISE 2   **CREATE SUPPORTING POINTS FOR A MAIN POINT**

1. **Work in pairs.**
2. **Using the same format as the ten items in the exercise above, create three of your own examples on any topics you choose. (Use the blank forms below.)**
3. **Write your examples on the board. Test your classmates on their ability to determine what, if anything, is wrong with them.**

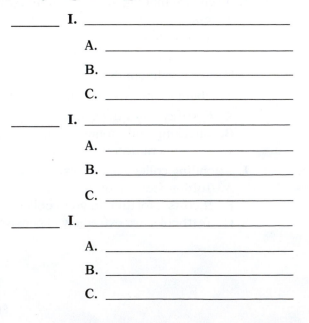

_____ **I.** _____

   A. _____

   B. _____

   C. _____

_____ **I.** _____

   A. _____

   B. _____

   C. _____

_____ **I.** _____

   A. _____

   B. _____

   C. _____

REWRITE SUPPORTING POINTS

What is wrong with the outlines below? Rewrite each one so that it meets the four basic requirements of a good outline. (Answers can be found on page 271 of Appendix II.)

- Each supporting point relates to the main point.
- Each supporting point contains only one idea.
- Supporting points are not repeated or restated.
- Each supporting parallel point has an equal level of importance.

1. **I.** Since it lasts longer and costs less, polyester is better than silk; in addition, it is easier to care for.
   - **A.** It may be washed twice as many times before wearing out, and its color doesn't fade as quickly.
   - **B.** It doesn't have to be dry-cleaned, and ironing is unnecessary.

2. **I.** The United States exports products to countries on several continents. These include South America, Brazil, Argentina, and Asia.
   - **A.** Other places receiving U.S. exports are Japan, China, and Colombia.
   - **B.** Europe, Spain, France, and Germany receive U.S. exports.

WRITE AN OUTLINE

The following paragraphs represent the first major section (I) of the body of a speech.

1. **Read the speech.**
2. **Outline the information in the speech by filling in the blanks of the skeleton provided below. Two outline units are already provided for you.**

(Answers can be found on page 272 of Appendix II.)

There are many things to do on a visit to Mexico City, including going shopping and visiting interesting places. You will enjoy visits to Chapultepec Park, the Aztec pyramids in Teotihuacán, the world renowned Museum of Anthropology, and the Palace of Fine Arts, where you can see art exhibitions and the Ballet Gran Folklórico de México.

You can shop for native crafts such as colorful embroidered blouses, handwoven rugs, and handmade pottery.

You can also shop for items of onyx such as ashtrays, vases, and bookends. Silver lovers can buy beautiful sterling silver pieces such as serving trays, picture frames, and key chains. They can also buy lots of silver jewelry including bracelets, necklaces, and rings.

I. _____

    A. <u>Visit interesting places</u>

        1. _____

        2. _____

        3. _____

        4. _____

           a. _____

           b. _____

    B. _____

        1. <u>Native crafts</u>

           a. _____

           b. _____

           c. _____

        2. _____

           a. _____

           b. _____

           c. _____

        3. _____

           a. _____

           b. _____

           c. _____

           d. _____

              i. _____

              ii. _____

              iii. _____

Transitions make it easy for your listeners to follow your plan for your speech. They remind your audience where you've been and say where you're going.

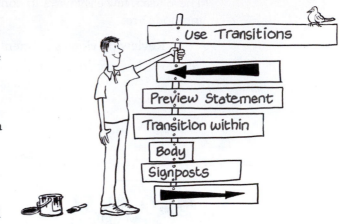

Think of transitions in a speech as "signposts" along a highway as you travel from one city to another. For example, let's say that you and a friend are en route from Miami to Disney World in Orlando. After driving for an hour, you see a sign that says "Welcome to Ft. Lauderdale." Shortly after that you see another sign that says "Orlando, 200 Miles." You know where you've been and how far you are from your destination. The signposts reassure you that you are on the right road, and they help you to stay on track.

Just as signposts on a highway are important, so are transitions in a speech. Transitions tell your audience that something new or important is about to happen in your speech.

TRANSITION AFTER THE INTRODUCTION

Every speech needs a transition after the introduction. This transition should signal that the main part of the speech is about to begin. For example, look at the outline for "A Fabulous Fantasia Cruise" on pages 56–58. After the introduction, the following transition signals the first section of the body:

First, you'll be pleased to learn about the comfortable cabins that will be your rooms for the week.

TRANSITIONS WITHIN THE BODY

Transitions are also needed between each section of the body. This kind of transition generally consists of two separate sentences that provide two important functions:

- to review the information just presented
- to preview the next section

USING TRANSITIONS

There are a few easy ways to construct transitions. The two most common methods are:

- Review previous statement; then preview the next statement.
- Review previous statement; then ask a rhetorical question.

1. Review Statement; Then Preview Statement

Example A

REVIEW

1. Analyze the Audience

"I have talked about how to analyze the audience."

PREVIEW

2. Choose a Topic

"Next, I will talk about how to choose a topic."

Example B

REVIEW

3. Gather Information

"We have seen all the places you can search for information about your topic."

PREVIEW

4. Prepare Visual Aids

"Now let's look at preparing visual aids."

2. Review Statement; Then Ask a Rhetorical Question

Example A

REVIEW	QUESTION
1. Analyze the Audience	2. Choose a Topic
"I have talked about how to analyze the audience."	"Now, how do you choose a great topic?"

Example B

REVIEW	QUESTION
3. Gather Information	4. Prepare Visual Aids
"We have seen all the places you can search for information about your topic."	"Next, how can you prepare effective visual aids?"

Now take a look at the outline for "A Fabulous Fantasia Cruise" on pages 56–58. After talking about guest accommodations, the following transition is used before talking about the ship's facilities:

Now you can see how comfortable you'll be while in your cabin. However, the ship has many facilities for you to enjoy when you leave your cabin.

After talking about the ship's facilities, this next transition is used before discussing ports of call:

As you can see, the ship has many facilities for you to enjoy while onboard. You will need to get off the ship in order to visit the four exciting ports of call.

After discussing ports of call, the following transition is used before introducing shore-visit activities:

You now know which exotic places you'll be visiting. You will have a choice of many fun things to do while on shore.

Finally, after talking about shore-visit activities, the transition below is used before discussing shipboard activities:

We hope the shore-visit activities won't tire you out too much. You'll need your energy, because once you're back on the ship, many other activities await you!

TRANSITION BEFORE THE CONCLUSION

Every speech needs a transition before the conclusion. This last transition acts as a signal that the speech is about to end. For example, look at the outline for "A Fabulous Fantasia Cruise" that begins below. The last section is about shipboard activities. The following transition links the body and the conclusion:

With all these great onboard activities, you might not even want to leave the ship at all!

EXERCISE 1   ### COMPLETE THE OUTLINE

The partial outline below includes the introduction and conclusion of a speech entitled "A Fabulous Fantasia Cruise." Some of the headings and supporting ideas have already been filled in. Use the list of Missing Headings and Supporting Ideas on page 58 to complete the outline. (Answers can be found on pages 272–274 of Appendix II.)

INTRODUCTION

I. Are you wondering what to do for your next vacation? I have the perfect solution for all of you. Why not take a cruise?

II. I'm going to tell you about five highlights you can expect on a fabulous Fantasia Cruise.

    A. Luxurious guest accommodations

    B. Excellent shipboard facilities

    C. Exotic ports of call

    D. Interesting shore-visit activities

    E. Fun shipboard activities

TRANSITION: *First, you'll be pleased to learn about the comfortable cabins that will be your rooms for the week.*

BODY

I. _____

    A. Fully air-conditioned cabins

    B. _____

    C. _____

    D. _____

TRANSITION: *Now you can see how comfortable you'll be while in your cabin. However, the ship has many facilities for you to enjoy when you leave your cabin.*

II. Ship's facilities

   A. _____

   B. Swinging dance club open all night

   C. _____

   D. _____

TRANSITION: *As you can see, the ship has many facilities for you to enjoy while onboard. You will need to get off the ship in order to visit the four exciting ports of call.*

III. _____

   A. _____

   B. _____

   C. _____

   D. Cozumel, Mexico

TRANSITION: *You now know which exotic places you'll be visiting. You will have a choice of many fun things to do while on shore.*

IV. Shore-visit activities

   A. _____

   B. Activities for sports lovers

      1. _____

         a. Waterskiing

         b. _____

         c. _____

      2. Land sports

         a. _____

         b. _____

   C. _____

TRANSITION: *We hope the shore-visit activities won't tire you out too much. You'll need your energy, because once you're back on the ship, many other activities await you!*

V. _____

    A. Afternoon and evening bingo in captain's lounge

    B. _____

    C. Competitive games

        1. _____

        2. _____

    D. _____

    E. _____

TRANSITION: *With all these great onboard activities, you might not even want to leave the ship at all!*

CONCLUSION

  I. I'm sure you will now agree that a Fantasia Cruise would be the perfect vacation.

    A. The guest accommodations are second to none.

    B. The ship has wonderful facilities for you to enjoy.

    C. You'll visit four unforgettable places.

    D. There are many shore-visit activities.

    E. There are many things for you to do while aboard the ship.

 II. Your dream vacation awaits you. Make your reservation soon and cruise to paradise with Fantasia!

Missing headings and supporting ideas

Casino open twenty-four hours a day	Porthole in every cabin
Olympic-size swimming pool	Guided tours of each port
King-size bed in every cabin	Port-au-Prince, Haiti
Color TV in every cabin	Three elegant restaurants
Shipboard activities	Visits to four exotic places
Water sports	Sailing
Nightly shows in ship's nightclub	Ping-Pong tournaments
Puerto Plata, Dominican Republic	Costume party
Poolside shuffleboard tournaments	Hiking
Georgetown, Grand Cayman	Passenger talent show
Horseback riding	Shopping for native crafts
Fishing	Guest accommodations

EXERCISE 2   PREPARE AN INTRODUCTION, A CONCLUSION, AND TRANSITIONS

Choose one of the speech outlines from "Recognize What Makes a Good Outline" on pages 49–50 (be sure to correct it), or create your own outline for a hypothetical speech. Then prepare the following sections and transitions.

1. an introduction
2. a conclusion
3. a transition between the introduction and the body
4. a transition between the body and the conclusion
5. transitions between each section of the body

Example (based on #3)

INTRODUCTION

I. Do you have extra cash that you don't know what to do with? Is your money burning a hole in your pocket? Don't just spend it on more things you don't need. Invest it and watch it grow!

II. There are many good ways to invest your money.
   A. Stocks
   B. Mutual funds
   C. Real estate
   D. Corporate bonds

TRANSITION 1: *If you have a tolerance for some risk, you might want to consider investing money in the stock market.*

BODY

I. Stocks

TRANSITION 2: *Buying and selling stocks is only one way to invest your money. You might consider purchasing mutual funds.*

II. Mutual Funds

TRANSITION 3: *Now you know about some of the different types of mutual funds. You might also consider investing in real estate.*

III. Real Estate

TRANSITION 4: *As you can see, real estate has excellent potential for appreciation. If you are more conservative, you might like to invest in corporate bonds.*

IV. Corporate Bonds

TRANSITION TO CONCLUSION: *You could always divide your funds between corporate bonds and one of the other types of investments.*

CONCLUSION

I. As you can see, there are a variety of investments you could make.
   A. Stocks
   B. Mutual funds
   C. Real estate
   D. Corporate bonds

II. Start investing today. If you choose your investments carefully, you could be a millionaire by the time you retire!

EXERCISE 1

The ending *-ed* always sounds like [t] when the last sound in the present tense verb is voiceless. The sounds [p], [k], [f], [s], [ʃ](as in *wash*), and [tʃ] (as in *watch*) are voiceless.

Examples: talk**ed**   cross**ed**   laugh**ed**

Read the following words and sentences aloud. Be sure to pronounce the *-ed* in the past tense verb like [t].

1. look**ed**
2. miss**ed**
3. stopp**ed**
4. work**ed**
5. pick**ed**
6. wish**ed**
7. Mom bak**ed** a pie.
8. He finish**ed** early.
9. Tara stopp**ed** singing.

EXERCISE 2

The ending *-ed* always sounds like [d] when the last sound in the present tense verb is voiced. All vowels and the consonant sounds [b], [g], [v], [m], [n], [l], [r], and [ð](as in *breathe*) are voiced.

Examples: liv**ed**   turn**ed**   play**ed**

Read the following words and sentences aloud. Be sure to pronounce the *-ed* in the past tense verb like [d].

1. lov**ed**
2. stay**ed**
3. fill**ed**
4. burn**ed**
5. fibb**ed**
6. cri**ed**
7. We play**ed** a game.
8. He mov**ed** again.
9. I mail**ed** a letter.

EXERCISE 3

The ending *-ed* always sounds like the new syllable [Id] when the last sound in the present tense verb is [t] or [d].

Examples: want**ed**   rest**ed**   end**ed**

Read the following words and sentences aloud. Be sure to pronounce the *-ed* in the past verb like [Id].

1. end**ed**
2. add**ed**
3. hunt**ed**
4. want**ed**
5. need**ed**
6. paint**ed**
7. I rest**ed** at home.
8. The car start**ed**.
9. He avoid**ed** his boss.

CHAPTER 4

Speaking to Inform

Informative speaking is all around us. Any speech is an informative speech if it presents information to an audience. A report, a teacher's explanation, and a talk at a group meeting are all examples of informative speeches.

When do we make informative speeches? We make them all the time. Whenever we give a stranger directions, explain a problem to a mechanic, or describe an illness to a doctor, we are speaking to inform.

The goal in giving an informative speech is to state ideas simply, clearly, and interestingly. If you achieve this goal, the audience will understand and remember your speech. In this chapter, you will learn how to build an informative speech.

PREPARING FOR THE INFORMATIVE SPEECH

You build an informative speech the way you build a house. For both constructions, you first need a blueprint, a vision of what you want to build. The steps for preparing an informative speech are:

1. Analyzing your audience
2. Choosing your topic

3. Narrowing your topic
4. Gathering information
5. Preparing visual aids
6. Organizing your speech

If you follow these steps, or this blueprint, you will create an informative speech that is well organized, interesting, and memorable.

1. ANALYZING YOUR AUDIENCE

Start preparing for your informative speech by getting as much information about your audience as you can. This information will help you prepare a speech that is relevant and interesting to your listeners. What do you need to know about your audience in order to be able to do this?

Age Range

What is the age range of your audience? What topics would interest them? If they are young, an appropriate speech topic might be choosing a career. However, if they are middle-aged, a good topic might be planning for retirement.

Gender

What is the gender of your audience? If there are both men and women, choose a topic that is interesting to both. On the other hand, if there are only men or only women, you can choose a topic of specific interest to that group.

Occupation(s)

Is your audience made up of college students who don't work? Or do most of your classmates have jobs? If they have jobs, where do they work? What do they do? If members of your audience have occupations in common, you could build your speech on this shared background.

Economic Level(s)

What is the financial position of your audience? You would not, for example, try to inform the average college student about how to negotiate the purchase of a luxury yacht. However, it might be a great topic for a group of wealthy retirees.

General Background

What are the general backgrounds, attitudes, and religious beliefs of your audience? It would not be appropriate, for example, to talk to vegetarians about the best steak restaurants in Buenos Aires. Similarly, people who are against smoking would probably not be interested in a speech about different types of cigars. Other questions should also be considered in order to choose a topic that is of interest to everyone.

- Are your listeners married?
- Do they have children?
- What are their racial and ethnic backgrounds?

It is also important to avoid statements that may offend people in your audience. For example, senior citizens might not like to be called "the elderly," and women may object to being called "girls." To be on the safe side, avoid biased generalizations based on sex, occupation, economic level, or general background.

ACTIVITY

SURVEY YOUR CLASSMATES

Your classmates will be your audience for most speeches. You should have a good idea about the makeup of your class. They already shared autobiographical information in the self-introduction speeches presented earlier.

1. Your teacher might ask you to complete the following Personal Information Survey anonymously. He or she will compile the results and share them with the class. The information will help you analyze your audience.

Personal Information Survey

1. How old are you?

_____

2. Where were you born?

_____

3. How long have you lived here?

_____

4. Where else have you lived?

_____

5. What languages do you speak?

_____

6. What countries have you visited?

_____

7. What are you majoring in?

_____

8. If you have a job, what do you do?

_____

9. What is your marital status?

_____

10. Do you have any children? How many? How old are they?

_____

_____

11. What are your special interests or hobbies?

_____

_____

---

2. **Use the form below to record information about your classmates. This will help you prepare your future speeches.**

ANALYSIS OF AUDIENCE	
Age Range	
Gender	
Occupation(s)	
Economic Level(s)	
General Background	

2. CHOOSING YOUR TOPIC

2. Choose a Topic

When asked to choose a topic, your first question might be "What should I talk about?" A quick and easy way to find a good topic is to choose something that you know a lot about or that really interests you. For example:

An Experience You Remember Vividly

Example

A student who had gone for a hot-air balloon ride while on vacation in Australia spoke enthusiastically about hot-air balloons.

Something You Care a Lot About

Example

A student who had come to the United States from Poland at the age of eighteen gave an excellent speech about problems facing immigrants in a new country.

Something at Which You Are Skilled or Experienced

Example

Having worked for her father, a businessman who bought and sold emeralds in Colombia, a student gave a terrific speech about emeralds.

Something About Which You Are Knowledgeable

Example

A student who had been collecting stamps since he was nine years old made an excellent speech about the history of the postage stamp.

The informative speeches described above were particularly good because the students chose topics they were really interested in and that they already knew something about. Think about your special interests, hobbies, or personal experiences, and you will have no trouble choosing a topic.

3. NARROWING YOUR TOPIC

3. Narrow the Topic

The next step is to narrow your topic. If you picked a topic that you know a lot about, you probably know more about it than your audience. Although being knowledgeable is important, be careful not to tell everything you know about your topic. Doing so is a bad idea for two reasons:

1. It is impossible to say everything there is to say about a topic in a short amount of time. For example, if you have five minutes to talk about soccer, it is impossible to say everything about soccer in five minutes. You would only be able to discuss broad generalizations about the sport. You would have to limit your talk to something like:
   - the history of soccer or
   - the basic rules of soccer or
   - the worldwide popularity of soccer

2. Your audience cannot remember too many details after one five-minute speech. Limit your topic so that your audience can understand and remember it. For example, if your topic is Mexico City and you try to cover its history, climate, geography, social and political problems, restaurants, and museums in five minutes, your audience will never remember it all. However, they will remember more if you limit your topic to:

- shopping in Mexico City or
- popular tourist attractions or
- the Aztec influence in Mexico City or
- famous museums in Mexico City

How do you narrow an informative speech topic effectively? It may help to remember that a good informative speech topic:

- is specific
- contains only one idea
- is achievable

Is Your Topic Specific?

Limit your topic to one particular aspect of the topic. For example, the topic "hurricanes" is too general, but the topics "preparing for hurricanes" and "dangerous effects of hurricanes" are specific.

Does Your Topic Contain Only One Idea?

Make sure your topic has just one idea. For example, the topic "choosing a hotel and buying a car in a foreign country" has two ideas, but the topics "choosing a hotel in a foreign country" and "buying a car in a foreign country" each contain one idea.

Is Your Topic Achievable?

Make sure the audience is actually able to do, understand, or remember something after your speech is over.

Example A

If you give a "how to" speech, like "how to weave an Oriental rug," your audience will not be able to weave an Oriental rug after hearing your speech. Such a complicated task is not achievable after a brief speech. However, the topic "how to buy an Oriental rug" is achievable since your audience would be able to use this information if they ever went shopping for an Oriental carpet.

Example B

After hearing a speech about building a personal computer, most people would not be able to build a personal computer. However, after hearing a speech about the use of computers in education, they would be able to remember valuable information about the topic.

ACTIVITY

EVALUATE THESE TOPICS

1. **Indicate whether each of the topics is appropriate by labeling it as follows:**

   a too general

   b contains more than one idea

   c not achievable in a brief speech

   ✓ good topic

(Answers can be found on page 277 of Appendix II.)

Examples

    _a_   South America

    _c_   How to Become a Concert Pianist

    _✓_   The Significance of Dreams

    1. Electronic Watches and Calculators

    2. How to Buy a Used Car

    3. Musical Instruments

    4. Writing a Résumé

    5. Child Abuse

    6. How to Fly an Airplane

    7. Applying for a Bank Loan

    8. Ecuador

    9. Birds

    10. Snakes

    11. Choosing and Caring for a Parrot

    12. Basic Techniques of Dog Training

    13. Life-Saving Uses of Snake Venom

    14. The History of Hawaii and Alaska

    15. The Best Way to Lose Weight

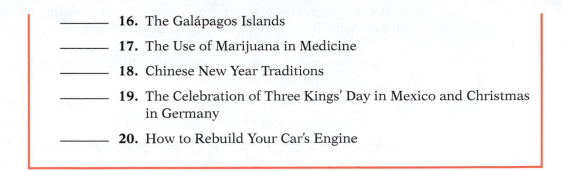

16. The Galápagos Islands

17. The Use of Marijuana in Medicine

18. Chinese New Year Traditions

19. The Celebration of Three Kings' Day in Mexico and Christmas in Germany

20. How to Rebuild Your Car's Engine

2. Now discuss your answers with your classmates and teacher.

4. GATHERING INFORMATION

4. Gather Information

Now that you have

- analyzed your audience
- chosen your topic
- and narrowed it

you need to gather information so you can prepare the actual speech. There are two places to look for material for your speech:

- Within yourself: Write down what you already know about the topic.
- Outside yourself: Interview people who know something about your topic, or do research in the library or on the Internet.

Find more information about your topic than you can use. You will then be able to choose which information to include in your speech instead of having to "stretch" your facts to fill time when you don't have enough. This extra knowledge may also be helpful if you are asked to answer questions after your presentation.

Interviews

Consult people who know something about your topic. In every college or university and in every community, experts who can help you are available. Your peers, teachers, or other people you know may also have specialized knowledge about your topic. You may decide to interview some of these people.

Before you interview anyone, decide what questions you will ask and how you will ask them. There are five basic types of questions that you can use:

1. **Open-ended questions (or general information questions requiring the respondent to elaborate):**
   - *How do you feel about the recent scandal in our city government?*
   - *What do you think about this new "foolproof diet" on the market?*

2. **Closed-ended questions (or *yes/no* questions):**
   - *Do you think the new city manager should be removed from office just because she has been indicted on corruption charges?*
   - *Have you ever been on a diet that didn't work?*

3. **Scale questions:**

   How would you rate our city government?

   Poor   Fair   Average   Good   Excellent

4. **Directive questions (specific information questions):**
   - *Could you give me two reasons why people fail on most diets?*
   - *Who is the mayor of New York City?*

5. **Multiple-choice questions:**

   How many diets do most people try in a lifetime?

   ___*None*   ___*Two to five*   ___*Eleven to twenty*

   ___*One*   ___*Six to ten*   ___*Over twenty*

Library Research

College and university libraries are great places to find books, magazines, newspaper articles, and journals about your topic. The *Readers' Guide to Periodical Literature* can refer you to relevant magazine articles. Indexes for major newspapers (e.g., *The New York Times Index*) can lead you to pertinent newspaper articles. And journals published by professional organizations (e.g., the *AMA Journal*, published by the American Medical Association) often have more specific information. Dictionaries and encyclopedias give general information about most subjects and can be useful for defining terms and concepts. Encyclopedic dictionaries may include idiomatic expressions and famous quotations that you can use in your speech as well.

Books are cited alphabetically by author, by title, and by subject. You can use the computer terminals in the library to find where books are located. If you can't find what you're looking for, ask the reference librarian. He or she is there to help.

It's helpful to record every piece of information, fact, or quotation you find on a separate 4" × 6" note card. Be sure to write down the important bibliographical information about your source. This includes:

- the author's name
- the author's credentials
- the title of the book / the name of the magazine or newspaper and article

That way, you have all the information you need at your fingertips to cite your sources aloud during your speech. Listeners are often skeptical; they like to know the source of a speaker's information as well as the qualifications of the source. You establish your own credibility as a speaker when you tell your audience where you found your information.

Let's say you were preparing a speech about identity theft. You did your research and found many good sources of information. One of your bibliography cards might look like this:

Book Title:	Identity Theft
Author:	John R. Vacca
Credentials:	Security consultant and computer security official for NASA and the International Space Station Program; internationally known author of 30 books and 400 articles in area of Internet security.
Publisher:	Pearson Education, Inc. 2003
Quote:	"Identity theft is the appropriation of an individual's personal information to impersonate that person in a legal sense."

During the presentation of your speech, you should cite this source. Be sure to mention the book title, author's name, publisher, and date. Here is a source citation from a student's speech about identity theft.

Some of you might be wondering, "What exactly is identity theft?" Internationally known author and security consultant John R. Vacca defines this crime in his book entitled Identity Theft, *published by Pearson Education in 2003. He states, "Identity theft is the appropriation of an individual's personal information to impersonate that person in a legal sense."*

By citing your sources of information during your presentation, you give credit to those whose ideas you are using. You also establish your own reputation as an ethical speaker and a responsible researcher.

TIP: Arrange a set of your bibliography note cards in alphabetical order.

- After your speech, a listener may ask for more information about one or more of your sources.
- You can look through your note cards and quickly find information about your source's credentials.
- You will impress your audience by showing that you cited highly qualified and credible sources of information.

Internet Research

The Internet is a great source of current information about most topics. Please refer to Chapter 6, Using the Internet, to help you gather information for your speeches.

5. PREPARING VISUAL AIDS

Why use visual aids? The answer is that visual aids—objects, models, pictures, charts, diagrams, and even physical demonstrations—help make a speech clear and interesting. They add variety, capture attention, illustrate concepts, and provide entertainment. Visual aids help your audience to actually see and experience what you are talking about.

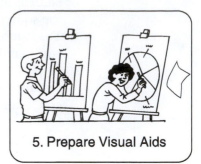

5. Prepare Visual Aids

Example A

In a speech about funeral customs in Japan, this picture of an actual Japanese funeral made the speech more interesting:

Example B

In a speech about the increasing population in the United States, the following bar graph helped the listeners to "see" and remember the statistics:

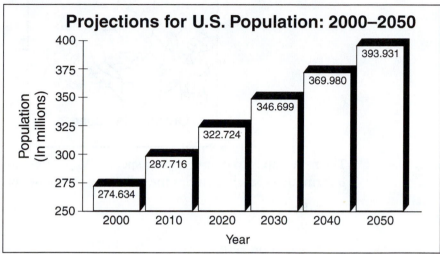

Source: U.S. Census Bureau

Example C

In a speech about asthma, a student conducted a demonstration that involved the whole class. She gave the audience drinking straws and instructed them to place the straws between their lips and to inhale and exhale through them. They were extremely uncomfortable breathing this way and felt like they would suffocate. The student explained that this is how people with asthma usually feel when attempting to breathe due to the constricting and narrowing of their trachea. This demonstration helped the audience to "experience" the information as well as to understand and remember it long after the speech ended.

Creating and Using Visual Aids

Visual aids are helpful in three ways:

- They help the speaker get organized.
- They help the audience understand the information.
- They help the audience remember the speech.

Not only is it important to find or to create helpful visual aids, it is also important to use them effectively during your speech. Please refer to Chapter 5, Using Dynamic Visual Aids, for in-depth guidelines to create and use visuals that will enhance your speeches.

6. ORGANIZING YOUR SPEECH

6. Organize the Speech

The next step is to organize your speech. As pointed out in Chapter 3, a good informative speech includes the following components:

- Body
- Preview
- Attention-getting opener
- Summary
- Memorable concluding remarks

Step 1: Prepare the Body

First, prepare the body of your speech. Arrange the points of your speech in a clear, logical manner. That way, your audience can follow you, understand your information, and remember what you have said. In order to do this, it is important to choose an organizational pattern that fits your topic.

Read about the eight organizational patterns below. Then choose the best one for your particular topic.

1. **Past-Present-Future.** Use this pattern to discuss how something once was, how it has changed, and how it will be in the future. For example, in discussing the Olympics, you might organize your information under the following three headings:

   I. The history of the Olympics

   II. The Olympics today

   III. The future of the Olympics

2. **Time.** Use this pattern to describe how processes, personal experiences, events, or activities happen by the hour, part of the day, week, month, or year. It can also be used to explain the steps in a process. For example, in speaking about making a speech, you might organize your information under the following headings:

   I. Choosing a topic

   II. Gathering information

   III. Making an outline

   IV. Presenting the speech

3. **Problem-Solution.** Use this pattern to speak about a specific problem and ways to solve it. (Note: A problem isn't always a negative situation, such as crime or child abuse. It can also be a positive situation, such as choosing a career or deciding where to go on vacation.) For example, in speaking about the problem of choosing the college that's right for you, you might present the following solutions:

I. Read the different college catalogues.

II. Visit campuses of different colleges.

III. Talk to people who attend various colleges.

IV. Talk to teachers at the colleges you are considering.

4. **Location.** Use this pattern to divide a topic into different geographical locations. For example, in speaking about interesting marriage customs, you might use the following sequence:

I. Marriage customs in Japan

II. Marriage customs in Saudi Arabia

III. Marriage customs in the United States

5. **Cause-Effect.** Use this pattern to describe a particular situation and its effects. For example, in speaking about the effects of cigarette smoking, you might discuss:

I. The effects of smoking on pregnant women

II. The effects of secondhand smoke

III. The effects of smoking on people with allergies

6. **Effect-Cause.** Use this pattern to describe a particular situation and its causes. For example, in speaking about reasons for drug addiction, you might discuss:

I. The easy availability of drugs

II. The need to escape from the pressures of work

III. The lack of education about harmful effects of drugs

7. **Related Subtopics.** Use this pattern to divide one topic into different parts, or subtopics. For example, in speaking about false advertising, you might discuss:

I. False advertising on television

II. False advertising in magazines

III. False advertising on the radio

8. **Advantage-Disadvantage.** Use this pattern to talk about both positive and negative aspects of a topic in a balanced, objective manner. For example, in speaking about the death penalty, you might discuss:

I. Advantages of capital punishment

II. Disadvantages of capital punishment

RECOGNIZE ORGANIZATIONAL PATTERNS

Indicate the organizational pattern of each speech described below by labeling them as follows:

a. Past-Present-Future		**e.** Cause-Effect
b. Time		**f.** Effect-Cause
c. Problem-Solution		**g.** Related Subtopics
d. Location		**h.** Advantage-Disadvantage

(Answers can be found on page 277 of Appendix II.)

Examples

___c___ In a speech about high school dropouts, Mary presented a series of suggestions for parents and teachers to follow in order to help teenagers do well in high school. She also suggested that students should help and encourage each other to graduate from high school.

___f___ José also spoke about high school dropouts. He discussed some reasons why students drop out of school. He pointed out that some students don't receive encouragement at home, while others need money to help support their families so they leave school to get jobs. Also, some would rather "hang out" with friends than go to class.

_____ **1.** In Kim's speech about looking for a job, he explained that the first thing to do is to prepare a résumé. The second thing to do is to read the employment section in the newspaper or to visit an employment agency. Kim said the last thing to do is to schedule job interviews and pray a lot.

_____ **2.** In Michelle's speech about gambling, she chose three states in which certain types of gambling are legal—Florida, New York, and Nevada. She then described the different forms of gambling permissible in each state.

_____ **3.** In a speech about automobiles, Jean described cars of sixty years ago and how hard they were to drive. She then talked about the automatic cars we have today with their many modern features. Finally, she said that someday cars would be driven by computers so that the "drivers" can relax and enjoy the ride.

_____ **4.** In a speech about saving money, Hector said that saving money is a problem because most products are very expensive. He suggested that some good ways to save money are to comparison-shop for the best prices, buy things on sale, and eat less expensive foods.

_____ **5.** In a speech about a day in the life of a teacher, Luisa talked about early-morning preparation, classroom teaching, and after-school activities.

_____ **6.** In a speech about entertainment in his city, Claude talked about entertainment for music lovers, entertainment for art lovers, and entertainment for theater lovers.

_____ **7.** In a speech about pets, Kimiko spoke about the problems people have with pets as well as the joy pets can give their owners.

_____ **8.** In a speech about depression, Leonardo described the disorder and many of its symptoms. He then discussed how drugs and psychological counseling are used to treat depression.

_____ **9.** In a speech about obesity in the United States, Nancy talked about its characteristics. She said that people are obese because they don't exercise, don't eat right, and lack the motivation to go on diets.

_____ **10.** In a speech about diamonds, Antoine stated that diamonds are classified by the three C's: cut, color, and clarity. He then explained each of these characteristics in more detail.

ACTIVITY

DEVELOP OUTLINES FROM TOPICS

This will help you gain practice in developing speech topics into outlines and show you there are many ways to approach and develop speech topics. Work in a small group with 3 or 4 classmates.

1. Choose one of the following topics.
2. Working with your group members, prepare an outline of 3–5 main headings for the topic. You will have 20 minutes for this activity. Feel free to use your imagination and make it funny if you like.
3. Share your ideas with the rest of the class.

Sample Topics

Ways to Survive with No Money

Disadvantages (or Advantages) of . . .

- Being An Only Child
- Traveling Alone
- Being Married or Being Single
- Owning a Car or Not Owning a Car
- Having Children
- Living with a Roommate
- Being a Working Student
- Having a Boyfriend or Girlfriend
- Living Alone

Disadvantages (or Advantages) of . . .

- Living in a Large Metropolitan City
- Living in a Small Town or Village
- Retiring
- Owning a Home
- Owning a Pet
- Getting Fired from a Job

Example

"Ways to Survive with No Money"

(One of our students provided this humorous example.)

  I. Ask friends to invite you to dinner every night.

  II. Save money in restaurants.

    A. Order hot water.

    B. Pour ketchup into the hot water to make tomato soup.

  III. Ask teachers to let you sleep in their offices to save on rent.

  IV. Borrow clothes from a friend.

  V. Hitchhike to school to save bus fare.

Step 2: Prepare a Preview

After deciding on an organizational pattern and determining the main headings in the body of your speech, you next need to prepare a preview. You should tell your audience what you're going to cover before you actually begin the body of your speech. This should be easy because you have already determined what you will cover in your headings.

Example A

My purpose today is to tell you what to do in the event of a hurricane. I will cover three major areas:

  A. First, how to prepare for a hurricane

  B. Second, what safety measures to take during a hurricane

  C. Third, what to do after the storm is over

Example B

In discussing left-handed people, I will explain three interesting facts:

  A. First, I'll explain why left-handed people have more accidents than other people.

  B. Second, I'll inform you about the four most common problems that left-handed people face.

  C. Third, I'll tell you about some world-famous "lefties."

In each example, the speaker clearly stated the purpose and numbered the subpoints. The audience thus knows exactly what the speaker is going to discuss.

Step 3: Prepare an Attention-Getting Opener

At the beginning of your speech, it is very important to grab your audience's attention and make them interested in what you have to say. Four different ways to prepare an interesting, attention-getting introduction follow.

1. **Ask your audience a series of rhetorical questions.** Rhetorical questions are asked for dramatic effect with no answers expected. Your listeners will immediately be interested in knowing the answers. The following rhetorical questions were used to open a speech about the process of getting a tattoo:

    What can cost ten dollars or a thousand dollars?

    What can be every color of the rainbow?

    What can be with you as long as you live?

    What can you wear on your arm, your cheek, your leg, or even your back?

2. **Tell a story.** People love to listen to a story. They want to find out what it is about. This story was used to open a speech about the Gold Museum in Bogotá, Colombia:

    A guard took me into a square room with no lights. The room was so black, I couldn't even see my own feet. All of a sudden, a hidden electric wall closed behind me. There was no way out. I thought I was in a tomb. All at once, bright lights came on. I was surrounded by gold on all four sides!

3. **State a surprising fact.** The statement below was used to introduce a speech about the billion-dollar business of bartering. The speaker talked about ways to trade skills, services, or products to get almost anything you want without cash:

    You can get almost anything you want without cash! And you can begin today!

4. **State a well-known quotation.** This quotation from William Shakespeare's *Hamlet* was used to open a speech about the disadvantages of borrowing:

    Neither a borrower nor a lender be, for loan oft loses both itself and friend.

Step 4: Prepare a Summary

As explained in Chapter 3, every speech needs a summary of the information presented. Remind your audience of what you said by repeating the main points covered in the body of your speech.

Example A

Well, I've given you some very important information today. You now know:

- *how to prepare if a hurricane is coming.*
- *what safety measures to take during the storm.*
- *what to do after the hurricane is over.*

Example B

As you can see, the Olympic Games are very important to people all over the world. I hope you learned some interesting information about:

- *The history of the Olympics*
- *The Olympics today*
- *The future of the Olympic Games*

Step 5: Prepare Memorable Concluding Remarks

Again, as you learned in Chapter 3, every speech needs an ending that leaves the audience thinking about and remembering what was said. Like attention-getting openers, memorable concluding remarks can take the form of rhetorical questions, stories, surprising facts, or quotations. Many famous public speakers have appreciated the power of quotations.

Example A

President John F. Kennedy ended many of his speeches with this quotation from the poet Robert Browning: "Some men see things as they are, and ask, 'Why?' I dare to dream of things that never were, and ask, 'Why not?'"

Example B

Civil-rights leader Martin Luther King Jr. ended his famous "I Have a Dream" speech with words from an old spiritual song: "Free at last, free at last, thank God Almighty, we are free at last."

Say your memorable concluding remarks slowly and clearly, maintaining eye contact with your audience. Be as dramatic and confident as possible!

ACTIVITY

CHOOSE A TOPIC

Step 1: Come to class prepared with ideas for topics for your informative speech. Be sure your topic is specific, contains only one idea, and is achievable. Consider your audience, and choose topics that would be of interest to your classmates. List five possible topics below.

1. _____   4. _____

2. _____   5. _____

3. _____

Step 2: Work in a small group with 3 or 4 classmates. Take turns presenting your ideas for topics. Help one another each choose 2 or 3 topics that are the most interesting.

Step 3: When groups are finished, each student should show the teacher a list of 2–3 possible speech topics. Your teacher will help you choose the best topic for your speech.

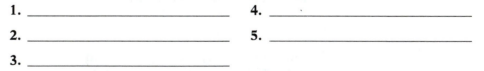

1. _____

2. _____

3. _____

OUTLINING AN INFORMATIVE SPEECH

The following outline shows how one student outlined an informative speech. The transcript of the sample speech follows the outline. Notice how the speech includes the following components:

- Attention-getting opener
- Preview
- Body
- Summary
- Memorable concluding remarks

Also, notice how transitions have been used to connect the components.

ATTENTION-GETTING OPENER

Every student in this room has something in common with famous astronauts, Olympic athletes, actors, politicians, and business executives. It's a common affliction that causes pain, suffering, and distress. Can you guess what it is? I'll tell you. It's called stage fright.

PREVIEW

Today we will be learning four major facts about stage fright.

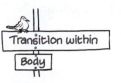

Preview Statement

Transition to Body

    I. Physical symptoms

    II. Causes

    III. Famous people who have had stage fright

    IV. Solutions

TRANSITION: *OK, let's get started on our investigation of stage fright by first looking at its six major symptoms.*

BODY

    I. Physical symptoms of stage fright

      A. Rapid breathing

      B. Rapid heart rate

      C. Dry mouth

      D. Butterflies in stomach

      E. Increased perspiration

      F. Trembling hands

TRANSITION: *Now you understand the symptoms of stage fright. Let's continue our investigation by examining the causes of stage fright.*

Transition within Body

    II. Causes of stage fright

      A. Fear of forgetting

      B. Looking silly

      C. Being disliked

      D. Lack of confidence about language skills

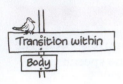
TRANSITION: *Now you are aware of some of the causes of stage fright. Let's continue our inquiry into stage fright by looking at a few famous people who have suffered from this affliction.*

III. Famous people who have had stage fright
   A. Winston Churchill (block of ice in stomach)
   B. Julio Iglesias (nervous about pronunciation in English)
   C. Jane Fonda (tremendous fear)
   D. Olivia Newton-John (shaking and crying before performance)

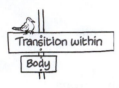
TRANSITION: *As you can see, you are in good company with famous people who have had stage fright. Now let's investigate what you can do to overcome this common problem.*

IV. Solutions for stage fright
   A. Short-term solutions
      1. Preparation and practice
      2. Start slowly
         a. Place notes on speaker's stand
         b. Establish eye contact
         c. Deep breathing
   B. Long-term solutions
      1. Remember stage fright is normal
      2. Get more experience
      3. Talk to friends

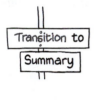
TRANSITION: *Now that you understand what you can do to reduce stage fright, our investigation is complete.*

SUMMARY

You should now understand four important facts about stage fright.

   I. The physical symptoms
  II. The causes
 III. Famous people who have had stage fright
 IV. What can be done about it

MEMORABLE CONCLUDING REMARKS

In conclusion, stage fright is like a lion in a cage. It's only dangerous if you allow it to roam free! Remember: As long as you are in control of it, your stage fright, like the lion, cannot harm you!

ACTUAL SAMPLE SPEECH

INTRODUCTION

I. Every student in this room has something in common with famous astronauts, Olympic athletes, actors, politicians, and business executives. It's a common affliction that causes pain, suffering, and distress. Can you guess what it is? I'll tell you. It's called stage fright.

II. Today we will be learning four major facts about stage fright.

    A. The physical symptoms of stage fright

    B. The causes of stage fright

    C. Famous people who have had stage fright

    D. Solutions to the problem of stage fright

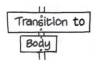

TRANSITION: *OK, let's get started on our investigation of stage fright by first looking at its six major symptoms.*

BODY

Stage fright affects everybody differently. However, most speakers and performers agree that they suffer from stage fright to some degree before facing an audience. There are a variety of physical symptoms of stage fright.

One of the symptoms of stage fright may be rapid breathing. Another symptom is a rapid heart rate. My heart feels like it is beating a thousand times a minute right now! Many speakers state that their mouth feels very dry when they are nervous. Others feel like they have butterflies in their stomach. Some people start to sweat a lot when they have to present before an audience. Almost everyone reports that their hands begin to shake while they are in front of a group.

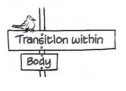

TRANSITION: *Now you understand the symptoms of stage fright. Let's continue our investigation by examining the causes of stage fright.*

There are a variety of different causes of stage fright. I'm sure you will be able to relate to one or more of them.

Many people are worried that they will forget what they want to say. Others are afraid that they will look silly in front of a lot of people. Some speakers or performers think that the audience won't like them and will want the money for their tickets refunded. Many international students lack confidence in their English language skills. They might be afraid that the listeners won't understand them.

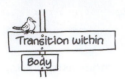

TRANSITION: *Now you are aware of some of the causes of stage fright. Let's continue our inquiry into stage fright by looking at a few famous people who have suffered from this affliction.*

Students and ordinary people aren't the only ones who suffer from stage fright. There have been many famous people of many different nationalities who have had stage fright also.

Winston Churchill was the prime minister of England during World War II. He once said that he thought there was a block of ice in his stomach each time he made a speech. Julio Iglesias, the famous Spanish singer, has revealed in interviews that he is nervous about his pronunciation when speaking English. Jane Fonda, the well-known American actress, has admitted to having a tremendous fear when she faces an audience. And last but not least, Olivia Newton-John, the famous Australian singer and actress, has admitted to shaking and crying before a performance.

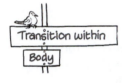

TRANSITION: *As you can see, you are in good company with famous people who have had stage fright. Now let's investigate what you can do to overcome this common problem.*

The good news is that there are some ways to help you relax and reduce the amount of stage fright you feel. There are some temporary solutions and some permanent solutions.

A very good temporary or short-term solution to stage fright is to be thoroughly prepared for a presentation. Practice your speech or performance many times. This will help you feel more confident. It is a good idea to take your time before you begin to speak. Gently place your notes on the speaker's stand. Be sure to look at your audience before you begin. When you see them looking at you with interest and giving you encouraging nods, you will feel much better. Take several deep breaths before you begin. This will also help calm your nerves a little.

A more permanent or long-term solution is to remember that stage fright is perfectly normal. Almost everyone experiences stage fright, and you are not alone in feeling this way. Look for opportunities to practice speaking in front of groups. Get as much experience as possible. The more experience you get, the less nervous you will begin to feel. A final long-term solution is to talk about stage fright with friends. Talking about your fears with others can be very helpful.

Conclusion

TRANSITION: *Now that you understand what you can do to reduce stage fright, our investigation is complete.*

CONCLUSION

I. You should now understand four important facts about stage fright.
   A. The physical symptoms of stage fright
   B. Different causes of stage fright
   C. Famous people who have had stage fright
   D. Some techniques you can use to help you overcome stage fright
II. In conclusion, stage fright is like a lion in a cage. It's only dangerous if you allow it to roam free! Remember: As long as you are in control of it, your stage fright, like the lion, cannot harm you!

ADD VISUAL AIDS

What types of visual aids might enhance this speech about stage fright? Work in small groups with 3 or 4 classmates to do the following:

1. Make a list of your ideas.
2. Decide which ones would work best.
3. Indicate where in the speech you would show visual aids.
4. Share your ideas with the rest of the class.

Assignment: *Give an informative speech.*

1. Using the Informative Speech Preparation Worksheet and Checklist on pages 86–87, prepare notes for your presentation.
2. Using the guidelines from Chapter 3: Putting Your Speech Together, outline your speech.
3. Your teacher may use the form on page 252 of Appendix I to evaluate your speech. Look it over so you know exactly how you will be evaluated.
4. Give a 4- to 5-minute informative speech.

INFORMATIVE SPEECH PREPARATION WORKSHEET

1. Choose three topics that interest you.

   a. _____

   b. _____

   c. _____

2. Narrow each topic.

   a. _____

   b. _____

   c. _____

3. Choose the topic that interests you the most. Divide it into three or four subtopics.

   a. _____

   b. _____

   c. _____

   d. _____

4. Prepare an attention-getting opener.

   _____

   _____

   _____

5. Prepare a preview.

   _____

   _____

   _____

6. Prepare a summary.

   _____

   _____

   _____

7. Prepare memorable concluding remarks.

   _____

   _____

   _____

   _____

You may want to use the checklist below. Check off each step as you prepare for your speech.

INFORMATIVE SPEECH PREPARATION CHECKLIST

Name: _____ Topic: _____

Due Date: _____

_____ Chose narrow, specific, achievable topic

_____ Consulted outside sources:

    _____ Interviews   _____ Dictionaries

    _____ Newspapers   _____ Professional journals

    _____ Encyclopedic dictionaries   _____ Magazines

    _____ Internet   _____ Encyclopedias

    _____ Books

_____ Chose organizational pattern

_____ Prepared outline

_____ Prepared body

_____ Prepared preview

_____ Prepared attention-getting opener

_____ Prepared summary

_____ Prepared memorable concluding remarks

_____ Prepared transition after introduction

_____ Prepared transition before summary

_____ Prepared transitions in body

_____ Prepared visual aids:

    _____ Objects   _____ Charts and diagrams   _____ Demonstrations

_____ Practiced speech with visual aids at least three times

EXERCISE 1   Read the following words aloud. Be sure you can feel the tip of your tongue protrude between your teeth when you pronounce [ð].

1. they	**9.** brother
2. then	**10.** either
3. that	**11.** bathe
4. those	**12.** smooth
5. there	**13.** clothe
6. other	**14.** soothe
7. mother	**15.** breathe
8. father	

EXERCISE 2   Read the following pairs of words aloud. Be sure to place your tongue between your teeth for [ð] and behind your teeth for [d].

	[ð]	**[d]**
1.	they	**d**ay
2.	then	**d**en
3.	there	**d**are
4.	breathe	bree**d**
5.	lather	la**dd**er

EXERCISE 3   Read the following phrases and sentences aloud. Be sure to place your tongue between your teeth for [ð] in each of the boldfaced words.

1. a. **mother** and **father**

   b. **This** is my **mother** and **father**.
2. a. **other brother**

   b. Will your **other brother** be **there**?
3. a. get **together**

   b. Let's get **together another** day.
4. a. **bathe the** baby

   b. **Grandmother** must **bathe the** baby.
5. a. **than the other**

   b. **This** is better **than the other** one.

CHAPTER 5

Using Dynamic Visual Aids

It is an established principle of psychology that people learn far more when information is presented through two or more senses. Tell listeners something and they will remember some of it; tell and *show* listeners and they will remember most of it!

Audiences enjoy eye-catching, colorful visual aids. Visual aids enhance a presentation by helping the audience to more easily understand and remember your information. There are many different types of visual or presentational aids that good speakers can use to enhance a speech. In this section we will:

- Provide you with some general guidelines for using visual aids
- Describe the different types of presentational aids
- Provide you with some practical tips for effective use of PowerPoint

GENERAL GUIDELINES

Any presentational aids you use should portray Americans as being a diverse group. As long as you depict people of different ages, genders, races, and religions favorably and in good taste, almost anything goes. The following are some general guidelines to observe when using any type of visual aid:

1. **Design your visual aid to have a specific purpose or to support an important point in your speech.**

2. **Visual aids should be LARGE enough for everyone to see.** Measure the distance in feet from your visual aid to the back of the room and divide by twenty. This number—the quotient —should be the minimum letter height (in inches) of any words used in your visual aid. For example, if the last row is forty feet from your visual aid, divide forty by twenty. Your minimum letter height should be two inches.

3. **Keep charts, maps, and graphs very simple and uncluttered.** Don't try to show too many details in one visual aid. Less is more!

4. **Practice your presentation while using or showing the visual aids BEFORE you actually deliver the speech.** Become familiar with your visuals by practicing when, where, and how you will use them.

5. **Be sure to look at your audience, not at your visual aids.** You must maintain eye contact with your listeners while explaining or displaying your visuals. Do not talk to your visual aid. Talk to the listeners.

6. **Cover all visual aids when you are not using them and put them away after you have finished showing them.** For example, if you are starting to speak about the Temple of Heaven in Beijing, don't leave up a picture of the Great Wall of China that was used in an earlier section of your speech.

7. **Never pass out objects, photos, or papers during your speech.** If your audience is looking at objects or reading papers, they will not be listening to you.

8. **You may want to ask an assistant to handle your aids so you can concentrate on your audience.** Be sure to arrange this with a classmate before the day of your speech. Explain exactly what you want your helper to do.

THINK ABOUT LECTURES YOU HAVE HEARD

1. Did your teachers use any visual aids?
2. Did they help you understand and remember the information better? How?
3. What particular aids might have helped improve the class?
4. Discuss your ideas with the rest of your class.

It is helpful to think of visual aids in three categories:

- No-tech visual aids
- Low-tech visual aids
- Hi-tech visual aids

I. NO-TECH VISUAL AIDS

A. Flip charts, posterboard, or blackboards

These can be used to display a variety of visual aids, including:

- sketches or diagrams
- graphs
- charts
- maps
- photographs

1. Sketches or diagrams

Use a sketch to display a simple illustration that calls attention to points you want to emphasize.

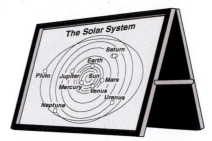

2. Graphs

Bar graph. Use a bar graph to compare rankings. In this graph, the North ranked highest in the first quarter, while the East ranked lowest for the same period.

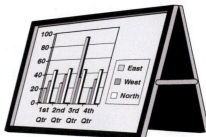

Pie graph. Use a pie graph to compare percentages.

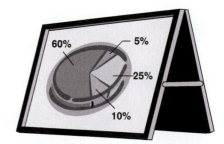

Line graph. Use a line graph to show how a trend has changed over time.

3. Charts

Flow Chart. Use a flow chart to explain the sequence of steps in a process.

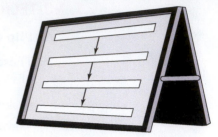

Bullet Chart. Use a bullet chart to show key points.

4. Maps

Use a map to show location or physical arrangement of places.

5. Photographs

Use an actual photograph to show realistic details of your object or topic.

B. Physical objects

These, along with personal demonstrations, can be used as visual aids.

1. **Actual objects and/or personal demonstrations.** For example: scuba equipment; paintball equipment; cooking utensils for demonstrations; mannequins, large dolls, or an actual person to demonstrate something.

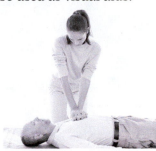

2. **Actual animals.** Some students bring in pet parrots, hamsters, snakes, etc., in their cages as visual aids for speeches.

3. **Models of objects.** Use a model of the object if the object is too large to display, like an airplane; impossible to display, like the human brain; or too small to display, like a molecule.

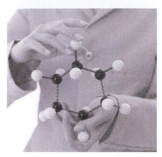

How to Explain Your Visual Aid

1. Tell your listeners what kind of visual aid you are displaying.
2. Explain exactly what the visual aid is designed to do or show.
3. Emphasize what the listeners should focus on.

Example

- Tell your listeners what kind of visual aid you are displaying:
  These are pictures of victims receiving CPR.
- Explain exactly what the visual aid is designed to do or show:
  They show the correct techniques for administering CPR.
- Emphasize what the listeners should focus on:
  Notice how the victim's head is tilted back in the first picture.
  Notice the placement of the rescuer's hands while doing chest compressions on the victim in the second picture.

II. LOW-TECH VISUAL AIDS

A. Overhead transparencies

These are images printed on clear plastic sheets and projected onto a white screen or wall using an overhead projector. Transparencies are very simple and inexpensive to prepare. Speakers use them to present graphs, pictures, diagrams, etc.

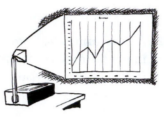

- You can create text using a typewriter or computer and print it out directly onto a transparency.
- You can also photocopy photos and drawings from books directly onto a transparency.
- You can write on transparencies with markers while you are speaking. This is helpful when you want to emphasize important information by drawing circles around key words or underlining key terms.

Tips for Using Transparencies

1. Text must be large enough to be seen from the back of the room. All letters and numbers should be at least one-half inch tall.

2. Use colored markers to emphasize key points and create visual interest.

3. Keep transparencies simple and uncluttered. Use them to highlight a few important points. Listeners will be distracted if they are too complex.

4. Use the "Progressive Conceal/Reveal Method."

   a. Display information on the transparency little by little rather than all at once.

   b. Use a heavyweight piece of paper or cardboard to cover the transparency.

   c. Slide the paper or cardboard down to show each point you want your audience to see when you are ready to disclose it.

B. Films and videotapes

If you have access to a TV set with a DVD or VHS player, showing a film or videotape segment illustrating your subject matter can be very effective. Keep your film clip short—30–45 seconds or less. A film segment over that is too long for relatively brief speeches of, for example, less than seven minutes.

Tips for Using Films or Videotapes

1. Always set up your tape or film segment before the day of your speech. Never make an audience wait while you are rewinding or fast-forwarding to the segment you want to show.

2. Explain to your audience exactly what they are going to see and why you are showing them this film segment.

Example A

In her speech, "Techniques of Dog Training," one student explained that positive reinforcement was necessary in obedience training. She then told the audience that she would show them a film segment demonstrating this. She played a brief home videotape of her brother using positive reinforcement to teach her Doberman the basic obedience commands "sit" and "stay."

Example B

In a speech entitled "Autism," a student explained several characteristics of autistic adults. She then showed a segment from the movie *Rain Man* in which actor Dustin Hoffman portrayed an autistic adult.

A Word About Audio Aids

Sound effects can be very effective while making presentations. Audio can be used for humor, for drama, to create a mood, to clarify how something or someone sounds, etc. Audio effects can be played for the audience using CDs, cassette players, or musical instruments. Your film or video segments may have accompanying audio. PowerPoint presentations can even be created with accompanying sound effects. Some audio effects you might consider using in your presentations include:

- music
- sound of drums beating or rolling
- recordings of voices
- sound effects (for example, doors slamming, bells ringing, tires screeching, wind blowing, ocean sounds)

PRACTICE ENHANCING A SPEECH WITH VISUALS

Work in small groups with 3 or 4 classmates.

1. **Choose a topic from the list below, and describe what types of visual aids and audio effects might enhance a speech about it.**

how to make a great cup of coffee	giving CPR
the need to reduce highway speed limits	the health-care crisis
drunk driving	global warming
the need for prison reform	boating safety
learning disabilities	interviewing for a job

2. **Share your ideas with the rest of the class.**

Example

Audiovisuals for an anti-smoking message

- Overhead transparencies making fun of Joe Camel in a hospital bed
- Cartoons of smokers puffing and coughing outside an office building
- Pictures from a textbook showing the difference between a smoker's lungs and a nonsmoker's lungs
- A recording of the hoarse, husky voice of a longtime smoker
- Photos of famous people who have died because of lung cancer due to smoking

III. HI-TECH VISUAL AIDS

A. Image galleries

You can find virtually any pictures or photos you need for your visual aids on the Internet. There are several wonderful sites for finding hundreds of thousands of images, pictures, and illustrations in all categories. Most important, they are free of charge! These sites include:

> http://images.google.com
>
> http://images.yahoo.com
>
> http://www.lycos.com/picturethis

Keyword search: Use keywords that are as specific as possible, and you will find exactly what you are looking for.

Example A

Let's say you need a picture of the *Mona Lisa* for a speech about the art of Leonardo da Vinci or you need a picture of the Eiffel Tower for a speech about Paris. Just enter "Mona Lisa" or "Eiffel Tower" in the search box. In moments you will see hundreds of pictures of the *Mona Lisa* or the Eiffel Tower that you can print out to use as a visual aid in your speech.

Example B

In a speech to persuade the class that animal abusers should receive mandatory jail sentences, one student showed horrifying photos of abused animals. She found hundreds of photos on the topic by typing the words "animal abuse" in the search box of the image database sites.

B. PowerPoint

PowerPoint is a very powerful tool for helping speakers deliver dynamic presentations.

- Over 90 percent of all professional speakers use PowerPoint during their speeches.
- At least 90 percent of all multimedia presentations in the United States are created with PowerPoint.

We hope you have the chance to use PowerPoint in one or more of your class speeches. Unfortunately, PowerPoint is not always used effectively. A careless PowerPoint presentation can hurt more than it helps by confusing or distracting the listeners. If you are going to use this technology to your best advantage, you need to learn some basic tips and tactics for:

- creating great PowerPoint slides and
- delivering your speech using PowerPoint.

CREATING GREAT POWERPOINT SLIDES

There are three major aspects to creating an effective PowerPoint slide:

- Content (text and art)
- Color
- Font (type and size)

How to Design Great PowerPoint Slides

❏ Content (text and art)

❏ Color

❏ Font (type and size)

1. Content

Text and art are the most common elements of PowerPoint slides. They can be used alone or in combination, depending on the idea you want to communicate.

a. Text. Don't fill up a slide with too much text. Use a maximum of twenty words on a slide. If you have a lot of information, divide it among two or more slides.

- Simplify text. Create keywords and easy-to-remember phrases.

An Ineffective Slide

Hurricane Preparedness

Always prepare for a hurricane. It is important to have plenty of bottled water on hand just in case the water supply is contaminated.

A good rule of thumb is to have at least 1 gallon of water per person per day.

Be sure to have plenty of non-perishable canned foods. Also, be sure to fill doctors' prescriptions for medicines before the hurricane hits.

An Effective Slide

Hurricane Preparedness

- 1 gallon of water per person daily
- Prescription medicines filled in advance
- Sufficient canned foods

- Simplify text. Round off numbers.

An Ineffective Slide

2004 Identify Theft Statistics

— The FTC received 635,192 identity theft complaints.

— Consumers reported losses from fraud of more than $547,000,000.

An Effective Slide

2004 Identity Theft Statistics

- FTC reports over 635,000 complaints
- Consumers lost approximately $550 million

b. Art. Clip art, pictures, and photographs that represent common objects and ideas will greatly enhance your message. Art can be entertaining or humorous. Just don't overdo it. Use a maximum of three pieces of art per slide. Keep illustrations simple.

This sample slide shows a combination of text and clip art. Notice the short phrases and simple illustrations.

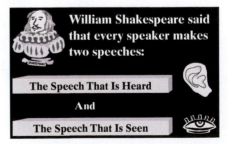

2. Color

You will need to choose one color for the background of your slide, one color for titles, and one color for the text. Be consistent and use the same color combinations for all your slides.

a. Background color. The best background is dark—black or dark blue work best as background colors. A dark background eliminates the bright whiteness of the LCD projector light and focuses your audience's attention on the content of the slide.

b. Title and text color. Select light colors that contrast well against a dark background. Shades of yellow or white show up best against dark blue or black backgrounds. Avoid using blues, greens, or reds for text or titles. They won't show up well.

3. Font Type and Size

You will need to choose a font for your slide titles or headings, and text. PowerPoint has approximately 100 fonts to choose from. Many are not effective for visual aids. Fancy, decorative, and cursive writing fonts are hard to read and can be very distracting. You want to use font types and sizes that are easy to see and easy to read.

a. Font type

- If you prefer Roman style fonts (called serif fonts because they have little feet or tails on each letter), choose fonts such as Times New Roman, Bookman Old Style, or MS Reference Serif.
- If you prefer the sans-serif fonts (no feet or tails on the letters), choose fonts such as Arial, Verdana, or MS Reference Sans Serif.
- Use the same font on all your slides throughout the entire presentation.

b. Font size

- Make slide titles and main headings a minimum of 36–46 points. Subheadings should be a bit smaller than main headings and larger than text.
- Text should be a minimum of 24 points in size.
- Use uppercase and lowercase letters. ALL CAPS are difficult to read.

Tips for Using PowerPoint

Delivering your speech with PowerPoint requires careful preparation. You need to be very familiar with your slides. It is important that you coordinate them with your words, maintain eye contact with your audience, and speak clearly and extemporaneously at the same time. Follow these tips:

1. **Face your audience at all times.**

   Position the computer monitor so that it faces you. Look at your monitor to see which slide you're on. There is no need to turn around to look at the large screen.

2. **Focus all of the attention on YOU occasionally.**

   Black out the screen and your audience will automatically look at you. Simply press "B" on your keyboard and the projector screen will go black. This will give you a chance to deliver other segments of your speech, make spontaneous comments, answer questions, etc., without the audience being distracted by the continuous display of an unwanted slide.

3. **Use PowerPoint slides sparingly.**

   PowerPoint slides are most effective when they supplement your speech. Some speakers use PowerPoint to illustrate the entire presentation. They end up reading the speech to the audience as the slides are displayed. Avoid overloading your speech with too many slides. Remember: *You* are supposed to be the focus of the presentation, not your PowerPoint slides!

4. **Back up your PowerPoint presentation.**

   Murphy's Law states, "If anything can go wrong, it will." Despite all your hard work and practice, you might be horrified to discover that the equipment hasn't arrived or that the computer or projector doesn't work. There are many ways that technology can disappoint you.

You need to be prepared with a backup plan in case you are unable to use PowerPoint. We recommend two safety nets:

- **Make copies of all your PowerPoint slides by printing them out on overhead transparency film.** If PowerPoint is unavailable for some reason, you can use an overhead projector to display your transparencies in an emergency. Overhead projectors are readily available everywhere.

- **Print out your presentation.** Make a hard copy of your PowerPoint presentation. That way, if the electricity fails, you can still deliver your speech. Your notes and printed copies of your slides will act as your outline to trigger your memory, and you will still be able to deliver your talk.

EXERCISE 1

The following words contain the most common three-member consonant clusters in English. Be sure to enunciate each cluster carefully.

Consonant Clusters at the Beginning of Words

[spr]	[spl]	[skr]	[skw]	[str]
spry	splash	screen	squad	strap
spray	split	scream	square	stray
spring	splinter	scrape	squint	street

Consonant Clusters at the End of Words

[sps]/[lps]	[spt]/[lpt]	[skt]/[kst]	[rkt]
wasps	gasped	asked	parked
helps	helped	fixed	worked

EXERCISE 2

Read the following sentences aloud. Carefully pronounce all the consonant clusters in the boldfaced words.

1. I **fixed** the **cracked masks**.
2. **Spray** the **strong** perfume **sparingly**.
3. We **strolled through** the **streets**.
4. The **strong** man **worked** at the factory.
5. I **scream**, you **scream**, we all **scream** for ice **cream**!

Look at the scrambled words. Write the correct word in the blank. Use the clues below each word to help you figure out the scrambled word. Read the sentences aloud carefully pronouncing all the consonant clusters.

1. E A L S T

   It's a crime to _____.

2. R I P A S E

   To _____ someone is to pay them a compliment.

3. S K A

   To make a request is to _____.

4. S P W A

   A _____ is an insect that stings.

5. A T R S M E

   The children went swimming in the _____.

CHAPTER 6

Using the Internet

The Internet consists of millions of computers, from those belonging to multinational corporations, world governments, colleges, and universities to those belonging to your friends and family.

The World Wide Web is part of the Internet. It is a vast universe of information about most topics. It is often called the world's largest library. There is a wealth of information to be found on the Internet. Unfortunately, finding the information you want can be frustrating. Often the information you find is not accurate or credible. It is important to use reliable and trustworthy sources. This chapter will guide you. We will provide some general principles and guidelines for using the Internet for research and show you how to cite Internet sources in your speeches.

There are a variety of search tools to help you find information about your topics. Two major types are search engines and meta-search engines.

SEARCH ENGINES

Search engines enable you to find information by entering a word or phrase related to your topic. The search engine then searches through the Internet and provides a list of links to relevant websites. You might not find the information you are looking for right away. What one search engine finds may not show up on another. That's why it is a good idea to use more than one search engine. Some of the most popular search engines include:

Google at www.google.com

Alta Vista at www.altavista.com

Yahoo at www.yahoo.com

Excite at www.excite.com

Virtual Library at www.vlib.org

META-SEARCH ENGINES

Meta-search engines are search engines that look through several search engines simultaneously.

- This allows you to access more relevant links to websites on one try than a single search engine.
- This is very helpful when you are looking for information about an uncommon or obscure topic.

Popular meta-search engines include:

Ask Jeeves at www.askjeeves.com

Dogpile at www.dogpile.com

MetaCrawler at www.metacrawler.com

Mamma at www.mamma.com

UNDERSTANDING URL EXTENSIONS

URL stands for "Uniform Resource Locater." This is simply the address of a web page or Internet site. The last three letters of the basic URL are called extensions. URL extensions give you important information about the type of Internet site they represent. The following chart explains what the various extensions mean.

URL Extension	Types of Organizations	Example Sites
.com or .net	Businesses or for-profit commercial sites	www.amazon.com www.bellsouth.net
.org	Nonprofit groups	www.unitedway.org www.breastcancer.org
.gov	Government agencies	www.fda.gov www.irs.gov
.edu	Educational institutions	www.harvard.edu www.mdc.edu
.mil	Military groups	www.army.mil www.navy.mil

Nonprofit organization websites provide a lot of information about their activities. For example:

- Professional associations inform you about their specific professions.
- Political groups inform you about their positions on issues.
- Charities educate you about the work they do or types of people they help.

EXERCISE 1   **VISIT NONPROFIT ORGANIZATION WEBSITES**

Part 1: Visit any three of the following websites.

www.asha.org   www.madd.org   www.bbb.org
www.ama-assn.org   www.add.org
www.uwint.org   www.unicef.org

1. Be prepared to discuss in class:
   a. what the URLs stand for
   b. what kind of organization the site represents
   c. what the main functions of the organization or association are
2. Use the worksheet on the next page to record your information.

Example

www.apa.org

a. This URL stands for the American Psychological Association.

b. The APA represents the largest professional and scientific association of psychologists worldwide.

c. According to the site, the APA exists to advance psychology as a science and as a means of promoting health and human welfare.

Nonprofit URL #1: _____

a. _____

b. _____

c. _____

Nonprofit URL #2: _____

a. _____

b. _____

c. _____

Nonprofit URL #3: _____

a. _____

b. _____

c. _____

Part 2: Visit www.idealist.org. (This site contains a large directory of links to nonprofit organizations.) Choose three nonprofit groups and visit their websites.

1. Be prepared to discuss:
   a. the kind of organization the site represents
   b. its mission or purpose
2. Use the worksheet on the next page to record your information.

Example

http://deeproots.org

   a. Deep Roots is a nonprofit scholarship organization. _____

   b. Its purpose is to provide educational support to talented youth in developing nations. _____

Nonprofit URL #1: _____

a. _____

b. _____

_____

Nonprofit URL #2: _____

a. _____

b. _____

_____

Nonprofit URL #3: _____

a. _____

b. _____

_____

Government agency websites provide a lot of information about the specific areas for which they are responsible.

- Websites exist for virtually every government agency at the local, state, and national levels.
- They provide many facts and statistics that you could use in presentations.

EXERCISE 2 **VISIT GOVERNMENT AGENCY WEBSITES**

Part 1: Visit any three of the following websites:

www.irs.gov   www.va.gov   www.fbi.gov

www.fda.gov   www.census.gov   www.nasa.gov

www.nps.gov   www.dhs.gov

1. Be prepared to discuss in class:
   a. what the URLs stand for
   b. what the main functions of the government agency are
2. Use the worksheet on the next page to record your information.

Example

www.osha.gov

    a. This URL stands for the Occupational Safety and Health Administration (OSHA).

    b. According to the site, OSHA exists to assure the health and safety of America's workers by setting and enforcing safety and health standards in the workplace.

Government Agency URL #1: _____

a. _____

b. _____

_____

_____

_____

Government Agency URL #2: _____

a. _____

b. _____

_____

_____

_____

Government Agency URL #3: _____

a. _____

b. _____

_____

_____

_____

Part 2: Visit www.fedworld.gov. Click on "Top Government Websites." (This website provides information compiled by the federal government about everything imaginable.)

1. Choose any three government agencies. (These may be called by other names such as "Department," "Administration" or "Center," etc.) and visit their websites.

2. Answer the same two questions as before. Use the worksheet below to record your findings.

Government Agency URL #1: _____

a. _____

b. _____

Government Agency URL #2: _____

a. _____

b. _____

Government Agency URL #3: _____

a. _____

b. _____

SUBJECT, KEY WORD, AND PHRASE SEARCHES

Once you have selected a speech topic, you are ready to search for information. You need to conduct a "search." The three most common search methods are:

- Subject search
- Keyword search
- Phrase search

Each method has different advantages depending on your topic and the type of information you want to include in your speech.

SUBJECT SEARCH

A subject search is effective when you want to look through broad categories of information on the Internet. Several search engines provide links to many general categories of information. Yahoo's homepage includes a section labeled "Web Directory." Its general categories include:

Arts	Education	News
Business	Entertainment	Recreation
Computers	Health	Science

Just click on one of these general categories. You will get a screen with a list of sub-categories. Decide which sub-category is the most relevant and click on it. Eventually you will find a screen with websites you want to visit.

Example

Let's say you are making a speech about distance learning courses in community colleges. Here is how a Yahoo subject search might work:

1. Access the Yahoo homepage. Click: Education.
2. This brings you to another screen. In the Top Categories list, click: Higher Education.
3. This brings you to a third screen. Click: Distance Learning.
4. This takes you to a fourth screen. Click: Community Colleges.
5. Bingo! Yahoo targets 31 sites you could visit for information.

KEYWORD SEARCH

When you search by a keyword, the program finds virtually all available information with the word you entered. You need to use keywords that are as specific as possible to help you filter out literally thousands of useless links. It will help you increase your chances of finding information that you really want.

Example

Suppose you want to use www.google.com to find information for a speech about Mexican Talavera pottery. If you enter the keyword *pottery* in the search box, Google will provide you with approximately 17,300,000 websites. If you type *ceramics* in the search box, Google will recommend 13.5 million links for you to check out.

Most of these links will not have information relevant to your needs. If you type the specific word *Talavera* in the search box, Google will recommend 800,000 links for you to check. This is still far too many links to follow up in a reasonable amount of time. To narrow the list of links from thousands of sites to a realistic number, you need to do a specific phrase search. Enter *Talavera Pottery*, and you will get 16,500 links compiled by Google. Enter *Talavera Ceramics*, and you will get 4,360 links. Enter *Mexican Talavera Ceramics*, and Google recommends a manageable 24 sites.

Read on! The next section will help you to better understand this business of phrase searches.

PHRASE SEARCH

As seen in the "Mexican Talavera Pottery" example above, phrase searches improve the accuracy of searches and reduce the number of useless search results. Surrounding a group of words with quotation marks tells the search engine to only find documents in which those exact words appear together. Phrase searching, used effectively, is a powerful method for significantly limiting your search results. Use it as often as possible. Be sure to:

- identify search terms,
- think of alternative search terms, and
- narrow and broaden search terms as necessary.

Example

Let's say you want to use www.google.com to find information for a speech to persuade listeners not to buy any products that were tested on animals.

1. **Identify search terms.** Possible search terms might be:
   - *"Animal testing"* (produced 531,000 links)
   - *"Animal experimentation"* (produced 166,000 links)

2. **Think of alternative search terms.** Other search terms might include:
   - *"Animal cruelty"* (produced 466,000 links)
   - *"Mistreatment of animals"* (produced 11,000 links)

3. **Narrow or broaden search terms as necessary.** The above search terms produced too many links for you to be able to browse through in a reasonable amount of time. Think of ways to narrow your phrases. Possibilities include:
   - *"Cosmetic testing on animals"* (produced 4,500 links)
   - *"Product testing on animals"* (produced 1,720 links)

Let's say you want to limit your talk to products tested on dogs only. Narrow your search further:
   - *"Animal experimentation on dogs"* (produced 0 links)

In a case such as the one above, you need to think of an alternative search term:
   - *"Animal experiments on dogs"* (produced 11 links)

Sometimes a phrase in quotations is too narrow and you need to broaden your search.
   - *"Product testing on dogs"* produced NO links, but
   - *Product testing on dogs* (no quotation marks) produced half a million links.

You might also need to use alternative terms simultaneously with narrowing or broadening your search phrase. Let's say you wanted to narrow your search to the testing of just cosmetics on dogs.
   - *"Cosmetics testing on dogs"* produced only 1 website, while
   - *"Cosmetic testing on dogs"* produced 6 relevant websites, and
   - *Cosmetics testing on dogs* (no quotation marks) found 71,000 links.

As you can see, searching for relevant and worthwhile information on the Internet is a trial-and-error process. You must be persistent and try many combinations of words and phrases with and without quotation marks.

PRACTICE CREATING SEARCH TERMS

Choose a topic from the list on the next page.

1. **Think about a way to narrow your search through the use of a subtopic, and create an appropriate search term.**
2. **Develop two alternative search terms for this subtopic.**

inflation	drug use among athletes	Alzheimer's disease
plagiarism	the Internet	travel
résumés	space travel	world hunger
sex education	school violence	cloning
terrorism	stem cell research	school uniforms
culture shock	self-esteem	study habits
identity theft	credit card fraud	credit card debt
illiteracy	homelessness	hobbies
animal ethics		

3. Use the worksheet below to record your search terms.

Example A

Topic: _inflation_

Subtopic = search term #1: _"ways to fight inflation"_

Alternative search term #2: _"fighting inflation"_

#3: _"how to reduce inflation"_

Example B

Topic: _starving children_

Subtopic = search term #1: _"causes of world hunger in children"_

Alternative search term #2: _"reasons for childhood starvation"_

#3: _"why there are starving children worldwide"_

Topic: _____

Subtopic = search term #1: _____

Alternative search term #2: _____

#3: _____

TRY OUT DIFFERENT SEARCH ENGINES

1. Choose three different search engines and conduct a parallel search for information on the search terms you developed in the preceding activity. Try them with and without quotation marks. Repeat the search using your alternative terms to see if you can get better results.

2. Be prepared to discuss the following questions in class:

  a. Were there differences in the number of links produced by each search engine?

  b. Were there differences in the number of links produced when you used the alternative search terms?

  c. Were there differences in the number of links produced when you enclosed the search phrase in quotation marks?

  d. Which search engine did you like best? Why?

EVALUATE A WEBSITE

You now know how to search for material on the Internet. But how reliable is the material you find? Many websites provide inaccurate, biased propaganda disguised as "good" information. It is important to learn how to evaluate the quality of the websites you visit in order to decide if the information seems to be trustworthy or false.

The following guidelines for evaluating Internet sources are adapted from materials developed by the libraries at the University of South Carolina–Lancaster and the University of Wisconsin–Eau Claire.*

  A. Authorship/Sponsorship

  1. Find out what person(s) or organization is responsible for the information on the website.

    a. Who wrote the information?

    b. What qualifications does this person have on the topic?

    c. Do other researchers cite information from this author or organization?

  2. A good way to get information about the author or sponsorship of material on the Internet is to:

    a. Look for links on the site you found to other documents or information about the author.

    b. Enter the author's or organization's name, enclosed in quotation marks, in one of the search engines listed on page 104.

    c. Analyze what you find: If the author or sponsor of a website seems to be a credible authority, the information is most likely accurate. If you can't find any other information about the author or organization, be suspicious about the information you found!

  B. Purpose

  1. Try to determine why the information was written.

    a. Was it written to sell something?

    b. Was it written to advance a cause or controversial policy?

    c. Was it written to convince you to change your beliefs?

---

*"Using the World Wide Web: A Self-Guided Tutorial" developed at Medford Library at the University of South Carolina–Lancaster, http://usclancaster.sc.edu/library/WebTutorial/evaluating.html, and the "10C's for Evaluating Internet Sources" developed at McIntyre Library at the University of Wisconsin–Eau Claire, http://www.uwec.edu/library/Guides/tencs.html.

2. Decide if the information seems to be impartial or if it appears biased to represent the agenda or commercial interests of a particular group or person.

C. **Content**

Analyze the information provided by the website.

    a. Is there bibliographic or other documentation? (A site with a list of references or an explanation of how the information was compiled is likely to have accurate information.)

    b. Is the information current? (Look for evidence that the site is current. The date is usually found at the bottom of the page. Look for it. If the date is not recent, the information might no longer be relevant or valid.)

    c. Does the site contain spelling or grammatical errors? (A site full of careless errors often contains content errors.)

D. **Review: Evaluating the Quality of a Website**

    1. A credible person/sponsor is responsible for the information.

    2. The site provides links to other sites.

    3. The information appears to be objective and is not presented to directly or indirectly benefit any person or organization.

    4. The site/information is current.

    5. The site/information is free from careless errors.

EXERCISE

EVALUATE A WEBSITE

Choose any topic that interests you.

    1. Enter the topic in a search engine. Click on one of the sites that the search engine finds for you. Click on any links to better evaluate the content of the entire site.

    2. Does the site you visited appear to be one of quality? Be prepared to discuss specific elements indicating the quality of the site.

    3. Take notes on the form below. Be prepared to share your impressions about the quality of the site in class.

Topic: _____

Website URL: _____

Who is responsible for the information?

_____

Does the site provide links to other sites? Which ones?

_____

Does the information appear to be objective? How can you tell?

_____

How current is the information on the site? When was the site last updated?

_____

Did you find any careless errors on the site? If so, what types of errors?

_____

A WORD ABOUT PLAGIARISM

The _Longman Dictionary of American English_ defines plagiarism as "the act of taking someone else's words, ideas, etc. and copying them, pretending that they are your own." In other words, plagiarism is stealing; it is a crime for which you could be expelled from any college or university. While many students realize the importance of giving credit to authors of actual books and newspaper or magazine articles, they often forget to cite sources when they use information from the Internet in their presentations. You will be guilty of plagiarism if you don't credit your Internet sources of information.

CITING INTERNET SOURCES

As mentioned, it is imperative that you cite sources of the facts, statistics, and other information you present in your speech. This holds true for Internet research as well as for information obtained from print media such as books, magazines, and newspapers. When citing Internet sources, be sure to specify the author's name when available and website, the date, and the URL for each citation. It is not enough for you to simply say, "According to the Internet" or "I found the following information on the World Wide Web." You must be more specific.

Example

Here is an excerpt from our student Luis's informative speech about identity theft. He cited two Internet sources early in the speech, using the first for his attention-getting introduction.

INTRODUCTION

According to the Web pages of the Federal Reserve Bank of Boston at www.bos.frb.org, the FBI calls identity theft one of the fastest growing crimes in the United States. The FBI estimates that 500,000 to 700,000 Americans become identity theft victims each year.

PREVIEW

Today I'd like to make you aware of an international problem that could affect you. It's called identity theft. I will present four important aspects of this serious situation.

1. How identity theft occurs
2. How identity thieves use your personal information
3. How to prevent identity theft from happening to you
4. Steps to take if you are a victim of identity theft

TRANSITION

I will begin by explaining how identity thieves are able to steal your personal information. I found this information on the official website of the Federal Trade Commission at www.ftc.gov.

1. They steal wallets containing your identification and credit cards.
2. They steal your mail including bank and credit card statements.
3. They complete a change-of-address form to divert your mail to another location.
4. They use personal information you share on the Internet.
5. They rummage through your garbage for personal data.

In both cases, Luis made it very clear where he found his information. Be sure you cite your sources—both print media and Internet—in your speeches. In the case of Internet research, it is also a good idea to give the date that you got the information. Websites are not as permanent as printed materials, and they can disappear.

Remember: There is a wealth of information on the World Wide Web, if you know where to look. Be sure to:

- Use different search engines.
- Use specific phrase or keyword searches.
- Be persistent. Keep trying to find quality information by using different words/phrases and by visiting many different sites until you find what you need.
- Use the Internet wisely. There is a lot of bad information on the World Wide Web. Try to discriminate between the good information and the misinformation!
- Be sure to correctly cite your Internet sources of information and give credit where credit is due.

PRONUNCIATION TIP
SYLLABLE STRESS IN COMPOUND NOUNS

It's important to stress the correct syllables of words when speaking. Unfortunately, English does not use written accent marks the way some other languages do to tell us which syllable to stress. However, stress is usually placed on the first part of compound nouns.

EXERCISE 1   Practice saying the following compound nouns aloud. Be sure to stress the first part of each compound noun.

1. **bed**room
2. **ice** cream
3. **base**ball
4. **grape**fruit
5. **drug**store
6. **school**house
7. **foot**ball
8. **air**plane
9. **key**hole
10. **sun**tan
11. **stop** sign
12. **book**store
13. **suit**case
14. **doll**house
15. **light** bulb

EXERCISE 2   Write twelve more compound nouns. Practice saying them aloud. Be sure to stress the first part of each compound noun.

1. _____
2. _____
3. _____
4. _____
5. _____
6. _____

7. _____
8. _____
9. _____
10. _____
11. _____
12. _____

EXERCISE 3   Write ten sentences using compound nouns from Exercises 1 and 2. Practice saying the sentences aloud. Be sure to stress the first part of each compound noun.

1. _____
2. _____
3. _____
4. _____
5. _____
6. _____
7. _____
8. _____
9. _____
10. _____

Speaking to Persuade

Persuasive speaking is all around us. Any speech is persuasive if its purpose is to convince others to change their feelings, beliefs, or behavior. A salesperson trying to convince someone to buy a product, a political leader trying to get someone to vote a certain way, and a teacher lecturing about why a history class should be required are all speaking to persuade.

When do we make persuasive speeches? We make them all the time. When we ask a friend to lend us money, ask our teacher for a higher grade, try to convince a sibling to lose some weight, or try to persuade a parent to buy us something, our goal is to try to change or influence others.

In this chapter, you will learn how to build a persuasive speech.

PRACTICE YOUR PERSUASIVE SKILLS

Find a partner and role-play a situation in which you practice persuasion.

1. Choose one of the persuasive-speaking situations below (or think of a different persuasive-speaking situation):

   - Convince your parents to let you go on a camping trip with friends.
   - Convince your younger brother (or sister) to do his (or her) homework.
   - Convince a friend that watching TV is (or isn't) a waste of time.
   - Convince your boss to give you a promotion or a raise.
   - Convince your parents that you are (or aren't) too young to get married.
   - Convince your teacher that you did not get help writing a composition.
   - Convince students to vote for you to be president of the class.
   - Convince a friend to smoke less.
   - Convince a salesclerk to let you return something you bought.
   - Convince your parents to let you get a part-time job.
   - Convince clients to invest in your new company.
   - Convince your parents to buy you a car.
   - Convince your parents to abolish your curfew.

2. Your teacher will give you and your partner 10 minutes to plan your scenario.

3. Role-play the situation in front of the class.

4. Speak persuasively about the topic for 2–3 minutes. Present at least three compelling reasons why the person should do what you want them to do. Be prepared to counter any objections they might have.

Example: You are trying to convince your parents to buy you a car.

Several persuasive points for you to develop might be:

a. Public transportation is not safe. There have been a lot of muggings at your local bus stops.

b. Public transportation is not reliable. You are always arriving late to class and missing important information that you need to get good grades.

c. Because of the poor bus service, you were fired from your job for consistently arriving late to work. If you had a car, you could get a job and keep it. This would help you pay for your school expenses.

d. If you had a car, you could volunteer to do more errands for your parents and drive them places when their cars were in for repairs.

PREPARING FOR THE PERSUASIVE SPEECH

As with the informative speech, you build a persuasive speech step by step. The persuasive-speech blueprint below will help you create persuasive presentations that are interesting and effective.

The steps for preparing a persuasive speech are:

1. Choosing your topic
2. Determining your specific purpose
3. Analyzing your audience
4. Gathering information
5. Preparing visual aids
6. Organizing your speech

1. Choose a Topic
2. Determine the Specific Purpose
3. Analyze the Audience
4. Gather Information
5. Prepare Visual Aids
6. Organize the Speech

1. CHOOSING YOUR TOPIC

1. Choose a Topic

As with your previous speeches, your first question may be "What should I talk about?" Several suggestions about how to choose appropriate topics for your persuasive speech follow.

Choose a topic that really interests you.

It is easy to think of ideas if you choose a topic that you feel strongly about.

Example A

A student who had been in a serious car accident and suffered only minor injuries because he was wearing a seat belt gave a speech entitled "The Use of Seat Belts in Cars Should Be Required by Law."

Example B

A student who had a brown belt in karate gave a speech entitled "Everyone Should Learn Karate as a Form of Self-Defense."

Suggest a change that isn't too large.

It is much easier to convince an audience to change their opinions, feelings, or behavior a little than to persuade them to change their minds completely.

Example A

It would be very difficult to convince a heavy smoker to stop smoking completely. However, you might be able to persuade him or her to cut down to one pack a day.

Example B

It would be unrealistic to try to persuade a very religious person to convert to a different faith. However, you might be able to convince him or her to read a book about different religious customs.

Choose a topic that is controversial.

Do not choose a point of view that most people already agree with.

Example A

"Exercise Is Good for You" is not a good topic. Most people already agree with this statement. However, "Jogging Is Healthier than Swimming" or "Everyone Should Enroll in an Exercise Class" are topics that are controversial since not all people agree with these claims.

Example B

The topic "English Is Spoken All Over the World" is not controversial. However, the topic "Everyone Should Learn English as a Second Language" and "English Should Be Required in South American Schools" are topics that could be argued since many people might not agree with these opinions.

FORMULATE PERSUASIVE CLAIMS FOR TOPICS

Write down three persuasive speech topics that you might like to use. Several general topics are listed below. What are your views about these topics? If you have a strong opinion about one, that may be a good topic for your persuasive speech.

Abortion	Separation of church and state
Racial equality	College entrance requirements
Prostitution	Legalization of marijuana
Capital punishment	Boycotting the Olympic Games
Arranged marriages	Opportunities for the handicapped
Nuclear weapons	Smoking in public places
Gun control	Living together before marriage
Donating money to charity	The legal drinking age
Working mothers	Punishment for dishonesty
Drunk drivers	Mercy killing
Animal experimentation	Violence on TV
Pornography	Highway speed limits
Women's rights	Required college courses
Sex education	Students evaluating teachers
Stem cell research	Homosexual marriages
Cell phones	Cloning of animals
Human cloning	Electric cars
In vitro fertilization	Surrogate mothers

Possible Persuasive Speech Topics:

1. _____

2. _____

3. _____

Now that you have selected possible general topics, you will need to form related specific persuasive claims. There may be more than one specific persuasive claim related to a general topic.

Example A

General Topic: School Dress Codes
Possible Specific Persuasive Claims:

- High school students should not be required to wear uniforms to school.
- School uniforms should be required in public elementary schools.
- Private schools should abolish student dress codes.

Example B

General Topic: Capital Punishment
Possible Specific Persuasive Claims:

- Capital punishment should be abolished nationally.
- Capital punishment should be legal in every state.
- Criminals convicted of armed robbery should receive the death penalty.

ACTIVITY

NARROW DOWN YOUR TOPIC

Choose one of the general controversial topics that interested you in the preceding activity. Think of three possible specific persuasive claims related to that topic. Choose one for your persuasive speech.

General Topic: _____

Specific Persuasive Claims:

1. _____

2. _____

3. _____

Your Choice: _____

2. DETERMINING YOUR SPECIFIC PURPOSE

2. Determine the Specific Purpose

The general goal of persuasive speaking is to convince your listeners to change something. The first step in this is to decide what you want them to change—a belief, an opinion, or their behavior.

To Change Audience's Belief (That Something Is True or False)

In this case, your specific purpose is to convince the audience of one of the following:

- a reported fact is either true or false
- something will or won't happen
- an event was represented accurately or inaccurately

Examples

Mexico City (or Tokyo) is the largest city in the world.

The defendant committed (or did not commit) the crime.

Capital punishment is (or is not) a deterrent to crime.

There is (or is not) life after death.

To Change Audience's Opinion (About Something's Value)

In this case, your specific purpose is to convince the audience that something is one of the following:

- good or bad
- important or unimportant
- fair or unfair
- better or worse (than something else)
- helpful or not helpful

Examples

It is fair (or unfair) for foreign students to pay higher tuition.

Required courses in college are important (or unimportant).

Dogs make better (or worse) pets than cats.

New York is more (or less) interesting than San Francisco.

To Change Audience's Behavior

In this case, your specific purpose is to convince your listeners to either:

- do something they are not doing now
- stop some behavior they currently practice

Examples

You should donate blood at the campus blood drive.

You should stop drinking coffee.

You should limit the amount of TV you watch to a maximum of one hour daily.

You should learn to scuba dive for a hobby.

ACTIVITY **DIFFERENTIATE FACTS VS. OPINIONS**

This activity is designed to help you understand the difference between statements of fact and statements of opinion. Work individually for 5–10 minutes and follow the steps below.

1. Think of any place (city, state, country, continent, etc.) in the world beginning with the first letter of your first name. (Pablo chose Panama.)

2. State two objective, indisputable facts about the place. ("Panama is in Central America." "Panama is an isthmus.")

3. Now think of a product, an animal, or an object beginning with the first letter of your first name. (Pablo chose perfume.)

4. State two subjective opinions about the product, animal, or object. ("Perfume makes people more attractive." "Perfume smells nice.")

5. When you are finished, your teacher will ask you to come to the front of the room and share your "facts" and "opinions" with the rest of the class. (You might be surprised to find that what you stated as "facts" are really "opinions.") Your teacher will help you be the judge.

ACTIVITY **IDENTIFY SPECIFIC PURPOSE**

Write the letter of the specific purpose next to each persuasive speech topic. (Answers can be found on page 282 of Appendix II.)

a. Change audience's belief (that something is true or false)
b. Change audience's opinion (about something's value)
c. Change audience's behavior

_____ 1. Everyone should learn to give artificial respiration.

_____ 2. Airplane travel is the safest way to travel in the U.S.

_____ 3. Soccer is a more exciting sport than baseball.

_____ 4. The government should prohibit all cigarette advertising.

_____ 5. Lower highway speed limits save lives.

_____ 6. Single parents should be allowed to adopt children.

_____ 7. History is a more important subject than biology.

_____ 8. You should donate at least fifty dollars a year to your favorite charity.

_____ 9. Alcoholic beverages should not be sold on Sunday.

_____ 10. Parrots make wonderful pets.

3. ANALYZING YOUR AUDIENCE

3. Analyze the Audience

Audience analysis was briefly discussed in Chapter 4: Speaking to Inform. Audience analysis is especially important in persuasive speaking. It is necessary to learn as much as possible about your audience's feelings and opinions toward your topic. You need to know how they feel and why they feel a certain way in order to prepare an effective persuasive speech.

You can expect your listeners to feel one of three ways about the topic you choose for your persuasive speech. They might:

Agree completely: If your audience already agrees with your belief or point of view, you must choose a different topic for your speech.

Be indifferent: If your audience doesn't care about your topic, you must find out why they are indifferent to it. In your speech, you need to:

- interest them in your topic
- convince them that it is important
- persuade them to adopt your opinion

Disagree completely: If your audience does not agree with your point of view, they probably have definite reasons for feeling the way they do. You must find out why they disagree with your opinion in order to convince them that their reasons are not good.

SURVEY YOUR AUDIENCE

Interview your classmates to find out what they think about your topic. Use the opinion survey form below to record your findings.

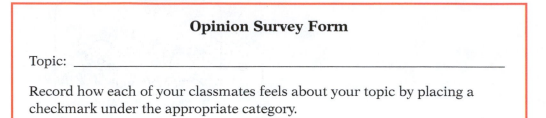

Opinion Survey Form

Topic: _____

Record how each of your classmates feels about your topic by placing a checkmark under the appropriate category.

Classmates' reactions to topic:

Disagree	Indifferent	Agree
✓_____	✓_____	✓_____
_____	_____	_____
Total = _____	Total = _____	Total = _____

If your classmates are indifferent, it is because (check all reasons given):

_____ They don't think your topic affects them.

_____ They have never heard of your topic.

_____ They have never given your topic any thought.

_____ Other:

_____

If your classmates disagree with your opinion, it is because (write all reasons given):

1. _____

2. _____

3. _____

4. _____

5. _____

4. GATHERING INFORMATION

4. Gather Information

The next step is to collect the information you need to create your speech.

1. Write down what you already know about your topic.
2. Think about your own related observations or experiences.
3. Gather additional necessary information by:
   a. conducting research
      - For suggestions regarding library research, see pages 70–71 in Chapter 4.
      - For Internet research, see Chapter 6.
   b. interviewing experts or people who have an interest in your topic

Example A

A student's persuasive topic was "The College Should Increase the School Library's Budget." She called the head librarian, who felt the library needed additional books, better computers, more staff, and longer hours to better serve the students' needs.

Example B

Another student tried to convince the class that more scholarships should be available for international students. He interviewed the financial aid director at the university. The director agreed with him and provided specific information about the limited funds available to help international students with their education.

When you are looking for information for a persuasive speech, the editorial pages of newspapers can be especially useful. They often include articles and letters that express different opinions about current controversial topics. The Internet may be of particular value as well: Often there are links to websites in which different opinions about the topic are expressed.

Whenever you quote specific people or use information from newspapers, magazines, books, or the Internet in your speech, be sure to tell your audience the source of your information.

- This will make your evidence and arguments more believable.
- You will also gain the respect of your listeners by showing them that you are a responsible researcher.

5. PREPARING VISUAL AIDS

As discussed in Chapter 5, visual aids—pictures, graphs, or objects—can make your speech more interesting and can be very powerful persuasive tools. An audience is more likely to be convinced if they can actually see the importance of what you are describing.

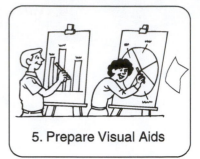

5. Prepare Visual Aids

Example A

In a speech to persuade a class to donate money to a charity that helps children with disabilities, this picture affected the audience emotionally and thus made them want to make a donation:

Example B

In a speech to persuade a class to pay off the balance on their credit cards and stop using them, one student explained that Americans are declaring bankruptcy more now than at any time in history, largely because of the misuse of credit cards. He then showed the following pie chart to illustrate the high percentage of Americans that carry credit card debt:

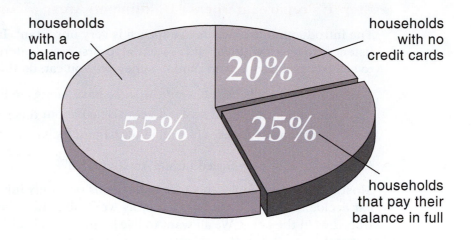

households with a balance

households with no credit cards

20%

55%

25%

households that pay their balance in full

Example C

In a speech to persuade a class to complain to university officials about the polluted lakes on campus, one student held up a large bottle of dirty brown water with a dead fish in it. He explained that the dead fish came from one of the nearby lakes. This convinced the students that his speech presented a serious problem.

6. ORGANIZING YOUR SPEECH

6. Organize the Speech

The next step is to organize your speech. A good persuasive speech includes the following components:

- Opener building on areas of agreement with audience
- Statement of purpose
- Preview of persuasive points
- Body
- Summary
- Memorable concluding remarks

Step 1: Prepare an Opener Building on Areas of Agreement

The introduction to a persuasive speech is very important. In order to convince listeners to agree with you, it is essential to first give them reason to trust you and to see you as a person who thinks as they do. You can do this by first discussing:

- common goals (we all want the same basic things in life)
- common problems (we are all concerned about this particular problem)
- common experiences (we all know what it is like to . . .)

Example A: "Highway Speed Limits Are Too High"

Most of us know people who have had friends or family injured or killed in terrible car accidents on the highways. Certainly we've all read or heard about these tragedies in the news. We all want to live long, happy, healthy lives and not worry about the possibility of accidents. No one wants to worry about whether they will arrive at their destination safely every time they get in a car.

Example B: "Capital Punishment Should Be Legal"

I'm sure everyone here is concerned about crime in our community. Many of us know that it isn't always safe to go out alone at night or even to walk through a dark parking lot to get to our car. All of us want to feel safe in our homes, in our cars, and on the streets. We would all like to see the amount of crime reduced.

Example C: "Donate Money to the Red Cross"

Although we take many things for granted, we all know how fortunate we are to have nice clothes to wear, a place to live, and plenty of food to eat. We all realize that many people in the world aren't so lucky. There are many starving and homeless people on every continent. Most of you would be willing to help people less fortunate than yourselves if you knew what to do.

Step 2: Prepare a Statement of Purpose

Now that you have shown your audience that you are a sensible person who shares their values and beliefs, the next step is to clearly state the specific purpose of your speech.

Example A: "Highway Speed Limits Are Too High"

The maximum speed limit on U.S. highways should be fifty miles per hour.

Example B: "Capital Punishment Should Be Legal"

Legalizing capital punishment can help prevent crime.

Example C: "Donate Money to the Red Cross"

Everyone in this class should donate five dollars to the Red Cross.

Step 3: Prepare a Preview of Main Persuasive Points

Now that your listeners know your specific purpose, the next step is to preview the main persuasive points you will present in the body of your speech.

Example A: "Donate Blood to a Hospital Blood Bank"

I hope to persuade you to donate blood to a hospital blood bank for several reasons.

    I. Blood donations save lives.
    II. It is perfectly safe and painless.
    III. It is very convenient.

Example B: "Casino Gambling Should Be Legal in Miami"

    I. The creation of new jobs will reduce unemployment.
    II. A proposed sales tax increase will not be necessary.
    III. The city will have more funds to improve public facilities.

Example C: "Capital Punishment Should Be Legal"

    I. Capital punishment reduces crime.
    II. Rehabilitation programs don't work.
    III. Prisons are expensive for governments to maintain.

Step 4: Prepare the Body

Now that your listeners know your main persuasive points, the next step is to present evidence that will convince them to agree with you. Your audience analysis can help at this stage. Review your opinion survey form before deciding how to convince indifferent or hostile listeners.

Indifferent listeners do not see how a topic relates to them

In order to persuade listeners with this attitude, you must convince them that your topic is:

- interesting,
- important, and
- relevant to them.

Example A

One student wanted to persuade the class to buy water purification systems. According to this speaker's opinion survey, his classmates were indifferent to this topic because they had never given it any thought and didn't believe it was important. However, he found a newspaper story claiming that the quality of water in their community was the worst in the United States. In the article, doctors warned that drinking this water could increase the risk of contracting cancer.

Example B

One student gave a speech entitled "Casino Gambling Should Be Legal in Miami." After doing her audience analysis, she found that her classmates were indifferent to her topic for several reasons. Some students said they don't gamble, while some international students said they will only live in Miami for a couple of years. The speaker explained that casino gambling would help the city's finances, so a proposed sales tax increase would not be necessary. If the sales tax wasn't increased, prices in all stores and restaurants would be lower. Then everyone (gamblers and non-gamblers, permanent residents, and students on temporary visas) would benefit.

Hostile listeners are those who completely disagree with your opinion or belief

In order to persuade such listeners, you need to learn their reasons for disagreeing with you and convince them that these reasons are not valid.

Example A

One student wanted to persuade the class to donate blood to a hospital blood bank. According to this student's audience analysis, there were two reasons why his classmates didn't want to be blood donors.

- They were afraid of catching a disease from a dirty hypodermic needle.
- They didn't have transportation to get to the hospital.

To refute the first reason, the student interviewed the nurse in charge of the hospital blood bank, who explained that individually wrapped and sterilized needles are used for every blood donor and thrown away after each use. Therefore, it is impossible to catch a disease from a dirty needle.

To refute the second reason, the speaker explained that it is very easy to get to the hospital because:

- A bus goes from campus directly to the hospital every fifteen minutes.
- The hospital offers a free transportation service to all blood donors.

Example B

One student gave a speech entitled "Capital Punishment Should Be Legal Throughout the United States." This student's audience analysis showed that his classmates strongly disagreed with his claim for several reasons:

- Some believed that capital punishment does not reduce crime.
- Some audience members believed that murderers should be rehabilitated.
- Some audience members felt that life imprisonment is more humane than the death penalty.

To refute the first reason, the student:

- presented evidence that there are fewer murders committed in states that have the death penalty than in states that do not, and
- quoted a law enforcement expert who stated that criminals are less likely to commit murder if they fear the death penalty.

To refute the second reason, the speaker reported:

- results of studies showing the ineffectiveness of attempts to rehabilitate criminals, and
- specific studies that showed that most lawbreakers released from jail after participating in rehabilitation programs continue to commit the same crimes.

To refute the third reason, the speaker cited a report in which prisoners claimed that the thought of spending the rest of their lives in jail was unbearable. In fact, they would rather receive the death penalty.

Step 5: Prepare a Summary

An effective persuasive speech includes a summary of the evidence presented. This will remind your audience of why they should agree with you. The examples below show how evidence was summarized in two speeches.

Example A: "Donate Blood to a Hospital Blood Bank"

I'm sure you now realize that you should donate blood.

   I. It's rewarding and worthwhile.
      A. Think of a dying person whose life you might save.
      B. Think of the great personal satisfaction you'll have.
   II. It's perfectly safe and painless.
      A. Donating blood doesn't hurt a bit.
      B. There is no chance of catching any kind of disease.
  III. It's very convenient.
      A. It will only take a few minutes of your time.
      B. Free round-trip transportation to the hospital is available.

Example B: "Casino Gambling Should Be Legal in Miami"

As you can now see, legalizing casino gambling in Miami would greatly benefit you and all residents of the city.

   I. A proposed sales tax increase will not be necessary.
      A. This will keep prices you pay in restaurants lower.
      B. This will keep prices you pay in retail stores lower.
   II. Miami's finances will improve.
      A. More money will be spent to improve the roads you use.
      B. More money will be spent to improve the public parks and beaches you enjoy.
      C. More money will be spent on educational materials for children in public schools.

Step 6: Prepare Memorable Concluding Remarks

The last part of your speech to prepare is the conclusion. The conclusion of a persuasive speech should remind the audience why they should change a belief, an opinion, or a behavior. An effective way to do this is to make them think about the future and to remind them to take some type of action.

Example A

You might be healthy now, but think about your health in a few months or in several years. We all know that the water in this city is unhealthy for us. With a home purification system, you'll never worry about drinking polluted water again. For less than seventy-five dollars, turn your kitchen faucet into an ocean of fresh water. It is in your best interest to install a purification system for your sink today.

Example B

Be the best you can be! Just think—in a few short weeks, a beautiful, slender, athletic body can be yours. Heads will turn as you walk down the street. Be sure to start an exercise program today.

SAMPLE PERSUASIVE SPEECH

Feng, a Taiwanese student, made his persuasive speech about acupuncture. Notice how the transcript of his speech below includes all the important components:

- Opener building on areas of agreement
- Statement of specific purpose
- Preview of main points
- Body
- Summary
- Memorable concluding remarks

Also, notice how transitions have been used to connect the components.

General topic: Acupuncture

Statement of specific purpose: Consider acupuncture when you are sick or in pain.

OPENER BUILDING ON AREAS OF AGREEMENT

We all know someone who has been sick or in pain at some point in their lives. Maybe you, a friend, or a family member has had painful surgery, or suffers from depression. Often, the medicines the doctors prescribe have side effects and make the patient feel even worse. No one likes to suffer. When we don't feel well, we would all like to recover and feel better as quickly as possible. Acupuncture might be the solution for what is ailing you.

STATEMENT OF SPECIFIC PURPOSE

Consider acupuncture when you are sick or in pain.

PREVIEW OF MAIN POINTS

There are many reasons you should consider acupuncture instead of traditional Western medicine.

A. Acupuncture is a medically proven treatment.

B. Acupuncture is safe and painless.

C. Acupuncture effectively treats many conditions.

TRANSITION: *Many of you might be skeptical about acupuncture because you believe it is a new and unproven treatment. You will be amazed to learn that acupuncture has been used effectively for thousands of years and is medically respected in the United States.*

BODY

According to the *Encyclopedia Britannica*, acupuncture is an ancient Chinese medical technique for relieving pain and curing disease. It has been used successfully in Asian cultures for more than 2,500 years.

Acupuncture is endorsed by American mainstream medicine as well as by international organizations. In 1997, a panel of scientists and researchers at the National Institutes of Health determined that acupuncture had been clinically proven to be effective against a variety of medical problems and diseases. I will describe these later in my speech. A National Institutes of Health Conference on Acupuncture stated: "The data in support of acupuncture are as strong as those for many accepted Western medical therapies."

The Food and Drug Administration (FDA) reclassified acupuncture needles from "experimental devices" to the same category as medical and surgical instruments. This clearly shows that the FDA endorses acupuncture as a respected medical treatment. This is a picture of acupuncture needles.

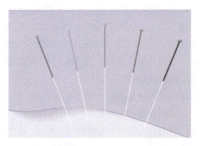

The World Health Organization (WHO) also endorses acupuncture as a medically proven treatment. They have endorsed the use of acupuncture as a medical therapy for over fifteen years.

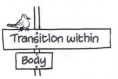
TRANSITION: *Many of you might be worried that acupuncture is not safe. You will be very pleased to learn that acupuncture is extremely safe and painless.*

According to the *Medical Acupuncture Online Journal*, acupuncture is extremely safe with virtually no chances of any side effects. Many patients become addicted to pain medicines which can have serious side effects. This won't happen with acupuncture. According to the book *Acupuncture for Everyone* by Dr. Ruth Kidsor, acupuncture is an effective treatment for pain, and it is not addictive. Also, there is absolutely no risk of catching any type of communicable disease from acupuncture needles. This is because modern acupuncturists use only sterilized, individually packaged needles which they throw away when they are done with each treatment. The same needles are never used twice.

You will also be happy to know that acupuncture treatments are painless. According to a book entitled *Acupuncture*, there may be a tingling sensation associated with the insertion of the acupuncture needles in some points, but the overall effect is very relaxing.

The author, Peter Mole, states that it is much like the effect you feel when receiving massage therapy. I'd like to show you a picture of a patient receiving an acupuncture treatment. Notice how relaxed and content the patient appears.

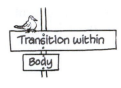

TRANSITION: *Some of you might think that acupuncture is helpful for only a few minor problems. I will now prove to you that acupuncture treats a wide variety of problems and diseases.*

Clinical studies have shown that acupuncture is effective in treating patients with chronic pain. The World Health Organization and the National Institutes of Health (NIH) have determined that acupuncture is effective in treating such painful conditions as headaches, arthritis, and back pain. It also reduces the pain of menstrual cramps, pain from surgery, and other musculoskeletal pains.

Acupuncture also treats a variety of diseases and other physical conditions. It has been proven to help people with allergies, asthma, and heart problems. It has allowed previously infertile couples to conceive a child. It even helps people with insomnia to sleep better at night. The NIH also specifically states that acupuncture has been proven to reduce a patient's nausea from surgery and chemotherapy.

Acupuncture also effectively treats many emotional or psychological problems. It has helped many people overcome tobacco, alcohol, and drug addictions. It helps people overcome eating disorders and obsessive behaviors. Acupuncture helps patients with anxiety disorders, and it alleviates stress. It has helped individuals with low self-esteem. Acupuncture also enables people who suffer from depression to feel better and to stop taking depression medication.

In general, acupuncture helps people's immune systems to function better. This helps them to avoid colds, the flu, and other respiratory infections. Many people simply use acupuncture as an effective form of preventative medicine.

SUMMARY

I hope I have convinced you to consider acupuncture as a medical treatment. Remember:

A. Acupuncture is a clinically proven and respected medical treatment.

B. Acupuncture is perfectly safe and painless.

C. Acupuncture treats a wide variety of physical and emotional problems.

MEMORABLE CONCLUDING REMARKS

Throw away those medicines that bother your stomach or make you sleepy. Remember: There is an alternative. The next time you aren't feeling well, acupuncture may be the way to go.

OUTLINE FENG'S SPEECH

Follow the steps below to get an idea of what the outline that Feng used for his speech looked like.

1. Using his speech as a guide, complete the skeleton outline below with the missing information.

2. Compare your completed outline with the sample outline on page 282 of Appendix II.

Example: *Feng's Persuasive Speech Outline*

INTRODUCTION

OPENER BUILDING ON AREAS OF AGREEMENT

I. We all know someone who has been sick or in pain at some point in their lives. Maybe you, a friend, or a family member has had painful surgery, or suffers from depression. Often, the medicines the doctors prescribe have side effects and make the patient feel even worse. No one likes to suffer. When we don't feel well, we would all like to recover and feel better as quickly as possible. Acupuncture might be the solution for what is ailing you.

STATEMENT OF SPECIFIC PURPOSE

II. Consider acupuncture when you are sick or in pain.

PREVIEW OF MAIN POINTS

III. There are many reasons to consider acupuncture instead of traditional Western medicine.

    A. _____

    B. _____

    C. _____

TRANSITION: *Many of you might be skeptical about acupuncture because you believe it is a new and unproven treatment. You will be amazed to learn that acupuncture has been used effectively for thousands of years and is medically respected in the United States.*

BODY

I. _____

    A. Acupuncture is an ancient Chinese technique.

        1. Relieves pain

        2. _____

        3. _____

B. Acupuncture is respected by known national and international health organizations.

    1. _____

        a. _____

        b. "The data in support of acupuncture are as strong as those for many accepted Western medical therapies."

    2. Food and Drug Administration (FDA)

        a. _____

        b. _____

        c. (Show visual aid—picture of acupuncture needles.)

    3. _____

        a. _____

        b. WHO has endorsed acupuncture use for over fifteen years.

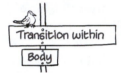
Transition within Body

TRANSITION: *Many of you might be worried that acupuncture is not safe. You will be very pleased to learn that acupuncture is extremely safe and painless.*

II. _____

    A. There are no side effects.

    B. Acupuncture is nonaddictive.

    C. _____

        1. _____

        2. _____

    D. Acupuncture is painless.

        1. _____

        2. _____

        3. (Show visual aid of patient receiving acupuncture treatment.)

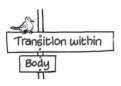
Transition within Body

TRANSITION: *Some of you might think that acupuncture is helpful for only a few minor problems. I will now prove to you that acupuncture treats a wide variety of problems and diseases.*

III. _____

    A. _____

        1. headaches

        2. _____

        3. _____

        4. _____

        5. _____

        6. _____

B. Physical problems and diseases

    1. _____

    2. _____

    3. _____

    4. _____

    5. _____

    6. _____

        a. _____

        b. chemotherapy

C. Emotional and psychological problems

    1. Addictions

        a. _____

        b. _____

        c. _____

    2. Eating disorders

    3. _____

    4. Anxiety disorders

    5. _____

    6. Low self-esteem

    7. _____

D. Helps the immune system function better

    1. _____

    2. _____

CONCLUSION

SUMMARY

I. I hope I have convinced you to consider acupuncture as a medical treatment.

    A. Acupuncture is a clinically proven and respected medical treatment.

    B. Acupuncture is perfectly safe and painless.

    C. Acupuncture treats a wide variety of physical and emotional problems.

MEMORABLE CONCLUDING REMARKS

II. Throw away those medicines that bother your stomach or make you sleepy. Remember: There is an alternative. The next time you aren't feeling well, acupuncture may be the way to go.

Assignment: Give a persuasive speech.

1. Using the Persuasive Speech Preparation Worksheet and Checklist on pages 142–144, prepare notes for your presentation.
2. Using the guidelines from Chapter 3: Putting Your Speech Together, outline your speech.
3. Your teacher may use the form on page 253 of Appendix I to evaluate your speech. Look it over so you know exactly how you will be evaluated.
4. Give a 4- to 5-minute persuasive speech.

PERSUASIVE SPEECH PREPARATION WORKSHEET

1. Choose three controversial topics that interest you.

    a. _____

    b. _____

    c. _____

2. Determine your purpose for speaking about each of the topics above.

    a. _____

    b. _____

    c. _____

3. Formulate a specific statement of purpose for each of the topics above.

    a. _____

    b. _____

    c. _____

4. Choose one topic, purpose, and specific persuasive claim.

    Topic _____

    Purpose _____

    Specific persuasive claim _____

5. Write three reasons why people might be indifferent or opposed to your topic.

    a. _____

    b. _____

    c. _____

6. Prepare an opener building on areas of agreement.

_____

_____

_____

_____

7. State your persuasive claim.

_____

_____

8. Write the main points of the body.

_____

_____

_____

_____

9. Prepare a summary.

_____

_____

_____

_____

10. Prepare memorable concluding remarks.

_____

_____

_____

_____

You may want to use the checklist below. Check off each step as you prepare for your speech.

PERSUASIVE SPEECH PREPARATION CHECKLIST

Name: _____   Topic: _____
Due Date: _____

_____ Chose topic about which the audience is indifferent or opposed
_____ Consulted outside sources:

_____ Interviews	_____ Books	_____ Magazines
_____ Newspapers	_____ Dictionaries	_____ Encyclopedias
_____ Encyclopedic dictionaries	_____ Professional journals	_____ Internet

_____ Prepared opener building on areas of agreement
_____ Prepared clear statement of purpose
_____ Prepared preview of main persuasive points
_____ Prepared outline for body
_____ Prepared summary
_____ Prepared memorable concluding remarks
_____ Prepared transition after introduction
_____ Prepared transition before summary
_____ Prepared transitions within body
_____ Prepared visual aids:

| _____ Objects | _____ Charts and diagrams | _____ Demonstrations |

_____ Practiced speech with visual aids at least three times

PRONUNCIATION TIP
STRESS IN NOUN/VERB PAIRS

In English, many two-syllable nouns and verbs are spelled alike. However, when spoken, they are pronounced differently. Most two-syllable nouns are stressed on the first syllable. Most two-syllable verbs are stressed on the second syllable.

Practice reading the following pairs of nouns and verbs aloud. Be sure to stress the first syllable of the noun and the second syllable of the verb.

Nouns	Verbs
1. **pre**sent (a gift)	pre**sent** (to give; to show)
2. **pro**ject (an assignment)	pro**ject** (to predict)
3. **con**vict (a criminal)	con**vict** (to find guilty)
4. **ob**ject (a thing; a purpose)	ob**ject** (to be against)
5. **re**cord (a written account; a recording)	re**cord** (to write down; to make an audio- or videotape)

Read the following sentences aloud. Be sure to stress the first syllable of each noun and the second syllable of each verb.

1. Please **recórd** the **récord**.
2. I **objéct** to that ugly **óbject**.
3. She will **presént** you with a **présent**.
4. We **projéct** that Mario will do well on the **próject**.
5. The judge will **convíct** the **ex-cónvict**.

Read the following sentences aloud. Then indicate whether the boldfaced word is a noun or a verb. Finally, circle the number of the syllable stressed.

Example

Enrique read *Reader's **Digest***.	<u>noun</u>	①	2
1. We rode camels in the **desert**.	_____	1	2
2. The **convict** escaped from jail.	_____	1	2
3. They signed the **contract**.	_____	1	2
4. Never **desert** a friend in trouble.	_____	1	2
5. Don't **convict** me of a crime I didn't do.	_____	1	2

CHAPTER 8

Listening

Know how to listen and you will profit even from those who talk badly.

—Plutarch, Greek historian

Nature has given to men one tongue but two ears, that we may hear from others twice as much as we speak.

—Epictetus, Stoic philosopher

Hearing is good and speaking is good, but he who hears is a possessor of benefits.

—Ptahhotep, Egyptian judge

Listening is one of the most important activities we engage in. People spend close to 50 percent of their waking time listening, and college students spend almost 90 percent of their class time listening. Most people realize that it is important to listen carefully when teachers lecture, friends talk, parents or advisers provide information, bosses explain things, or radio commentators report the news.

Unfortunately, some listening habits prevent people from fully understanding what they hear. By knowing what these habits are, you can avoid them and become better listeners. The exercises and activities in this chapter will help you improve your ability to listen effectively in a variety of situations.

Have you ever told a friend, child, parent, spouse, or anyone at all, "You don't listen!"? Has a teacher, friend, or anyone at all ever told you in frustration, "Why don't you listen?" Of course, we have all admonished others for not listening to us or been admonished for not paying closer attention to what someone was saying. Why is this? Why aren't people better listeners? Before we examine this more closely, it's important to objectively evaluate your own listening skills and target the specific areas you would like to improve.

EXERCISE

FIND OUT HOW WELL YOU LISTEN TO OTHERS

1. Work individually. Complete the "Listening Self-Evaluation" below. (The form continues on the next page.)
2. When everyone has finished, work in a small group. Take turns discussing your responses to the different questions.
3. Think of specific examples of situations in which you may have been guilty of not listening well. Share these examples with your group.
4. When all the groups have finished, share your observations with the class and think about how you can improve any bad listening habits. You will learn more about this in the next section.

LISTENING SELF-EVALUATION

How well do you listen? Check (✓) the box that best describes your listening habit in each situation described.

Listening Habit	Often	Sometimes	Seldom	Never
a. When I don't agree with what someone is saying, I tend not to listen to them.				
b. I pay attention to a speaker's appearance and don't listen to what they are saying.				
c. When someone is speaking, I tend to think about what I want to say, not what they are saying.				
d. When I am not interested in the topic being discussed, I tend not to listen carefully.				

Listening Habit	Often	Sometimes	Seldom	Never
e. I stop listening when I think I know what someone is going to say.				
f. At times my mind is somewhere else when I really should be listening.				
g. When I don't like or trust the speaker, I tend to block out what is being said.				
h. When I am listening to criticism, I tend to become annoyed or defensive and don't listen carefully to what the speaker is saying.				
i. I tend to pretend to be listening when I am not listening at all.				
j. I tend to focus on specific details of what a speaker is saying rather than on the main ideas or general purpose of the message.				
k. I tend to look at other people or objects in my surroundings rather than directly at the person speaking.				
l. I tend to hear what I want to hear or expect to hear instead of what the speaker is actually saying.				
m. I tend not to concentrate on what a speaker is saying if there is noise or other distractions.				
n. When I haven't been listening to someone speaking to me, I tell them I wasn't listening and ask them to repeat what they said.				

BAD LISTENING HABITS AND THEIR CURES

1. Being Distracted by the Speaker's Appearance or Delivery

Habit: Some people don't listen to what a speaker is saying because they are concentrating on the person's speech patterns, gestures, posture, clothes, or appearance. For example, a friend of John's father was explaining how to apply for a job with his company. John was so busy admiring the man's gold watch and expensive suit that he forgot to listen to what he was being told.

Cure: Concentrate on what the speaker is saying, not on how they look or sound. You can miss important information by thinking about a person's appearance or delivery style instead of paying attention to their words.

2. Deciding the Topic Is Boring

Habit: Some people decide in advance that they will be bored by what the speaker is going to talk about and use this prejudice as an excuse not to listen. For example, the president of a local bank came to speak to a group of college students about inflation. Emma decided that she wasn't interested in the topic and would be bored, so she brought a newspaper to read during the banker's speech. The speaker gave excellent suggestions about fighting inflation and saving money. All of Emma's friends thought it was a great speech with a lot of useful information. But she missed out because she wasn't listening.

Cure: Never take the attitude "I have to sit through another boring talk." Even if you are not interested in the topic at first, remember that some of the information could be important or interesting. Make an effort to listen for information that you could use later (e.g., in a college course, job, or conversation with friends or family). Adopt the attitude "I may as well listen since I'm already here."

3. Faking Attention

Habit: Some people pretend to be listening, but their minds are on other things. They might be looking directly at the speaker and even nodding their heads in agreement when, in fact, they are actually daydreaming, thinking about their own problems, or planning what they want to say in response to the speech. The speaker thinks the listeners are polite and interested, when they are really not paying attention. For example, Margaret Lane, author of a *Reader's Digest* article entitled "Are You Really Listening?", describes how faking attention cost her a job. When interviewing her for a job on a newspaper, the editor described his winter ski trip. She wanted to impress him by talking about a camping trip in the same mountains and started planning her own adventure story. The editor suddenly asked, "What do you think of that?" Ms. Lane (not having listened to him) answered, "Sounds like fun!" The annoyed editor replied, "Fun? I just told you I was in the hospital with a broken leg."

Cure: Don't just pretend to pay attention. Be sincere and take a real interest in the person speaking to you. If you are too busy to listen, ask the speaker if he or she can tell you later when you can really take the time to listen.

4. Looking for Distractions

Habit: Some people allow themselves to be distracted by their surroundings. They might look out the window or at the wall, play with a pencil or hair clip, or observe how people in the room are dressed. For example, one student failed a math test because she wasn't listening when the teacher told the class to be prepared for a quiz the following day. She was busy looking at a broken window shade and thinking that it was a shame that no one had bothered to fix it.

Cure: Concentrate! Refuse to allow distractions to take your mind off the speaker. Develop the willpower to ignore them.

5. Concentrating on Unimportant Details

Habit: Some people concentrate on specific details and miss the speaker's main points. For example, notice how the student missed the adviser's main points in the dialogue below.

ADVISER: On Friday May 10, Miss Martin, the Director of Financial Aid, spoke about applying for a scholarship.
STUDENT: May 10 was a *Thursday*, not a *Friday*.
ADVISER: I'll now summarize this important information for you. . .
STUDENT: It's not *Miss* Martin, it's *Mrs*. Martin.
ADVISER: Write to the address I gave you and send the application.
STUDENT: What address? What application?

Cure: When listening, pay attention to the general purpose of the message rather than to insignificant details. Listen for the main point of the talk first; then take note of any supporting facts.

6. Reacting Emotionally to Trigger Words

Habit: Some people ignore or distort what a speaker is saying because they react emotionally to "trigger words"—words or names of people that cause positive or negative emotional reactions. When this happens, their ability to listen decreases because they allow their emotions to take over. For example, if a favorite subject or person is mentioned, some people begin thinking about it and want to express their opinions. Similarly, if an unpleasant subject or person is mentioned, some people get upset or angry and stop listening to what the speaker is saying.

Example A

Pilar, a student from Argentina, was listening to her economics professor discuss the economy in South America. As soon as he mentioned Buenos Aires, Pilar became homesick and started to think about her friends and family still there. The mention of Buenos Aires caused her to have a pleasant emotional reaction. However, pleasant or not, the trigger word *Buenos Aires* caused Pilar to stop listening to her teacher's lecture.

Example B

Several students have reported that *terrorism* or *biological warfare* are their emotional trigger words. Upon hearing newscasters say these words, they become so preoccupied with the possibility of a terrorist attack that they stop listening to the rest of the newscast even when the commentator has started to discuss other topics.

Cure: Identify the trigger words that affect you. They may be names of certain people or they may be other subjects. Once you determine what they are, you can reduce their effect on you by recognizing them as soon as they are mentioned. This strategy will help you to remain objective and to concentrate on the speaker's message. Let the speaker finish what he or she is saying before you allow past memories to cause you to react emotionally.

ACTIVITY

THINK OF SOME PERSONAL TRIGGER WORDS

1. In the chart below, write the names of people or other subjects that trigger strong emotions in you.
2. When you have finished, discuss your responses in small groups. How do your classmates react when they hear each of these subjects or names?

	Negative Triggers	Positive Triggers
People		
Other Subjects		

ACTIVITY

EXPLORE THE EFFECTS OF BAD LISTENING

Step 1: Meeting in groups of 4 or 5 students, describe a situation in which you demonstrated one of the poor listening habits listed on pages 149–151. Discuss the following questions with your group members:

1. What was the consequence of your "bad" listening habit?
2. How can you improve this habit in the future?

Step 2: Describe a recent experience in detail. While you are talking, the other group members will purposely employ one of the bad listening habits described. After each member of the group has had a chance to be the speaker, discuss the following:

1. As a listener, how was your ability to listen affected by employing the bad listening habits?
2. As a speaker, how did you feel while your group members were demonstrating bad listening habits?

Step 3: Choose a member of your group to summarize the experiences of the group for the class.

EXERCISE

IDENTIFY THE PROBLEM

Next to each example, write the letter of one of the following bad listening habits that is demonstrated. (Answers can be found on page 286 of Appendix II.)

a. Being distracted by the speaker's appearance or delivery
b. Deciding the topic is boring
c. Faking attention
d. Looking for distractions
e. Concentrating on unimportant details
f. Reacting to emotional triggers

_____ 1. A Mexican tour guide was explaining the history of Chapultepec Castle to some American tourists. One of the tourists loved to hear the way Spanish speakers roll the letter *r* and paid more attention to the guide's pronunciation than to his explanation.

_____ 2. Linda was doing a crossword puzzle when her friend Rosa telephoned. As Rosa was talking, Linda kept saying, "Really?" and "I see" to make Rosa think she was listening. Linda was really working on her crossword puzzle.

_____ 3. Akiko's physical education teacher was explaining how to save the life of a heart attack victim through the use of CPR. As the teacher was speaking, Akiko was saddened by the memory of her grandfather who had recently died of a heart attack. All she could think about were the good times they had had together before he died.

_____ 4. Your friend is teaching you how to use his new camera. You want to learn to use the camera, but you notice he just bought an expensive stereo system with four speakers. While he is talking, you are looking at his new stereo, wishing you could afford one too.

_____ 5. Fernanda, a Brazilian student, told us that whenever someone mentions Brazil, she gets homesick. She immediately thinks of her family in São Paulo and starts to miss them terribly. She gets so emotional about being so far from her family that she doesn't listen to the speaker or follow the rest of the conversation.

6. A counselor was speaking about college graduation requirements. Lena decided that she didn't need to listen and would look up the information in the college catalogue. She wrote a letter to her boyfriend instead of listening to the speaker. She missed valuable information about new requirements that were not printed in the catalogue.

7. Your aunt is not a stylish dresser. You never really listen to what she says because, when you see her, you think about how her clothes don't match and how they look out of style.

8. A group of people were listening to a book review at their local library. One man was concentrating on remembering the exact ages and birthdays of all the book's characters; unfortunately, he missed much of the librarian's fascinating description of the novel's general plot.

9. Your academic adviser was explaining how to apply for financial aid or scholarships. You noticed that she bites her nails. You started thinking how ugly her nails looked and that she should stop biting them.

10. The school nurse was explaining the schedule for receiving free flu shots. She mentioned how many people get the flu each year. You were trying to remember the exact statistic and missed the information about when and where the flu shots would be administered.

ACTIVITY

PLAY TELEPHONE

Step 1: Play the game.

1. All students line up in the front of the room.
2. Your teacher will whisper a saying or quote to the first student. That student will whisper the saying to the next student, who in turn will whisper the saying to the next person in line and so on.
3. The last person in the line will announce the saying aloud.

Step 2: Discuss the following questions as a class:

1. Did the original saying that your teacher told the first student change?
2. Why did it change?

ACTIVITY

RETELL THE STORY

Step 1: Experience the retelling of a story.

1. Your teacher will ask four students to leave the room. They are not allowed to listen at the door!
2. Your teacher will read you a brief humorous anecdote or story from a newspaper or periodical such as *Reader's Digest*.
3. Your teacher will then call in the first student who is outside the room and ask one of the students in the room who heard the story to tell the story in their own words.

4. The second student from outside will be called in. The first student will tell this student the story in their own words.

5. Repeat this procedure with the third and fourth students.

6. When the fourth student has finished relating the story to the class, the teacher will reread the original story.

Step 2: Analyze how the story has changed from the original version.

1. Have details been added to the original story? Which ones?

2. Have details been omitted from the original story? Which ones were left out?

3. Have details been distorted? If so, how?

As you have seen, listening plays an important role in people's lives. It is a skill that can be learned and improved. However, listening is not a simple activity, especially in a second or foreign language. It involves a wide range of skills, many of which you will likely be addressing in other classes. It is beyond the scope of this text to teach all of the necessary listening skills. However, the following listening exercises will help you use what you are learning in this book to become a better listener:

- Comprehend main ideas and details.
- Take notes: outline main ideas and supporting details.
- Distinguish between facts, opinions, and inferences.
- Listen attentively to get the gist.
- Evaluate what you hear.
- Follow oral directions.

COMPREHEND MAIN IDEAS AND DETAILS

In the following two exercises, your challenge will be to listen for the main ideas as well as the details in a passage. (Answers can be found on pages 286–287 of Appendix II.)

EXERCISE 1   Your teacher will read an article entitled "Lying: Studies in Deception" two times. The first time, you will listen for main ideas; the second time, for details.

Step 1: Listen for the main ideas. Based on the information in the reading, write *T* if the statement is true and *F* if the statement is false. Wait until you have heard the entire article before answering the questions.

_____ 1. The ability to lie well is not a simple skill to learn.

_____ 2. An expert can easily detect a good liar.

_____ 3. Many companies and government agencies use polygraph tests each year.

_____ 4. Most experts agree that polygraph or lie-detector tests are reliable.

_____ 5. People have only recently become interested in attempting to detect lies.

Step 2: Your teacher will read the article again. This time, listen carefully for specific details. Complete the multiple-choice questions below by circling the correct responses.

1. The researcher who has studied lying is _____.
   a. an anthropologist from California
   b. a police officer from New York
   c. a psychologist from California

2. Lie-detector tests are also called _____.
   a. polygraph tests
   b. standardized tests
   c. psychological profiles

3. Who uses lie-detector tests? (Circle all correct responses.)
   a. police departments
   b. federal agencies
   c. private companies

4. How many times are lie-detector tests used?
   a. a million times a year
   b. a million times every five years
   c. a thousand times a year

5. How can lie detectors be fooled? (Circle all correct responses.)
   a. closing one's eyes
   b. using drugs
   c. hypnosis

Step 3: Discuss these questions as a class.

1. Do you think the "donkey tail" method of detecting liars was a good one? Why or why not?

2. Why was it assumed that the real liars would be the ones without soot on their hands?

3. Do you know of any other methods of detecting liars? If so, what are they?

EXERCISE 2

Your teacher will read you a passage about daydreaming two times. Once again, the first time, you will listen for main ideas; the second time, for details.

Step 1: Listen for the main ideas. Based on the information in the passage, write _T_ if the statement is true and _F_ if the statement is false. Wait until the reading is finished before answering the questions.

_____ 1. Almost everyone daydreams or fantasizes daily.

_____ 2. Daydreaming is a perfectly normal and enjoyable activity.

_____ 3. It is not normal for children to engage in fantasy play.

_____ 4. Although daydreaming has several advantages, it can be harmful.

Step 2: Your teacher will read the passage again. This time, listen for specific details. Decide if the statements are true _(T)_ or false _(F)_. Correct the false statements.

_____ **1.** Men daydream more than women.

_____

_____ **2.** Older people daydream a lot about the past.

_____

_____ **3.** Daydreaming helps children develop reading skills.

_____

_____ **4.** Daydreaming puts people to sleep when they are bored.

_____

_____ **5.** People have both realistic and unrealistic daydreams.

_____

_____ **6.** Most daydreaming occurs in company.

_____

Step 3: Discuss these questions as a class.

    1. What are the advantages of daydreaming? The disadvantages?
    2. When do you daydream or fantasize the most?
    3. What types of daydreams do you have?

TAKE NOTES: OUTLINE MAIN IDEAS AND SUPPORTING DETAILS

In the next three exercises, your challenge will be to take notes and organize the main ideas and supporting details in the passages you hear. (Answers can be found on pages 287–290 of Appendix II.)

EXERCISE 3

Your teacher will read a paragraph about the heart. The headings have been supplied in the outline below. Listen carefully and fill in the supporting details.

    I. Two General Facts About the Heart

        A. _____

        B. _____

    II. Living Beings with Four-Chambered Hearts

        A. _____

        B. _____

          1. ____Bears_____

          2. _____

          3. _____

        C. _____

III. Four Chambers of the Heart

    A. _____

    B. _____

    C. _____

    D. _____

IV. Heart Functions

    A. Functions of auricles

        1. _____

        2. _____

    B. Functions of ventricles

        1. _____

        2. _____

EXERCISE 4   **Your teacher will read a passage about umbrellas. Listen and fill in the main headings in the outline below.**

    I. _____

        A. Latin word

        B. Comes from <u>umbra</u>

        C. Means "shade"

    II. _____

        A. First person to use an umbrella

        B. Tied palm leaves together for shade

    III. _____

        A. Large

        B. Heavy

        C. Ribs made of whalebone

        D. Canvas-covered ribs

    IV. _____

        A. Lightweight

        B. Compact

        C. Ribs made of aluminum

        D. Waterproof material covers ribs

    V. _____

        A. Bus

        B. Train

        C. Cab

Your teacher will read you the body of a speech entitled "Sleep Deprivation in Night-Shift Workers."*

Step 1: Before you listen, try to predict what you will hear. Write down three major headings you think might be in the body of the speech.

1. _____

2. _____

3. _____

Step 2: Listen carefully and fill in the missing main headings and supporting details in the outline below.

I. _____

   A. _____

   B. Difficulty concentrating

   C. _____

   D. _____

II. _____

   A. Gastrointestinal disorders

   B. _____

   C. _____

III. Causes of sleep deprivation

   A. _____

   B. Run errands

      1. _____

      2. _____

   C. Set appointments

      1. _____

      2. auto repair

      3. home repair

   D. _____

---

*Night-shift workers are people who don't work during daytime hours. They usually work between 10:00 P.M. and 6:00 A.M.

IV. _____

    A. Make sleeping a priority

        1. _____

        2. _____

            a. 7:00–11:00 A.M.

            b. _____

    B. _____

        1. Create an environment conducive to sleeping

            a. _____

            b. _____

        2. _____

            a. _____

            b. making grocery lists

        3. _____

        4. Avoid alcohol

        5. _____

DISTINGUISH BETWEEN FACTS, OPINIONS, AND INFERENCES

Your challenge in the following exercise will be to practice critical thinking and listening. You will need to listen carefully to be able to identify whether the statements you hear are facts, opinions, or inferences.

Your teacher will discuss with you the characteristics of each of these to be sure you understand them. Before attempting this exercise, review the following information:

Characteristics of Facts

- Are known to be true
- May be based on something that has definitely happened
- May be based on direct observation
- Are not readily changed unless proven false
- Are objective and unbiased

Characteristics of Opinions

- Cannot be proven true or false
- Are subjective
- May be based on personal experiences
- Are often based on personal likes and dislikes

Characteristics of Inferences

- Are assumptions made without direct observation

  (An observer sees a person running from the scene of a robbery. The observer never actually witnessed the robbery but "infers" that the person running committed the crime.)

- Are assumptions made when we lack complete information

  (The police report the robber was tall and heavy. The listener "infers" that the person was a man.)

- Are assumptions based on connections we make between different pieces of information

  (A man waving a gun runs past a woman on the street. A necklace falls out of his pocket. The woman "infers" that the man just committed a robbery.)

- Can be proven or disproven

  (The police report the robber was tall and heavy. The listener "infers" the robber was a man. Eventually, an investigation by police will prove whether the robber was male or female.)

EXERCISE 6   Your teacher will read ten short passages. Each passage will be followed by three statements.

1. **Based on the information presented in each passage, decide whether the statements are facts, opinions, or inferences.**
2. **Check (✓) the appropriate box. (Answers can be found on pages 292–293 of Appendix II.)**

Example

You will hear, "Richard is a popular male name. Rick, Richie, and Dick are common nicknames for boys and men named Richard."

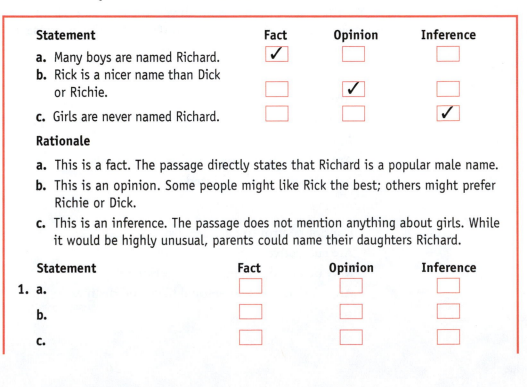

Statement	Fact	Opinion	Inference
a. Many boys are named Richard.	✔		
b. Rick is a nicer name than Dick or Richie.		✔	
c. Girls are never named Richard.			✔

Rationale

a. This is a fact. The passage directly states that Richard is a popular male name.

b. This is an opinion. Some people might like Rick the best; others might prefer Richie or Dick.

c. This is an inference. The passage does not mention anything about girls. While it would be highly unusual, parents could name their daughters Richard.

Statement	Fact	Opinion	Inference
1. a.			
b.			
c.			

Statement	Fact	Opinion	Inference
2. a.	☐	☐	☐
b.	☐	☐	☐
c.	☐	☐	☐
3. a.	☐	☐	☐
b.	☐	☐	☐
c.	☐	☐	☐
4. a.	☐	☐	☐
b.	☐	☐	☐
c.	☐	☐	☐
5. a.	☐	☐	☐
b.	☐	☐	☐
c.	☐	☐	☐
6. a.	☐	☐	☐
b.	☐	☐	☐
c.	☐	☐	☐
7. a.	☐	☐	☐
b.	☐	☐	☐
c.	☐	☐	☐
8. a.	☐	☐	☐
b.	☐	☐	☐
c.	☐	☐	☐
9. a.	☐	☐	☐
b.	☐	☐	☐
c.	☐	☐	☐
10. a.	☐	☐	☐
b.	☐	☐	☐
c.	☐	☐	☐

GET THE GIST

In the next two exercises, your challenge will be to listen to get the gist—in this case, the humor—of the anecdotes. (Answers can be found on page 294 of Appendix II.)

EXERCISE 7

Your teacher will read a humorous anecdote. Listen attentively to get the gist. Then discuss these questions as a class.

1. Why is this funny?
2. What information was in the story? What information did you bring to the story to "get" the joke?

EXERCISE 8

Your teacher will read another humorous passage. Again, listen attentively to get the gist. Then discuss these questions as a class.

1. What lines made this funny?
2. When the waiter said, "It's too bad you don't have pneumonia. They know what to do for that." What did he *not* say that you knew he was thinking?

In these last two listenings, in order to "get" the jokes, you had to use some background knowledge that you shared with the storyteller. This happens much of the time when we listen. In order to understand what someone is saying, we often need to bring some information from outside of the text to make sense of what we are hearing.

EVALUATE WHAT YOU HEAR

For this exercise, you will practice verbal comprehension and reasoning. You need to listen carefully and evaluate the information in each question before answering it. (Answers can be found on page 295 of Appendix II.)

EXERCISE 9

Your teacher will read you ten questions.

1. Think about each question carefully.
2. Then write your answer below. Be sure to answer each question immediately after hearing it.

1. _____
2. _____
3. _____
4. _____
5. _____
6. _____
7. _____
8. _____
9. _____
10. _____

FOLLOW ORAL DIRECTIONS

In this last exercise, your challenge will be to listen to verbal directions and follow them. (Answers can be found on pages 295–296 of Appendix II.)

EXERCISE 10

Your teacher will read ten directions.

1. **Listen to each complete direction.**
2. **Carry out the instructions immediately on the appropriate line below.**

1. 2   5   17   20   24   100   59

2. red   blue   chair   green   desk   table   black   seven   twenty

3. W   B   X   E   Z   C   U

4.

5.

6. apple   pear   corn   carrot   banana   paper   squash

7. _____

8.

9.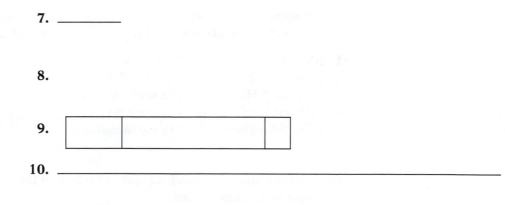

10. _____

_____

PRONUNCIATION TIP

LINKING

Linking sounds while speaking is necessary to speak English smoothly. Linking is the connecting of the last sound in one word to the first sound of the next word. The amount of linking in a person's speech varies from speaker to speaker. There are two situations in which English speakers regularly use linking.

When a word begins with a vowel sound, it is often pronounced as if it began with the final consonant sound of the previous word.

Examples

"Don't ask" sounds like "Don' task."

"We've eaten" sounds like "We'veaten."

When the same consonant sound that ends one word also begins the next word, that sound should not be pronounced twice. It should be pronounced one time, often with a slightly lengthened articulation.

Examples

"Warm milk" sounds like "war mmmilk."

"Five voices" sounds like "fi vvvoices."

EXERCISE 1 Read the following sentences aloud. Be sure to pronounce the words beginning with vowel sounds as if they begin with the last consonant sound of the previous word.

1. It's open.   (It sopen.)
2. Make a wish.   (Ma ka wish.)
3. Kiss Aunt Alice.   (Ki saun talice.)
4. Let's eat now.   (Let seat now.)
5. Leave him alone.   (Leave hi malone.)

EXERCISE 2 Read the following sentences aloud. Be sure to pronounce the identical consonant letters in the adjacent words as *one* sound.

1. Get two tickets.   (Ge two tickets.)
2. Stop pushing me.   (Sto pushing me.)
3. It's less serious.   (It's le serious.)
4. My mom made lemon pie. (My mo made lemon pie.)
5. Will Linda be there?   (Wi Linda be there?)

CHAPTER 9

Participating in Group Discussions

In group discussions, people exchange and evaluate ideas and information in order to better understand a subject or to solve a problem. It is an active and dynamic experience in which all members of the group interact and listen to each other.

When do we participate in group discussions? We participate in them all the time. In today's world, we often get together to share information, solve a common problem, or present a variety of different viewpoints to an audience. We participate in group discussions:

- at book clubs
- at civic groups
- at PTA meetings
- at lunch with friends
- while serving on jury duty
- during meals with our families

Group discussion is an important part of speech communication because we participate in it so often. In this chapter, you will learn how to lead and participate in a problem-solving group discussion.

BRAINSTORMING

Brainstorming is an important technique that you will need to use when discussing a problem and trying to figure out ways to solve it. Brainstorming can help you produce many ideas for the group to consider. Once you have lots of ideas, you can later narrow down the list and choose the best ones. Most of the steps in the path to successful problem solving will involve brainstorming. As you brainstorm, follow these guidelines:

- Choose a group member to write your topic on the blackboard, flip chart, or piece of paper. This person will write in list form all the ideas the group produces.
- Think of as many ideas as you can. Anyone may contribute ideas at any time. The more ideas, the better.
- Say anything about the topic that pops into your head. Don't worry if it seems ridiculous or silly.
- Do not criticize or evaluate ideas at this point. Even a "bad" idea may provoke a better one from someone else.
- Remember: The more ideas, the better. Everyone in the group should participate.

It's very important to remember that everyone must feel free to contribute as many ideas as they can think of. Do not criticize anyone's ideas during this brainstorming process by saying things like, "That will never work," or "Forget that idea. It's silly," etc.

EVALUATING THE IDEAS

When you can think of no more ideas, it is time to evaluate the ideas the group has produced and choose the best ones. Start by eliminating the ideas that are the least popular. The best way to do this is:

1. Group members read through the entire list of ideas generated by the brainstorming session.
2. Each member approaches the blackboard or flip chart and puts a checkmark next to two of their favorite ideas.
3. A person designated to be the group recorder will cross out all ideas that have received no checkmarks.
4. Group members then begin the process of evaluating the remaining ideas.

PRACTICE BRAINSTORMING

Work with 4 or 5 classmates and follow the directions below.

1. Read the following situations and choose one.

   a. Two sisters, Jane and Susan, were invited to their friend Ann's party. They accepted the invitation even though they really didn't want to go. They didn't go to the party. The next day, Ann wanted to know why they didn't show up. They had trouble thinking of a good reason they could give her for not going.

   b. Harry is always asking his friend Sergio to loan him money. He often forgets to pay back what he owes. Sergio can never think of an excuse not to loan him money.

2. Brainstorm explanations that Jane and Susan can give Ann for not attending her party or excuses that Sergio can give Harry for not loaning him money. Use your imagination, and be as silly as you like thinking of reasons. Try to think of a minimum of fifteen ideas.

   • The sisters might say, "A spaceship landed in our backyard and Martians kidnapped us last night."

   • Sergio might say, "A pickpocket stole my wallet this morning in the parking lot," or "I gave all my money to a homeless man today."

3. Choose someone to write down everyone's ideas in list form.

4. When all the groups have finished, share your ideas with the class. Discuss the advantages or disadvantages of each excuse.

PATH TO SUCCESSFUL PROBLEM SOLVING FOR GROUP DISCUSSIONS

A successful group discussion is one that accomplishes objectives and improves a situation. Frequently, its purpose is to solve a problem. However, many discussions are not productive because the participants wander aimlessly from point to point without any plan. In order to have a successful group discussion, it is essential to have a logical and organized plan.

The following path to successful problem solving will help you organize a group discussion into a logical sequence of events so that all participants can find one or more solutions to a problem.

Step 1: Identify a Problem

Choose a problem that interests all participants. The discussion will be much livelier if all group members feel personally involved and committed to solving the problem.

ACTIVITY

PRACTICE IDENTIFYING PROBLEMS

- Come to class prepared to suggest problems that you think would be of interest to the group. Staying informed about current events will give you lots of ideas. Read the newspaper or news magazines such as *Time, Newsweek,* etc.
- In small groups, brainstorm and make a list of specific problems for each category in the "Problems for Group Discussion" chart that follows.

PROBLEMS FOR GROUP DISCUSSION

Campus Problems

Examples

auto thefts

limited access for handicapped

_____

_____

Community Problems

Examples

an unsafe intersection

unsolved hate crimes

_____

_____

City Problems

Examples

lack of housing

unreliable transit systems

_____

_____

State Problems

Examples

unemployment

insufficient funding for education

_____

_____

National Problems

Examples

drug abuse

illiteracy

_____

_____

International Problems

Examples

air pollution

human rights abuses

_____

_____

Example

One group of students chose the national problem of children in the United States being less physically fit than ever before.

Step 2: Prove the Problem Exists

Present evidence that your group's problem truly exists.

- Find statistics.
- Refer to your own personal experiences or the experiences of people you know.
- Quote expert sources.
- Give specific incidences of the problem that have been reported in the news.

Example

Children in the United States are less physically fit than ever before.

1. The Harvard School of Public Health research has found alarming increases in the rate of obesity since 1960.
   a. Fifty-four percent increase among six- to eleven-year-olds
   b. Thirty-nine percent increase among twelve- to seventeen-year-olds
2. A Chrysler Fund Amateur Athletic Union (AAU) study found the average weight of twelve- to thirteen-year-olds has increased eight pounds over the past decade with only a slight increase in height.
3. The AAU study found that the percentage of children reaching minimal standards on four fitness tests had declined from 43 percent to 32 percent.
4. Research from the National Institutes of Health (June 2002) confirms childhood obesity is rising.
   a. The number of overweight children has doubled since 1980.
   b. Currently one in five children is overweight.
5. The American Health Foundation reports that 30 percent of children three to eighteen years old have above-average blood cholesterol levels.

Step 3: Explain the Causes of the Problem

- Your research and readings can help you discover this information.
- Personal opinions are also valuable, and brainstorming can be a useful way to facilitate an exchange of ideas.

Example

Children in the United States are less physically fit than ever before.

1. Their diets are high in fat, salt, and sugar.
2. Pollution and/or crime make it unsafe for children to play outside.
3. TV and video games also encourage children to remain indoors.
4. Physical fitness instruction in schools has deteriorated.

Step 4: Predict Possible Future Effects of the Problem

Predict what is likely to happen if the problem is not addressed.

- Explain how people or society in general might be affected.
- Again, share the results of your research as well as personal opinions.

Example

Children in the United States are less physically fit than ever before.

1. There will be increased physical problems in adulthood causing much human suffering.
2. Billions of dollars will be spent on medical problems.
   a. Medical insurance premiums will become higher.
   b. People will have to pay more out-of-pocket medical expenses.
3. There will be lower productivity due to increased absenteeism from work.

Step 5: Present Possible Solutions to the Problem

Brainstorm ways this problem might be solved.

- Present suggestions made by authorities and concerned individuals.
- Give your opinions about how to solve the problem.

Example

Children in the United States are less physically fit than ever before.

1. Pressure local schools to offer daily physical education classes for elementary and high school students.
2. Pressure the schools to put more emphasis on good nutrition.
3. Encourage parents to limit their children's TV and video game time.
4. Encourage parents to substitute low-fat, healthier foods for junk food.
   a. Whole-wheat crackers instead of potato chips
   b. Baked potatoes instead of french fries
5. Pressure local law enforcement officers to better patrol public playgrounds so that children and their parents are not afraid to use them.

Step 6: Select the Best Solutions

1. Ask the following questions as you discuss the advantages and disadvantages of each proposed solution. (If you can answer yes to the first two questions, and no to the last question, you may have found a winning solution!)
   a. Will this solution eliminate one or more of the causes of the problem?
   b. Will this solution eliminate the predicted future effects of the problem?
   c. Will this solution create more problems?
2. Select the best solution(s). Remember: While some solutions may not be perfect, they might still be the best solutions to the problem.

ACTIVITY

PRACTICE FINDING SOLUTIONS

1. In small groups, examine the possible solutions to the problem of children in the United States being less physically fit than ever before.
2. Brainstorm some other solutions to the problem. Come up with as many as you can. Choose one group member to write down what your group suggests.

3. Now analyze all the possible solutions to the problem. Consider the ones in the book and the ones your group brainstormed.

   a. Discuss the solutions one at a time.

   b. Think of as many possible advantages and disadvantages to each solution as you can.

   c. Choose another group member to write down all the advantages and disadvantages for each solution.

4. Choose the best solutions.

5. Discuss your conclusions with the entire class to see if they agree with you.

ACTIVITY

EVALUATE CAUSES, EFFECTS, AND SOLUTIONS

Consider the following scenario:

Hundreds of cats are roaming free throughout the campus of your school. They approach people and expect to be fed. They pounce on unsuspecting birds and eat them. They spray everywhere and leave their awful scent. They have frequent cat fights and make a lot of noise. They are a terrible nuisance. Something must be done.

Brainstorm, listen, and discuss ideas as outlined below.

1. Your teacher will divide the class into three groups: A, B, and C. Each group in succession will have a chance to sit in a circle and brainstorm for ten minutes while the rest of the class observes.

   a. Group A will brainstorm to identify causes of the cat problem.

   b. Group B will brainstorm for future effects of the problem.

   c. Finally, Group C will brainstorm for solutions to the problem.

2. Each group designates a recorder to write their ideas on the blackboard.

3. After all ideas are written on the blackboard, the group is to eliminate the least popular ideas by using the evaluating method described on page 166.

4. When the small groups have finished the activity, the entire class should discuss the process.

   a. Did the groups successfully brainstorm for ideas? Why or why not?

   b. Did group members work well together? Did everyone participate?

   c. How can group members work more effectively together in the future?

PATH TO BEING AN EFFECTIVE GROUP LEADER

Every successful group discussion needs an effective group leader. The following path to being an effective group leader shows how to assure the success of the group discussion.

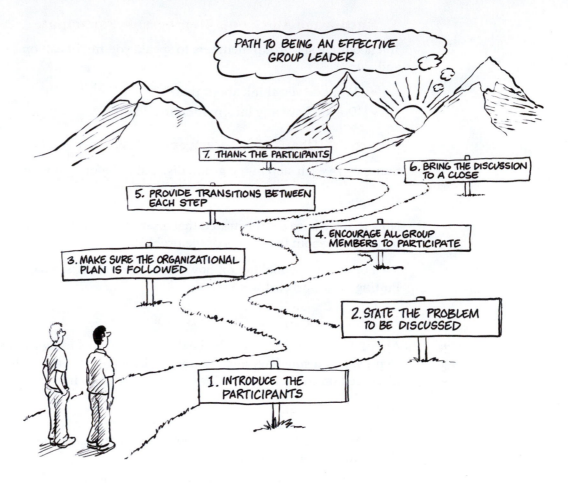

1. Introduce the Participants

Introduce the members of the group to one another and to the audience.

2. State the Problem to Be Discussed

This is similar to introducing a speech by providing a preview and an attention-getting opener, as discussed on pages 78–79 of Chapter 4: Speaking to Inform.

- Introduce the problem to be discussed.
- Briefly explain the organizational plan to be followed.

3. Make Sure That the Organizational Plan Is Followed

Make certain the group follows the organizational plan in order and does not skip steps. If a group member goes off on a tangent, it's your job to get him or her back on track. For example, you might say:

- "Let's get back to that point later," or
- "That's an interesting comment, but let's finish what we are currently discussing."

4. Encourage All Group Members to Participate

To encourage shy group members to speak, you might call on them by name and ask:

- "What do you think about that?"
- "Do you have any information to add?"

5. Provide Transitions Between Each Step

Summarize each step in the group discussion before going on to the next step.

Example

Now that we have demonstrated that a serious problem exists, why don't we move on and talk about the causes of the problem?

For detailed guidelines on how to use transitions, see pages 53–56 of Chapter 3: Putting Your Speech Together.

6. Bring the Discussion to a Close

After 20–25 minutes, conclude the discussion. Concluding a discussion is similar to providing a summary and memorable concluding remarks for a speech, as discussed on pages 79–80 of Chapter 4: Speaking to Inform.

7. Thank the Participants

- After concluding the discussion, be sure to thank the participants for their time and hard work.
- If an audience is present, thank them for listening.

PATH TO BEING A RESPONSIBLE GROUP MEMBER

In addition to having an effective group leader, every group discussion needs responsible and enthusiastic participants who are committed to the discussion's success.

- Each participant should prepare by reading and thinking about the topic beforehand.
- During the discussion, participants should feel free to comment, ask questions, and share information.
- All participants must be prepared and alert during the entire discussion. The following path to being a responsible group member will help assure an animated and productive group discussion.

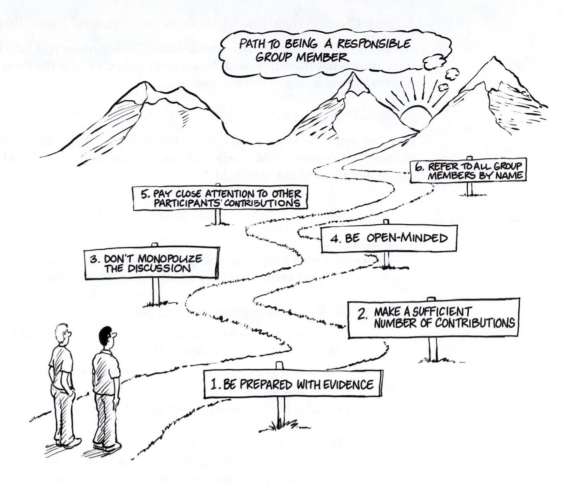

1. Be Prepared with Evidence

Prepare for the discussion by researching quotations, facts, statistics, and examples. Write possible contributions for each step of the discussion on note cards so that you can refer to them as needed during the discussion.

2. Make a Sufficient Number of Contributions

Contribute at least three times during each step of the discussion. Your comments don't need to be lengthy. Talk when you have a thought to share, a question to ask, or when you feel a point needs to be clarified for the audience.

3. Don't Monopolize the Discussion

Don't interrupt other group members while they are speaking. Give all participants a chance to speak and express themselves.

4. Be Open-Minded

Acknowledge other people's opinions and their right to express them. If you disagree with someone's opinion, let the person express the idea completely without interrupting. If you want to introduce a contrary point of view, do so politely. For example, you could start by saying, "I see your point. However, . . ."

5. Pay Close Attention to Other Participants' Contributions

Listen carefully to other participants' ideas. Taking notes will help you to remember what they have said. You may be asked to help the group leader summarize each step in the discussion.

6. Refer to All Participants by Name

Whether you refer to them directly or indirectly, use participants' names. For example, don't point to Marisela and say, "I'd like to add to what *she* said." Say, "I'd like to add to what *Marisela* said."

ACTIVITY

PRACTICE YOUR PROBLEM-SOLVING SKILLS

Before researching a topic for your group discussion assignment where your teacher will evaluate your performance, try an informal practice group discussion.

1. Work in a small group of 4 or 5 people.
   - Follow the Path to Successful Problem Solving and the Path to Being a Responsible Group Member.
   - Choose a group leader, who should follow the Path to Being an Effective Group Leader.
2. Consider the following situation and discuss the question below:

   Mr. Larry Adams is the owner of a business employing thirty people. Profits have been falling the past year because of petty theft on the part of the employees. Some of the workers have been taking home supplies (such as staplers, tape, paper clips, envelopes, stationery) for their personal use. Others have been running their personal mail through the company's postage meter to save money on stamps. Some of the employees have been making personal long-distance telephone calls from the office. Almost all the employees have been dishonest to some degree. Mr. Adams knows who the guilty workers are and what they have done.

   Question for discussion: What are the possible ways that Mr. Adams might deal with this situation? Brainstorm as many different options as you can and write them below.

   a. _____

   b. _____

   c. _____

   d. _____

   e. _____

3. Share your solutions with the entire class. Choose one student to write all the different ideas that the groups brainstormed on the blackboard.

4. Choose one student to lead the class. Discuss the advantages and disadvantages of each of the proposed solutions. Work together to reach consensus regarding the best way to handle the problem.

Group consensus: What is the best way for Mr. Adams to stop the petty theft occurring in his business?

Assignment: Have a group discussion on a topic of your choice.

1. In small groups, choose a leader.

2. Choose a specific problem that interests all group members and can be researched easily.

3. On your own, research the problem.

4. Complete as much of the Group Discussion Worksheet that follows as possible. If you are the group leader, also complete the Group Leader Worksheet on page 179.

5. Your teacher may use the forms on pages 254–256 in Appendix I to evaluate individual members, the group leader, and the group as a whole. Look the forms over so you know exactly how you will be evaluated.

6. Using the steps on pages 168–171, discuss the problem for 20–25 minutes. Write any additional information on the Group Discussion Worksheet.

GROUP DISCUSSION WORKSHEET

1. Identify a problem that interests all group members.

   _____

2. Summarize proof that the problem exists.

   _____

   _____

   _____

   _____

3. Explain the causes of the problem.

_____

_____

_____

_____

4. Predict possible future effects of the problem.

_____

_____

_____

_____

5. Present possible solutions to the problem.

_____

_____

_____

_____

6. Determine the advantages and disadvantages of each solution.

Solution A: _____

   Advantages: _____

   Disadvantages: _____

Solution B: _____

   Advantages: _____

   Disadvantages: _____

Solution C: _____

   Advantages: _____

   Disadvantages: _____

Solution D: _____

   Advantages: _____

   Disadvantages: _____

7. Select the best solutions.

_____

_____

_____

GROUP LEADER WORKSHEET

1. Prepare the introduction. (Introduce the participants.)

   _____

   _____

2. Prepare the preview. (State the problem to be discussed and the organizational plan to be followed.)

   _____

   _____

3. Prepare the first transition (between Identify a Problem and Prove the Problem Exists).

   _____

   _____

4. Prepare the second transition (between Prove the Problem Exists and Explain the Causes of the Problem).

   _____

   _____

5. Prepare the third transition (between Explain the Causes of the Problem and Predict Possible Future Effects of the Problem).

   _____

   _____

6. Prepare the fourth transition (between Predict Possible Future Effects of the Problem and Present Possible Solutions to the Problem).

   _____

   _____

7. Prepare the fifth transition (between Present Possible Solutions to the Problem and Select the Best Solution).

   _____

   _____

8. Prepare memorable concluding remarks.

   _____

   _____

EXERCISE 1

The words in each of the following rows sound the same if their final consonant sounds are left off. Read each row aloud. Exaggerate your pronunciation of the final consonant in each word.

1. cat	cap	cab	can	calf
2. rack	rat	rap	rag	ran
3. soup	soon	suit	sued	Sue's
4. week	weep	wheat	weed	weave
5. robe	rode	wrote	rope	roll

EXERCISE 2

Read the following sentences aloud. Exaggerate your pronunciation of the final consonant in each boldfaced word.

1. **Have** you **had ham**?
2. I **like bright light**.
3. The **sign** is on the **side**.
4. **Doug** ate a well-**done duck**.
5. The **bag** on his **back** was **black**.

EXERCISE 3

Choose any paragraph in this book. Circle all the words that end in consonant sounds. Read the paragraph aloud. Be sure to pronounce all final consonant sounds.

CHAPTER 10

Understanding Interpersonal Communication

Interpersonal communication is all around us. It occurs any time people exchange messages—when they express their opinions, ask and answer questions, express how they feel, talk about what they like and dislike, or say what they want and don't want.

When do we communicate interpersonally? We do it all the time. Whenever we talk to friends, parents, children, teachers, employers, waiters, doctors, salesclerks—in short, anyone—we are communicating interpersonally. Sometimes our communication is successful and we feel very good about it. However, sometimes it is not so successful. We may have an unpleasant argument or misunderstanding that causes us to feel angry, confused, or upset.

In this chapter, you will learn how to avoid misunderstandings in interpersonal communication. You will learn techniques of effective interpersonal communication that will help you feel good about yourself and your interactions with others.

LEARN HOW OTHERS PERCEIVE YOU

Work in small groups.

1. Choose a group leader.

2. On a blank sheet of paper, write:

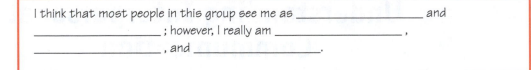

I think that most people in this group see me as _____ and _____; however, I really am _____, _____, and _____.

3. Fill in the blanks with adjectives or descriptive phrases. Don't let anyone see your responses and don't write your name on the paper.

4. Give your paper to the group leader.

5. As the leader reads each statement, try to guess who wrote each one. Explain your reasons.

6. When everyone has finished guessing, identify which statement you wrote.

7. As a class, discuss whether you were surprised by what any of the group members wrote. If so, which ones? Why? Do you think people perceive you differently from how you perceive yourself? If so, why?

APPRECIATE OTHER PEOPLE'S VALUES

We all have beliefs—some correct, others incorrect—about other people and their values. In this chapter, you will learn how to improve interpersonal communication and how to avoid misunderstandings. In Chapter 11, you will learn how beliefs, values, and behavioral patterns differ across cultures and how these differences may affect communication.

This activity will enable you to better understand and appreciate the different personal values and feelings of your classmates.

Before class, select a coin from your country that you feel represents you as a person.

Possible reasons for choosing the coin might be its:

value	size	shape
color	inscription	picture

1. Bring the coin to class. Your classmates will sit in a large circle. Explain your reasons for selecting the coin.

2. Select a classmate to whom you would like to give the coin. Possible reasons for choosing a classmate might be:
   - A feeling that you are very similar to that person
   - A feeling that you are very different from that person
   - A desire to better understand a classmate
   - An appreciation of that person's contributions to the class
   - A desire to encourage that person
   - A desire that the person change something about him/herself
   - Something about the coin reminds you of the person

3. Give your coin to the classmate you selected. Do this one student at a time, without speaking, until all students have given away their original coins.

4. Explain your reason for giving your coin to the recipient.

5. Discuss the following questions:
   a. How did you feel if you received coins?
   b. How did you feel if you didn't receive any coins?
   c. Why do you think you received (didn't receive) coins?
   d. What situations in life are similar to this exercise?
   e. What have you learned about your classmates from this exercise?
   f. What have you learned about other cultures from this exercise?
   g. If you had unlimited coins to give away, who would you give them to?

AVOIDING MISCOMMUNICATIONS

Misunderstandings happen to everyone. They occur between friends, coworkers, and family members. Communication breakdowns can be as harmless as showing up for an appointment a half-hour early or as inconvenient as waiting in the rain for two hours for someone who never shows up. They can be as devastating as a broken relationship or a divorce. They can even be a matter of life and death. For example, failure to communicate fuel shortages and other mechanical problems has been the cause of some airline disasters.

Miscommunication often occurs because listeners assume they understand what a speaker means when, in fact, the speaker had intended a completely different meaning from what was understood.

Example: Susana's Story

Susana was generally too shy to speak up in class. She finally had the courage to ask her psychology professor a question during a lecture. Before answering her, he replied, "Now that's an unusual query." Susana felt insulted, as she believed that her professor was implying that her question was foolish. She told the story to her speech communication professor in tears. Her speech communication professor was sure that the psychology professor hadn't intended to belittle Susana and encouraged her to ask him what he had really meant. The psychology professor was upset that Susana had misinterpreted his comment, as he had intended it to be a compliment. He had meant that her question was intelligent and insightful.

Sometimes, when listeners misunderstand what was said, they blame the speaker as being the source of the problem or misunderstanding without taking the time to ask the speaker for clarification. Other listeners simply ignore messages they don't understand or say the messages don't make any sense.

Much miscommunication can be avoided by determining what certain words mean before criticizing the speaker or the message. It's important to say to yourself:

- "I don't understand the message."
- "I had better ask some questions about it."
- "It might mean something else to another person."

COMPARE YOUR UNDERSTANDING WITH THE AUTHOR'S INTENT

Read this information about Donna and answer the following questions.

Donna was level-headed and giddy. She was kind and silly.
Donna was tiny but so large that everyone admired her.

1. What is your first impression of the above information? Write it below.

_____

_____

2. Be prepared to discuss your impression in class. Did you think the words were contradictory or nonsensical?

Think about this: With today's meaning of some words, this message does indeed sound like nonsense. However, in early English, many of the words used had completely different definitions from what they mean today.

- *Giddy* used to mean "enthusiastic" or "divinely possessed," derived from the same root as *God*.
- *Silly* once meant "happy," coming from the German word *soelig*.
- *Large* meant "good-hearted" or "generous."

If you substitute these definitions, the description means:

Donna was level-headed and enthusiastic. She was kind and happy.
Donna was tiny but so generous that everyone admired her.

Now that the words seem to make more sense, you are less likely to reject them, call them nonsense, or criticize the author. If people made a consistent effort to look beyond a speaker's actual words to find out what they mean, misunderstandings would occur much less frequently.

CLARIFYING THE SPEAKER'S INTENTIONS

Sometimes listeners jump to conclusions and blame their misunderstandings on speakers without first finding out their actual intentions. For instance, Susana jumped to the hasty conclusion that *unusual* meant "foolish" and that her professor was insulting her. Clarifying a speaker's message can help avoid misunderstandings and subsequent bad feelings.

Example: Peggy and Anne's Story

Peggy was expecting a delivery and knew she would not be home to accept it. She requested that the delivery service leave the parcel with her neighbor Anne. Happy to help, Anne brought the small package to Peggy's home after dinner. Peggy exclaimed, "I'm sure glad you didn't know what was in the box. Those are the diamond earrings my daughter sent for my birthday."

Anne's first reaction was to feel offended. She assumed that Peggy was implying that she was dishonest and that she would have stolen the package if she had known it was valuable. However, Anne realized she might have misinterpreted Peggy's remarks, so she asked, "Why are you glad I didn't know what was in the box?" Peggy replied, "Because had you known, you might have been unwilling to be responsible for such a valuable package." Anne was extremely relieved to learn that Peggy hadn't meant that she was untrustworthy. Had Anne not made the effort to clear up the misunderstanding, she would have harbored feelings of ill will toward Peggy. Their friendship would have deteriorated without Peggy ever knowing why.

Anne effectively avoided a miscommunication by asking Peggy to clarify what she had meant. If you are upset or confused about somebody's message, ask yourself, "Could I be misinterpreting what was said?" Getting the answer is as simple as saying, "I'm not sure what you meant. Would you please explain?"

ACTIVITY

DESCRIBE A MISCOMMUNICATION

1. **Think of a miscommunication you have had. Prepare answers to the following questions:**
   a. Why did the miscommunication occur?
   b. How might the miscommunication have been avoided?
   c. Was the misunderstanding resolved? If so, how? If not, what could be done now to resolve it?

2. **In small groups, describe the miscommunication, sharing your answers to the questions above. Be prepared to answer any other questions from the group.**

JUMPING TO CONCLUSIONS AND MAKING ASSUMPTIONS

We all make judgments and form conclusions based on information we read or hear. This is normal. However, we frequently jump to incorrect conclusions based on insufficient information without even realizing it.

ACTIVITY

THINK ABOUT HOW ASSUMPTIONS ARE MADE

1. **Read the following story.**
   A man went for a walk one summer day and met a friend whom he hadn't seen or heard anything about in over twenty-five years. The man greeted his friend, who was holding a child's hand, and asked, "Is this your daughter?" The friend replied, "Yes." The man asked the little girl, "What's your name?" The child replied, "It's the same as my mommy's." The man replied, "You must be Elizabeth."

2. **Write your answer to the following question.**
   Question: The man hadn't seen or heard from his friend in twenty-five years. He didn't know that his friend was married or had any children. How could he possibly know his friend's daughter's name?

_____

_____

(The correct answer is at the end of the chapter on page 195. Did you jump to a conclusion without realizing it?)

The tendency to jump to conclusions and make assumptions when we don't have all the information is a great barrier to interpersonal communication. It creates animosity between people, causes innocent individuals hardship or embarrassment, destroys friendships, and negatively affects interpersonal relationships. This happens when we make statements or draw conclusions that go beyond what we have actually observed, read, or heard.

Example: Where did the exercise equipment come from?

An elementary school principal in Miami decided to turn an empty storage area in his school into a gym for faculty and staff to use before classes started in the morning and at the end of the school day. Employees were thrilled when the slightly used state-of-the-art exercise equipment was delivered. A week later, the local newspaper printed a scathing article about the principal, accusing him of using school monies to fund an exercise room at his school. The outraged principal called the newspaper editor and explained that all the expensive equipment had been donated free of charge by the parents of some of the students.

ACTIVITY

TEST YOUR ABILITY TO EVALUATE EVIDENCE

Do you draw conclusions or make statements based on what you actually know to be true? Or do you draw conclusions or make statements that go beyond what you have actually observed, heard, or read? The following activity* will help you test your ability to differentiate between the two.

1. **Work in groups of 4–5 students.**
2. **Read the instructions carefully.**
3. **Discuss the story and the questions with your group. Work together to answer them.**
4. **When all the groups are finished, share your results with the entire class.**
5. **Which group got the most answers correct? Which group jumped to the most conclusions? Can you think of any real-life situations that relate to this activity?**

THE INFERENCE-OBSERVATION CONFUSION

Read the following little story. Assume that all the information presented in it is definitely accurate and true. Read it carefully because it has ambiguous parts designed to lead you astray! There is no need to memorize the story. You can refer back to it whenever you wish.

Next, read the statements about the story. Decide whether you consider each statement to be true, false, or ?. *T* means that the statement is definitely true based on the information presented in the story. *F* means that the statement is definitely false. *?* means that the statement may be either true or false and that you cannot be certain based on the information presented in the story. If any part of the statement is doubtful, mark it *?*. **Answer each statement in order; do not go back to change an answer later. Don't reread any statements after you have answered them. This will distort your score.**

---

*This test has been administered to thousands of students for over 50 years! It was included in an unpublished Ph.D. dissertation written by William V. Haney of Northwestern University, 1953.

Sample Story

You arrive home late one evening and see that the lights are on in your living room. There is only one car parked in front of your house, and the name "Harold R. Jones, M.D." is spelled in small gold letters on one of the car's doors.

Statements about Sample Story

1. The car parked in front of your house has lettering on one of its doors.   T   F   ?
2. Someone in your family is sick.   T   F   ?
3. No car is parked in front of your house.   T   F   ?
4. The car parked in front of your house belongs to a man named Smith.   T   F   ?

(Answers appear on page 195.)

So much for the sample. It should warn you of some of the kinds of traps to look for. Now begin the actual test. Remember: Mark each statement in order. Don't skip around or change answers later!

Story

Babe Smith has been killed. Police have rounded up six suspects, all of whom are known gangsters. All of them are known to have been near the scene of the killing at the approximate time that it occurred. All had substantial motives for wanting Smith killed. However, one of these suspected gangsters, Slinky Sam, has been positively cleared of guilt.

Statements about Story

1. Slinky Sam is known to have been near the scene of the killing of Babe Smith.   T   F   ?
2. All six of the rounded-up gangsters were known to have been near the scene of the murder.   T   F   ?
3. Only Slinky Sam has been cleared of guilt.   T   F   ?
4. All six of the rounded-up suspects were near the scene of Smith's killing at the approximate time it took place.   T   F   ?
5. The police do not know who killed Smith.   T   F   ?
6. All six suspects are known to have been near the scene of the foul deed.   T   F   ?
7. Smith's murderer did not confess of his own free will.   T   F   ?
8. Slinky Sam was not cleared of guilt.   T   F   ?
9. It is known that the six suspects were in the vicinity of the cold-blooded assassination.   T   F   ?

(The correct answers are in Appendix II on page 300.)

INTERPERSONAL COMMUNICATION STYLES

There are three possible broad approaches to the conduct of interpersonal relations. The first is to consider one's self only and ride roughshod over others. The second is always to put others before one's self. The third approach is the golden mean. The individual places himself first but takes others into account.

— Joseph Wolpe, M.D., *The Practice of Behavior Therapy*

The first interpersonal communication approach Dr. Wolpe describes is called the *aggressive* style. The second is called the *submissive* style. The third approach, the *golden mean*, is the one Dr. Wolpe recommends above all the others. It is referred to as the *assertive* style.

People who use the aggressive style of communication appear to be somewhat belligerent. They deliver their messages in loud, often hostile voices that convey the impression that they believe their opinions and feelings are more important than anyone else's. Intentionally or unintentionally, aggressive communicators tend to embarrass, insult, or intimidate their listeners in order to get their way.

People who use the submissive style of communication appear to put themselves last and seem to consider themselves inferior to others. This style encourages others to disregard their needs and to take advantage of them. Intentionally or unintentionally, submissive communicators often don't get what they want because they don't stand up for themselves.

People who use the assertive communication style appear to have a healthy self-image. They express their wishes in a clear and direct way that conveys the impression that they expect their rights to be respected and that they, in turn, respect the rights of others. Assertive speakers appear to be positive, fair, and self-confident.

The following chart illustrates the key characteristics of the three interpersonal communication styles.

Style	Characteristic
Aggressive	I'm important. You're not important.
Submissive	I'm not important. You're important.
Assertive	We're both important.

The following examples illustrate how people with submissive, aggressive, and assertive styles of interpersonal communication might respond to different situations.

Example A

A smoker asks if you object to his or her smoking in your car. You are allergic to smoke.

Aggressive Response: Yes, I most certainly do object. You are very rude and inconsiderate to even consider subjecting me to secondhand smoke. I refuse to allow smoking in my car.

Submissive Response: No problem. That's fine if you really want to.

Assertive Response: Thank you for asking. I'd prefer you didn't. It really bothers me. Would you like me to pull over so you could smoke a cigarette outside? I'd be happy to stop whenever you like.

Example B

You're next in line at a checkout counter and are in a hurry to leave. Somebody says, "Excuse me, I'm late for an important meeting. May I go ahead of you?"

> *Aggressive Response:* Absolutely not! Go to the end of the line like everybody else!
> *Submissive Response:* Sure, OK.
> *Assertive Response:* Actually, I'm also in a hurry. Why don't you ask someone in a different line?

Being aware of these three interpersonal communication styles will help you recognize your usual style and that of the people you know. With practice, you can become more skillful at using an assertive style—the *golden mean*—in your interactions with others.

EXERCISE

DISCOVER YOUR COMMUNICATION STYLE

For each response to the following situations, circle the letter of the communication style used. (Answers can be found on page 300 of Appendix II.)

> **A = aggressive   B = submissive   C = assertive**

1. You are in a restaurant and order your meal with a plain baked potato. The potato is served to you with butter and sour cream.

   a. You reprimand the server for not paying better attention to your order and for not checking the food before serving it.   A   B   C

   b. You remind the server that you had requested a plain potato and ask him or her to bring you another one.   A   B   C

   c. You either eat the potato as is or leave it uneaten on your plate without mentioning the error.   A   B   C

2. While waiting in line to buy movie tickets, someone cuts in front of you.

   a. You say nothing, hoping someone behind you will complain.   A   B   C

   b. You admonish the person for being rude and loudly tell him or her to wait like everyone else.   A   B   C

   c. You say that you had arrived first and point out the end of the line in case the person hadn't realized his or her mistake.   A   B   C

3. Your teacher returns your exam after grading it. He or she marked an answer wrong that you're sure is correct.

   a. You wait until after class and then show your teacher the exam. You explain that you don't understand why your answer was marked wrong and ask if it could be an oversight on his or her part.   A   B   C

b. When you notice the error, you interrupt the lecture. Waving your exam in the air, you say, "You made a mistake grading my paper. I want you to correct it right now."   A   B   C

c. You rationalize that the question was only worth three points and decide not to bring the error to your teacher's attention.   A   B   C

ACTIVITY

PRACTICE DIFFERENT COMMUNICATION STYLES

Read the following situations. Think of aggressive, submissive, and assertive responses to each one. Write them in the spaces provided. (Possible answers can be found on pages 300–301 of Appendix II.)

1. After waiting for your car to be serviced at the dealership, the service manager tells you it's ready. You go outside prepared to drive away. The car hasn't been washed, and the mechanics have left the windows and floor mats filthy. Handing you the keys, the service manager thanks you for your business.

   a. Aggressive Response: _____

   _____

   b. Submissive Response: _____

   _____

   c. Assertive Response: _____

   _____

2. A delivery person brings you a pizza loaded with anchovies, mushrooms, and sausage. You specifically ordered one only with double cheese.

   a. Aggressive Response: _____

   _____

   b. Submissive Response: _____

   _____

   c. Assertive Response: _____

   _____

3. You and a friend are seated in a crowded movie theater. All the seats are taken. The loud conversation of the couple sitting next to you is distracting.

   a. Aggressive Response: _____

   _____

   b. Submissive Response: _____

   _____

   c. Assertive Response: _____

   _____

4. Your roommates are pressuring you to move with them into a more expensive apartment. You really can't afford to pay more rent; besides, you like your current apartment. You're worried that they'll resent you if you don't agree to their request.

   a. Aggressive Response: _____

   _____

   b. Submissive Response: _____

   _____

   c. Assertive Response: _____

   _____

5. You are standing on line at the supermarket. Someone cuts in front of you. You are annoyed and feel the person should wait his/her turn like everyone else.

   a. Aggressive Response: _____

   _____

   b. Submissive Response: _____

   _____

   c. Assertive Response: _____

   _____

DIRECT AND INDIRECT COMMUNICATION STYLES

Many individuals are reluctant to state their feelings clearly and directly. They may have a tendency to hint at what they want, or "beat around the bush," by phrasing their needs and wants as questions rather than statements. This manner of communication can be very confusing and frustrating to listeners.

In an article for the *Washington Post*, Deborah Tannen, Ph.D., presents an illustration of how some people communicate indirectly by expressing their wishes as questions. A couple was having a conversation while riding in their car. The wife asked, "Would you like to stop for a drink?" Her husband answered "No," and they didn't stop. He was later frustrated to learn that his wife was annoyed because she had wanted to stop for a drink. He wondered, "Why didn't she just say what she wanted? Why did she play games with me?"

Phrasing your requests as questions can lead to confusion and misunderstanding. People will take your needs and wants much more seriously if you express them using a direct and assertive interpersonal communication style.

PRACTICE BEING DIRECT

Read each situation. Replace each question with a direct statement. (Possible answers can be found on page 301 of Appendix II.)

Example

Your younger brother is playing his stereo so loud that you can't concentrate on your studying. You go into his room and ask, "Don't you think the music is a bit loud?" You really mean,

"Please lower the volume. I'm studying for an exam."

1. You and a friend have gone out to dinner in a restaurant. You don't like the location of the table where the host or hostess is taking you. You ask, "Isn't this table stuck away in the corner?" You really mean,

   _____

   _____

2. You and your date have been at a party for hours. You feel very tired and want to go home desperately. You turn to your date and ask, "Are you ready to leave yet?" You really mean,

   _____

   _____

3. You're at a friend's house on a chilly winter day. Several windows are open and you are freezing. You ask your friend, "Isn't it a bit cold in here?" You really mean,

   _____

   _____

4. You're at the library trying to study. Several other students are carrying on a loud conversation that you find distracting. You go over to them and ask, "Isn't there someplace else you guys can go to have a conversation?" You really mean,

   _____

   _____

5. A passenger in your car lights a cigarette. You really don't like people to smoke in your car. You ask, "Do you have to smoke that in here?" You really mean,

   _____

   _____

PRACTICE BEING ASSERTIVE

Think of ten situations in which you might be reluctant to speak up or take action. Use the following situations or think of situations of your own.

- Speaking up about receiving a lesser product or service than you expected
- Sending back improperly prepared food in a restaurant
- Calling attention to an overcharge in a bill
- Declining an invitation to a social event or for a date
- Saying "no" to unwanted houseguests
- Asking a friend to return money that he or she borrowed
- Speaking up if someone cuts in front of you in line
- Returning a defective product to a store
- Speaking up to a colleague who calls you by a nickname you don't like
- Saying "no" to a friend's request to borrow a favorite possession

1. **Rank the situations from 1 to 10, 1 being the situation in which it is most difficult for you to assert yourself. Write them below.**

Rank	Situation
1	
2	
3	
4	
5	
6	
7	
8	
9	
10	

2. **In small groups, discuss the situations you wrote down and how you would like to respond to each one.**

Assignment: Role-play assertive interpersonal communication.

1. Choose a situation from the preceding activity.
2. With a partner, discuss what you'd like to do and say in that situation.
3. Role-play the situation with your partner. Practice responding assertively.
4. Present the role-play to the class.

PRONUNCIATION TIP

[s], [t], AND [θ]

A common error is to pronounce the sound [s] or [t] instead of the sound [θ] (as in *thin*). If you substitute [s] for [θ], **thank** will sound like **sank**. If you substitute [t] for [θ], **three** will sound like **tree**.

Pronounce [θ] by placing your tongue between your teeth. Pronounce [s] and [t] by placing your tongue behind your teeth. Look in a mirror and make sure you can see the tip of your tongue when you pronounce [θ]. Make sure you cannot see it when you pronounce [s] and [t].

EXERCISE 1

Read the following words aloud. Look in a mirror and make sure you can see and feel the tip of your tongue between your teeth.

1. thing
2. think
3. thought
4. through
5. Thursday
6. healthy
7. wealthy
8. something
9. bathtub
10. birthday
11. tooth
12. both
13. earth
14. faith
15. breath

EXERCISE 2

Read the following sets of words aloud. Be sure to place your tongue between your teeth when pronouncing [θ] and behind your teeth when pronouncing [s] and [t].

[θ]	[s]	[t]
1. three	see	tea
2. thin	sin	tin
3. thigh	sigh	tie
4. bath	bass	bat
5. faith	face	fate

Read the following phrases and sentences aloud. Be sure to place your tongue between your teeth when pronouncing [θ].

1. a. **thirty-third**
   b. **Thelma** had her **thirty-third birthday**.
2. a. **Thanksgiving**
   b. **Thanksgiving** falls on **Thursday**.
3. a. **through thick** and **thin**
   b. We remained friends **through thick** and **thin**.
4. a. **something** for **nothing**
   b. Don't **think** you can get **something** for **nothing**.
5. a. **author's theme**
   b. The **author's theme** is **thought**-provoking.

ANSWER TO THINK ABOUT HOW ASSUMPTIONS ARE MADE
(PAGE 185)

The man's friend was a woman. Her name was Elizabeth. Most people jump to the conclusion that the man's friend was also male.

Answers to Sample Story

1. *T* This is definitely true because it is clearly corroborated by the story.
2. *?* This might or might not be true. Perhaps Dr. Jones is just visiting you.
3. *F* This is definitely false because the story directly contradicts it.
4. *?* This may seem false, but you can't be sure: Perhaps the car has just been sold.

CHAPTER 11

Understanding Intercultural Communication

What is *intercultural communication*? In order to understand what this term means, it is important to first understand the term *culture*. Culture involves the beliefs, values, and behavioral patterns shared by large groups of people. It is learned from one's parents, family, friends, and other people one interacts with throughout one's life. No culture is better than another; it is simply different.

Intercultural communication occurs when people from different cultures exchange information, ideas, thoughts, and feelings with one another. They may do this through speaking, writing, or gestures. Sometimes, due to different beliefs, values, or behavioral patterns, miscommunication occurs. In order to communicate effectively across cultures, it is important to understand, respect, and appreciate the diverse beliefs and customs of people from different cultures.

The exercises and activities in this chapter are designed to help you gain an awareness of and appreciation for cultural differences so that you can communicate across cultures more effectively.

THINK ABOUT WHAT YOU VALUE IN A FRIEND

1. Write an anonymous "Friend Wanted" advertisement on a large poster-size paper. Specify the characteristics that you want in a friend.

2. Your teacher will collect the ads, number them, and display them around the room.

3. Read all the ads and decide which you like the best.

4. Your teacher will ask you which ad you would like to answer. Be prepared to answer such questions as:

   a. What attracted you to the ad?

   b. What kind of person do you think wrote the ad?

   c. Why do you think that person would be a good friend?

5. Your teacher will ask your classmates to identify which ads they wrote.

6. When everyone is finished, have a class discussion about the activity. Discuss:

   a. Do different cultures value different characteristics in friends? If so, what are the differences?

   b. Do different cultures value the same characteristics in friends? If so, what are the similarities?

EXPLORE YOUR CULTURAL BELIEFS

Find out more about beliefs, values, and behavioral patterns in different cultures.

1. In your culture, what is true about the people below? Complete the statements.

   Examples

   Men <u>are usually responsible for earning money.</u>

   Women <u>are usually in charge of family finances.</u>

   Young children <u>rarely help with the housework.</u>

   a. Men *are talkless*

   b. Women *are talking a lot.*

   c. Young children *are usually like to play*

d. Fathers _____

   e. Mothers _____

   f. Husbands _____

   g. Wives _____

   h. Brothers _____

   i. Sisters _____

   j. Grandparents _____

   k. Single men _____

   l. Single women _____

   m. Teachers _____

   n. Students _____

   o. Neighbors _____

2. In small groups, compare your statements. Discuss the following questions:

   a. Which of your statements were similar?

   b. Which of your statements were different?

   c. Which of your statements surprised you?

   d. Which of your classmates' statements surprised you?

ETHNOCENTRICITY

Ethnocentricity refers to the attitude that one's culture is better than any other culture. People who demonstrate cultural ethnocentricity look down on other cultures and believe them to be deficient in some way.

People can be ethnocentric about their country, looking down on people from other countries. They can be ethnocentric about religion or politics, believing themselves to be superior to those who have different views. They can even be ethnocentric about geography. For example, some city dwellers feel superior to those who live in rural areas, believing them to be less sophisticated and less educated.

Example: Belinda's Story

An American student, Belinda, described how she and her family moved from New York City to Montana. Belinda's friends felt sorry for her because she was leaving Fifth Avenue and Broadway behind. Belinda was unhappy because she thought she was moving to a primitive place. At first, her ethnocentric attitude prevented her from appreciating what Montana had to offer. Fortunately, after some initial adjustment, Belinda learned to love the beauty of the state, the friendliness of the people, and the other benefits of living in Montana.

STEREOTYPES

A *stereotype* refers to a preconceived idea about a person's gender, profession, race, religion, or culture. For example, statements like "All women love to shop," "All men like sports," "All accountants are boring," and "All New Yorkers are rude" are based on stereotypes. If you look closely at most stereotypes, you'll find that they are inaccurate and oversimplified. People from the same background all differ, and no two members of any culture behave alike all the time.

ACTIVITY

EXAMINE SOME STEREOTYPES

1. **Complete each statement with an adjective that describes your culture's reactions to these animals.**

    a. All snakes are _____

    b. All lions are _____

    c. All fish are _____

    d. All dogs are _____

    e. All cats are _____

    f. All pigs are _____

    g. All spiders are _____

    h. All birds are _____

    i. All rats are _____

    j. All horses are _____

    k. All cows are _____

2. **In small groups, compare your answers. Discuss the following questions:**

    a. Did you have difficulty completing each sentence with just one word? If so, why?

    b. Did everyone agree on the same adjective for any of the statements? If so, which one(s)?

    c. Were any animals given many different adjectives? If so, which one(s)?

In the exercise above, it may have been hard to fill in each blank with just one word because it is difficult to stereotype animals. Some snakes are poisonous; some are harmless. There are many breeds of dogs, including poodles, Doberman pinschers, cocker spaniels, and sheepdogs, each of which is often given a stereotype. Some are presumed to be sweet and lovable while others are reputed to be vicious and mean. It's unreasonable to describe *all* snakes, *all* spiders, or *all* dogs with one adjective, yet *all* members of one culture are often ascribed the same quality. Unfortunately, this quality is often a negative one.

DISCUSS THE IMPACT OF STEREOTYPES

How do cultural stereotypes affect intercultural communication?

Step 1: Meeting in small groups, explain a stereotype that others have of people from your culture.

Step 2: Discuss these questions:

1. Do you think this stereotype is accurate? Why or why not?
2. What reasons can you give for this stereotype?
3. How do you feel about this stereotype? Why?
4. Does this stereotype ever interfere with effective intercultural communication? If so, how?

(A sample response to this activity is provided on page 303 of Appendix II.)

THINK ABOUT HOW WE INTERPRET BEHAVIOR

Stereotypes often occur when people misinterpret cultural differences. How would you interpret the behavior patterns in the following chart?

1. Write your answers in the spaces provided.
2. Then compare your answers in small groups.

Student's Behavior	Interpretation
Sits at the back of the classroom and does not participate in class discussions	
Acts extremely embarrassed when called on by the teacher	
Constantly apologizes	
Asks lots of questions	
Offers opinions frequently without being asked	
Never offers opinions, even when asked	
Doesn't look at other people when speaking	
Shrugs shoulders when asked questions	
Says "yes" to everything	

(Sample interpretations for this activity are provided on page 303 of Appendix II.)

COLOR SYMBOLISM ACROSS CULTURES

The way we respond to particular colors is based partially on our culture. Colors often have different symbolic meanings in different cultures. A color that evokes a particular association in one culture can provoke a very different reaction in another culture. For example, the color green is often associated with money in the United States. Green does not cause people to make this association in most other countries. In American fashion and decoration, blue is for boys, while pink is for girls. This is a symbolic use of color that is not shared by many cultures. In the Chinese culture, white is the traditional color for funerals, while in the United States black is associated with death. Black has also come to suggest formality and sophistication in the United States.

ACTIVITY

CONSIDER WHAT COLORS MEAN IN YOUR CULTURE

Think about the following questions, and discuss your responses as a class.

1. In your culture, what colors are associated with the following?
   a. mourning or funerals
   b. weddings
   c. the birth of babies
   d. wealth and prosperity
   e. anger
   f. happiness
   g. celebrations

2. What special significance, if any, do the following colors have in your culture?
   a. red
   b. black
   c. white
   d. blue
   e. yellow
   f. purple
   g. pink
   h. green

3. Can you think of any other colors that have particular meaning in your culture? Tell the class about these.

CULTURAL DIFFERENCES IN COMMUNICATION

Intercultural communication is really interpersonal communication between people from different cultures. Although individuals within a culture differ, similarities in communication styles exist within each culture. In some cultures, people are generally very direct. They value free speech and express their personal opinions openly and assertively, saying exactly what they mean. People from such countries as Israel, the United States, Canada, Australia, New Zealand, and Great Britain tend to communicate rather directly relative to people from other countries. On the other hand, people from such countries as Japan, China, Korea, Thailand, and Mexico tend to communicate relatively indirectly. In order to maintain harmony and avoid conflict, they rarely express disagreement or displeasure in public for fear they might offend someone. They value silence and tend to speak in roundabout ways that individuals from cultures with more direct communication styles find confusing.

If, for example, a person bought an item that turned out to be defective, his or her response to the situation would likely be influenced by his or her culture. A person from a culture with a direct communication style would likely show it to a customer service representative. He or she might say, "Excuse me, this product is defective. I would like a refund, please." If refused, the person might ask to see the manager and repeat the request. On the other hand, a person from a culture with a more indirect communication style might not even return the product to the store. If he or she did, that person might show it to a customer service representative, apologize for being a bother, and hope that the representative would take the initiative to offer a refund. Alternatively, that person might display the defective item and ask, "Is there something you can do about this?" in the hope of being offered a refund without directly requesting one. If that person's request were denied, he or she would probably thank the employee and leave the store without pursuing the matter further.

ACTIVITY

EXPERIENCE DIFFERENT COMMUNICATION STYLES

In this activity, you will role-play direct and indirect communication styles and then reflect on which feels more comfortable to you and which is more typical of your culture.

1. With a partner, choose one of the following situations:
   a. You are a university student. You want to get to know an attractive student in your class. You would like the student to join you for a cup of coffee after class.
   b. You are a loyal, hardworking employee. You have been working for the same company for two years and have not received a raise. You would like your boss to give you a raise.
   c. You are a student. Your classmate borrowed a book from you and hasn't returned it. You need the book to study for an exam. You would like your classmate to return the book.
   d. You are a newlywed. You are shopping for furniture with your spouse. Your spouse likes furniture that you think is ugly. You would like to buy different furniture.
   e. You are a student. Your teacher has made a mistake in calculating your grade on an exam so that you received 83 percent instead of 89 percent. You would like the mistake corrected.

f. You are a student. You just had a wonderful meal in a restaurant with your boyfriend or girlfriend. The waiter brings your bill, and you see he has overcharged you for your meal. You would like your bill corrected before you pay.

2. Prepare two skits about the situation you have chosen. In the first skit, role-play the situation using an *indirect* communication style. For example, hint at what you want or express your wishes as questions. In the second skit, role-play the situation using a *direct* communication style. For example, state your wishes explicitly.

3. Role-play the two skits in front of the class.

4. As a class, discuss the two skits.

a. Which style are you more comfortable with?

b. Which style is closer to that used in your culture?

c. How would the situation be handled differently in your culture?

NONVERBAL COMMUNICATION

Nonverbal communication—such as posture, facial expressions, eye contact, body movements, and gestures—also differs between cultures. These differences are discussed in detail in Chapter 2: Delivering Your Message. A lack of awareness about these differences can lead to frustration, annoyance, and misunderstandings.

Example: Ruth Ann's story

Ruth Ann was an American student in a freshman science class. Her teacher assigned her to work on a project with a partner. Her partner, an exchange student, was from a culture in which direct eye contact is considered rude and disrespectful. Whenever Ruth Ann tried to engage him in conversation, he looked down at the floor. She thought that her partner was not interested in what she had to say and became very frustrated. Finally, during a work session, she placed both of her hands on his shoulders and said loudly, "Look at me when I'm speaking to you!" This made her partner feel extremely self-conscious and uncomfortable.

Ruth Ann didn't realize that her classmate hadn't meant to slight her; he was simply displaying nonverbal behavior characteristic of his own culture. If she had been more aware of this, she probably wouldn't have gotten frustrated and made him uncomfortable.

ACTIVITY **OBSERVE DIFFERENT CULTURAL STYLES IN ACTION**

Read Tomiko's story and answer the questions that follow.

Tomiko was a Japanese student enrolled in Professor Johnson's class. One day Professor Johnson was coming out of a classroom after giving a workshop on listening. Tomiko timidly approached her without saying a word. Professor Johnson, in an effort to engage Tomiko in conversation, asked her, "Did you enjoy the workshop?" "Yes, yes, I very much enjoyed the workshop," replied Tomiko, who then continued to talk about how much she had gained from the workshop. Professor Johnson, carrying a full load of books and papers to grade, politely listened and thanked Tomiko for her compliments, but Tomiko continued to stand in front of her.

Professor Johnson was confused. She didn't want to seem rude, but she was frustrated and impatient because she had a lot of work to do, and Tomiko wasn't asking any specific questions. Finally, Professor Johnson asked Tomiko if she would like a schedule of upcoming workshops to be offered. "Yes," replied Tomiko shyly, with her head bowed. "I would like that very much."

1. Think about these questions, and discuss your answers with the class.

   a. How did Tomiko feel about her interaction with Professor Johnson?

   b. How did her cultural background influence her communication style?

   c. How did Professor Johnson feel about her interaction with Tomiko?

   d. How did her cultural background influence her communication style?

   e. What could Tomiko have done to communicate more effectively?

   f. What could Professor Johnson have done to communicate more effectively?

2. Look at the analysis of "Tomiko's Story" in Appendix II on page 304. How do your responses to the above questions compare with the analysis provided?

3. Have you experienced cross-cultural misunderstanding?

   a. Can you think of any situations in which you might have misunderstood someone's behavior because of his or her cultural background? If so, how could the misunderstanding have been avoided?

   b. How can similar misunderstandings be avoided in the future?

   c. What factors should be considered when trying to establish communication with a person from another culture?

| ACTIVITY | **DESCRIBE SOME OF YOUR CULTURE'S CUSTOMS** |

1. Think of a custom, common practice, or behavior that is characteristic of your culture or the culture of someone you know well. You might consider:

   a. gift giving and receiving customs

   b. extending invitations/accepting or declining invitations

   c. mealtime behaviors

   d. showing appreciation

   e. public displays of affection

   f. greetings and leave-takings (bowing, cheek kissing, handshaking, hugging, etc.)

   g. marriage customs

   h. funeral customs

   i. holiday traditions

2. Explain the custom, tradition, or practice to the class.

3. Describe how a person from another culture reacted or might react to the custom or practice.

Example: Opening Christmas Presents

My friend Mary's family doesn't open their Christmas presents on Christmas Day. They get together on Christmas Eve to exchange gifts. Mary's great-grandfather came from Norway. It is a Norwegian custom to open presents on Christmas Eve. This became the tradition in Mary's family. Mary's new husband, John, was surprised to learn about this and was not very happy at the prospect of making a change in a tradition he had grown up with. His family had always opened presents on Christmas Day. Mary and John decided to compromise and open half of their presents on Christmas Eve and the other half of their presents on Christmas Day.

CULTURE CONFLICT

When people travel to another place as tourists or come to live in another country, there are many adjustments that they must make to the new environment. Everything seems different: a new language, different technology (telephones, banking machines), different forms of public transportation, different styles of appropriate dress, eating customs, etc. In these circumstances, cross-cultural misunderstandings are inevitable.

Although cross-cultural mishaps can be very distressing, they can also result in some humorous experiences. In fact, they often provide wonderful opportunities to help newcomers to a culture develop a better understanding of that culture and how to adapt to it.

Assignment: Give a speech about a "culture conflict."

1. Think of a situation in which you or someone you know personally experienced a cross-cultural problem.
2. Using the Speech Preparation Worksheet on page 206, prepare notes for a speech about this experience. Be sure to include all the details that will help your audience feel your frustration.
3. Your teacher may use the form on page 257 of Appendix I to evaluate your speech. Look it over so you know exactly how you will be evaluated.
4. Give a 2- to 3-minute speech about your "culture-conflicting" experience.

Example: *Ish's Speech*

MAKING TEA!

INTRODUCTION

I am holding a tea bag. I'm sure most of you have seen one of these before. They are very popular in the United States. Using a tea bag is a quick and easy way to make tea. You are probably thinking, "Why is Ish showing us a tea bag? What does this have to do with a speech about culture conflict?" Well, a tea bag caused me to experience a little cross-cultural problem that was very embarrassing.

I had just arrived from rural India. The first school that I attended was the University of Florida. My new American friend, Josh, invited me to have lunch with him in the student cafeteria.

I ordered a cup of tea from the lady behind the counter. I had never used or even seen a tea bag. My mother always brews fresh tea using tea leaves. I didn't know exactly what to do, so I tore open the tea bag and emptied its contents into my cup of hot water. Josh stared at me in amazement and yelled, "Oh no! Ish, don't drink that!" I got scared because I didn't know what I had done wrong. Josh got me another cup of hot water and a new tea bag. He showed me how to dip the tea bag in the water. I told Josh I liked to drink sweet tea. He gave me a paper packet of sugar. Before Josh could stop me, I immersed the packet of sugar in the hot water. Josh kept shaking his head from side to side and started to laugh. He told me not to drink the tea. I didn't understand why. Josh got me another cup of hot water. He explained that I had to tear open the sugar packet first and throw away the paper.

I was very confused. It made no sense to me. I was supposed to dip the tea bag into my cup without tearing it open, but I was supposed to tear open the sugar packet before putting the sugar in my tea!

CONCLUSION

At the time, I was very confused and upset. I felt very silly because the other people at the table were laughing. Now I realize how funny it must have looked to them. I know that if any of you ever come to visit me in India, you, too, will experience culture conflict. I promise not to laugh!

Use the following worksheet to prepare your notes for your "Culture Conflict" experience.

CULTURE CONFLICT EXPERIENCE SPEECH PREPARATION WORKSHEET	
What type of experience was it?	
Where were you?	
When were you there?	
Who was with you?	
What were you doing?	
Why were you there?	
How were you feeling?	
Why did you feel that way?	
What happened exactly?	
How did you react?	
How did the story end?	
Why did you learn from this experience?	

Thanks to all the technological advances that have connected people from different countries, the world is becoming a smaller place. In the future, you will be communicating more and more with people from different backgrounds. Appreciating and valuing cultural differences helps to promote human understanding and successful interaction among people from diverse cultures. Practicing effective intercultural communication will prepare you for informed and compassionate involvement in our increasingly global society.

PRONUNCIATION TIP

CONTRACTIONS

A contraction is the short form of a word or words. For example, the contraction of **do not** is **don't**, and the contraction of **did not** is **didn't**. Contractions are frequently used in spoken English and are grammatically correct.

When participating in conversations, use contractions. They will make your speech sound smooth and natural.

EXERCISE 1 Write the contraction of each two-word expression. Read each expression and its contraction aloud.

Example: it is _____it's_____

1. does not _____
2. I am _____
3. should not _____
4. will not _____
5. he is _____

6. I will _____
7. cannot _____
8. we have _____
9. you are _____
10. is not _____

EXERCISE 2 Write ten sentences using contractions from Exercise 1. Read them aloud.

1. _____
2. _____
3. _____
4. _____
5. _____
6. _____
7. _____
8. _____
9. _____
10. _____

Read the following pairs of sentences aloud. Notice how smooth, natural, and informal the sentences with contractions sound compared to those using the uncontracted forms.

1. a. Omar **does not** know.
   b. Omar **doesn't** know.
2. a. I **do not** think she cares.
   b. I **don't** think she cares.
3. a. **You are** coming, **are you not**?
   b. **You're** coming, **aren't you**?
4. a. **She is** very tall.
   b. **She's** very tall.
5. a. Antonio **is not** a good cook.
   b. Antonio **isn't** a good cook.

CHAPTER 12

Thinking on Your Feet

Thinking is something people do all day long. "Thinking on your feet" means being able to organize one's ideas quickly and speak about a subject without advance time to prepare. This type of speech is often called an *impromptu speech*.

When do we make impromptu speeches? We make them all the time. Most of our conversations with friends, parents, teachers, and employers are really short impromptu talks. These impromptu talks might include answering questions, giving opinions, or sharing knowledge about the many topics we discuss with people on a daily basis. As you can see, you already have experience giving impromptu speeches.

In this chapter, you will learn how to think on your feet and give short speeches without advance preparation. One way to improve your ability to give impromptu speeches is to practice giving extended responses to questions. The following activities will develop your capability to think on your feet, organize your ideas quickly, and speak informatively and confidently about a variety of topics.

RESPOND TO SPECIFIC INFORMATION QUESTIONS

Practice giving a short impromptu speech in response to a specific information question. Elaborate on your response by anticipating what else the listener might like to know and providing that information.

1. Your teacher will ask you a specific information question. Possible questions are listed below.
2. Think about the question for a moment. Consider examples and reasons that will support your answer.
3. Be sure to elaborate on your response as you answer the question.

Possible questions:

- Who is the best teacher you've ever had?
- How many classes are you taking?
- What is your favorite city?
- What is your favorite holiday?
- What are you majoring in?
- What do you like best about living in this country?
- Who is your best friend?
- Where do you want to live when you graduate?
- What is your favorite time of year?
- What do you do in your free time?
- Do you prefer watching TV or reading books?
- Where do you like to go on vacation?
- How many siblings do you have?

Example

Question: *Who is the best teacher you've ever had?*

Answer A: *Mr. Johnston.* (This is a curt reply and gives the impression you don't want to talk.)

Answer B: *Mr. Mark Johnston. He was my sixth grade teacher. Mr. Johnston was always caring and took a personal interest in all his students. He was always patient and encouraged us to ask questions when we didn't understand something.* (This is a well-supported, elaborate response.)

RESPOND TO *YES/NO* QUESTIONS

Practice giving a short impromptu response to a *yes/no* question. Elaborate on your thoughts by anticipating what the listener might want to know and providing that information.

Example

Question: *Do you go to school?*

Answer A: *Yes.* (Again, this is a curt response and gives the impression that you don't want to talk.)

Answer B: *Yes, I'm a junior at Northeastern University, and I'm majoring in business administration. I like the facilities at the university a lot, especially the sports facilities. The program is challenging, but the professors are very helpful.* (This is an elaborate response.)

1. Your teacher will ask you a *yes/no* question. Possible questions include:
   - Do you go to school?
   - Do you like animals?
   - Do you live near here?
   - Did you study English before coming here?
   - Do you have any pets?
   - Are you a good cook?
   - Do you have any siblings?
   - Do you like to watch TV?
   - Would you like to have children one day?
   - Have you ever had a job?
   - Do you like to travel?

2. Think about the question for a moment. What follow-up information could you provide to make your response more interesting?

3. Answer the question as completely as possible.

PREPARING FOR THE IMPROMPTU SPEECH

The best preparation for an impromptu speech is to be well-informed about people, places, and news events in your city, state, country, and around the world. This type of information will enable you to speak informatively about many topics in different situations.

Assignment: Report on a news event.

The following assignments will help you become better informed. This will make you better able to speak about many topics when asked to make impromptu speeches. Choose one and be prepared to talk about it in class.

1. Watch the evening news on TV. Be prepared to describe the details of a news story.

2. Listen to a radio news station for ten minutes. Choose a news item that interests you. Be prepared to describe it and explain why you found it interesting.

3. Read the editorial page of your local newspaper. Be prepared to give an oral summary of an editorial about a controversial issue and explain why you agree or disagree with the editor's opinions.

4. From a national newsmagazine like *Time, Newsweek,* or *U.S. News and World Report,* choose an article that you feel is very important. Be prepared to talk about the article and explain why it is important.

5. Describe a news event to three different people outside of class. Ask them their opinions about what you read or heard. Be prepared to discuss their opinions about the news event.

ORGANIZING THE IMPROMPTU SPEECH

Good impromptu speakers know many different ways to organize their thoughts even before they know their topic. They quickly mentally review possible organizational patterns when they know they must speak in a few moments. Being familiar with such patterns will enable you to choose the best method of organizing ideas for your particular topic. It will make it easier for you to think of things to say and examples to present. You will be able to choose an organizational pattern and start developing it mentally or on paper in the few moments you have before getting up to speak.

As you learned in Chapter 4, possible organizational patterns include:

- **Past-Present-Future** to describe how something once was, how it has changed, and how it will be in the future
- **Time** to describe chronological events or processes in sequential order
- **Problem-Solution** to describe a problem and ways to solve it
- **Location** to divide a topic into different geographical settings
- **Cause-Effect** to describe a situation and its effects
- **Effect-Cause** to describe a situation and its causes
- **Related Subtopics** to divide a topic into different parts
- **Advantage-Disadvantage** to describe positive and negative aspects of a topic

For detailed information about these patterns, review pages 74–75 of Chapter 4: Speaking to Inform.

OUTLINING THE IMPROMPTU SPEECH

When preparing for an impromptu speech, it can be helpful to create an outline for your ideas. This outline can be a real outline, which you write on paper, or a mental outline, which you keep in your head. When you create an outline, try to choose an organizational pattern that fits your topic. When Marco was asked to give an impromptu speech on "Addictions," he quickly outlined his ideas on paper before speaking. He divided the topic into several parts. Notice how he used the pattern of related subtopics in the outline that follows.

Example: *Marco's Outline*

INTRODUCTION

I. I'll bet everyone in this room knows an addict! That's right, I said *addict*. Before you get angry, please let me explain.

II. When we hear the word *addiction,* we usually think of harmful substances like drugs or alcohol. We forget there are many other kinds of addictions. I'd now like to remind you of some.

I. Television addictions
  A. Soap operas
  B. Detective shows
  C. Sports
    1. Football
    2. Baseball
    3. Wrestling

II. Book addictions
  A. Romance novels
  B. Mysteries
  C. Science fiction

III. Eating addictions
  A. Ice cream
  B. Chocolate

IV. Other addictions
  A. Shopping
    1. Clothes
    2. CDs
    3. Antiques
  B. Hobbies
    1. Stamp collecting
    2. Photography
  C. Sports
    1. Golf
    2. Jogging
    3. Swimming

CONCLUSION

I. As you can see, not all addictions are bad for you. And, much to your surprise, you probably know someone who is an addict!

II. What kind of addict are you?

ACTIVITY

THINK ABOUT ORGANIZATIONAL PATTERNS

Work in small groups and discuss possible organizational patterns for speech topics. Use the space below to record your ideas.

1. Marco used the pattern of related subtopics to organize his speech on the topic of "Addictions." What other organizational patterns could be used for this topic?

_____

_____

_____

2. What subtopics could be used for each organizational pattern that you chose?

_____

_____

_____

_____

3. Think about how you could organize some possible impromptu speech topics.

    a. Choose any five of the following topics and write each one on a line below.

travel	stress	punctuality
friends	hobbies	working students
shopping	laws	heroes
rules	customs	free speech
habits	manners	communication
a story in the news		

    b. Which organizational patterns could be used for each topic you chose?

Topic	**Possible Organizational Patterns**
1. _____	_____
2. _____	_____
3. _____	_____
4. _____	_____
5. _____	_____

GUIDELINES FOR IMPROMPTU SPEAKING

The following guidelines will help you relax and speak confidently when giving an impromptu speech:

1. Stay calm and begin slowly in order to give yourself time to think. No one is expecting a perfectly prepared speech. The audience knows this is an impromptu speech.

2. Begin with an attention-getting opener that is related to your talk. For example, make a startling statement, use a quotation from a well-known person, or ask the audience a question. Don't begin your speech with "My topic is _____," or "Today I'm going to talk about _____."

3. If you get confused or forget what you want to say, don't apologize to the audience. Stop briefly and organize your thoughts, and then continue speaking as if nothing happened.

4. Finish your speech gracefully with words your audience will remember. Don't end your speech with "I can't think of anything else" or "That's it." Review the information on page 80 of Chapter 4: Speaking to Inform and pages 135–136 of Chapter 7: Speaking to Persuade for hints about preparing memorable concluding remarks.

Assignment: Give an impromptu speech.

1. Your teacher may use the form on page 258 of Appendix I to evaluate your speech. Look it over so you know exactly how you will be evaluated.

2. Your teacher will assign you an impromptu speech topic. Possible impromptu speech topics are suggested on page 214. Think about how to develop and organize your speech for a few minutes. Your teacher may allow you to write your ideas on an index card.

3. Give a 2- to 3-minute speech about the topic.

PRONUNCIATION TIP

[b], [v], AND [w]

A common error is to pronounce the sound [b] or [w] like [v], and vice versa. If you confuse [b] and [v], **vote** sounds like **boat** and **best** sounds like **vest**. If you confuse [w] and [v], **wine** sounds like **vine** and **vet** sounds like **wet**.

To pronounce [b], press your lips firmly together. To pronounce [v], place your top teeth over your bottom lip. To pronounce [w], round your lips and don't let your lower lip touch your upper teeth.

EXERCISE 1

Read the following sets of words aloud. Be sure to press your lips together for [b], place your top teeth over your bottom lip for [v], and round your lips for [w].

[b]	[v]	[w]
1. best	vest	west
2. bet	vet	wet
3. Barry	vary	wary
4. bent	vent	went
5. be	V	we

EXERCISE 2

Read the following sentences aloud. Concentrate on pronouncing [b], [v], and [w] correctly.

1. A **whale would** look silly **wearing** a **veil**.
2. That **vest** is the **best** in the **west**.
3. The **berry** tastes **very sweet**.
4. The **vet** got **wet** in the rain.
5. She **bent** the metal **vent**.

Circle all the words in the following poem that have the sound [v]. Then read the poem aloud. Be sure to place your top teeth over your bottom lip as you pronounce words with [v].

1052

I never saw a Moor—
I never saw the Sea—
Yet know I how the Heather looks
And what a Billow must be.

I never spoke with God
Nor visited in Heaven—
Yet certain am I of the spot
As if the Checks were given—

—Emily Dickinson

CHAPTER 13

Using Idioms and Proverbs

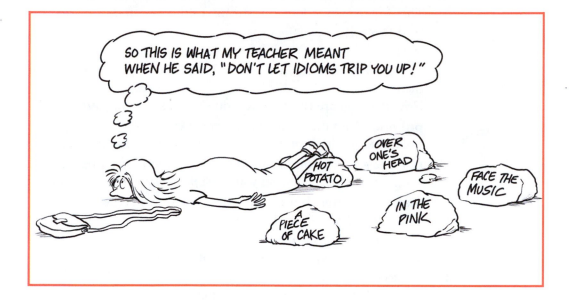

Every language has popular expressions that don't always mean what one would expect. These popular expressions are known as *idioms*. An idiom cannot be translated literally. Attempts to do so often lead to confusion and frustration. For example, the English idiom *you're pulling my leg* means "You're kidding or not telling the truth." It doesn't really mean that you are holding my leg and pulling it.

Every language also has popular expressions that express advice or wisdom. These expressions are known as *proverbs*. For example, the English proverb *Don't look a gift horse in the mouth* means "Don't be critical of a gift. Accept it graciously."

Improving your ability to understand and use these expressions will help improve your speech communication skills. It will enable you to better understand your English-speaking friends and express yourself in a natural, informal manner.

In this chapter, you will learn and use a variety of idioms and proverbs.

IDIOMS WITH BODY PARTS

The following idioms include names of body parts.

1. **pull someone's leg:** to joke about something or exaggerate
   Are you *pulling my leg?* Tell me the truth!

2. **not have a leg to stand on:** to not have proof or support for an idea or a decision
   Without a witness, you *don't have a leg to stand on.*

3. **on one's last legs:** in the last phase before collapse or death
   That horse doesn't look too strong. I think it's *on its last legs.*

4. **foot the bill:** to pay the expenses
   My father is *footing the bill* for my education.

5. **stand on one's own two feet:** to be independent or responsible for one's own life
   Now that you are twenty-one, you should *stand on your own two feet.*

6. **put one's foot down:** to take a firm stand
   My father *put his foot down* and said I couldn't use the car.

7. **put one's foot in one's mouth:** to say something embarrassing
   Think before you speak so you don't *put your foot in your mouth.*

8. **make one's mouth water:** to stimulate the appetite
   The smell of Mom's cooking *makes my mouth water.*

9. **melt in one's mouth:** to taste very good
   Grandmother's apple pie *melts in your mouth.*

10. **see eye to eye:** to agree completely
    We get along well because we usually *see eye to eye.*

11. **pull the wool over someone's eyes:** to deceive or trick someone
    My teacher didn't believe my excuse. I couldn't *pull the wool over her eyes.*

12. **butterflies in one's stomach:** a feeling of nervousness
    When I speak before large groups, I get *butterflies in my stomach.*

13. **over one's head:** too difficult to understand
    Stella can't understand the chapter; it's *over her head.*

14. **lose one's head:** to lose control
    After I got a small raise, I *lost my head* and bought an expensive car.

15. **out of hand:** out of control
    The poorly conducted meeting got *out of hand.*

16. **lend a hand:** to provide assistance
    I'll *lend a hand* and help you fix your car.

17. **one's heart is not in (something):** one is not interested in or enthusiastic about (something)
    My heart's not in doing housework today.

18. **by heart:** so that it is memorized
    I know the Pledge of Allegiance *by heart.*

19. **slap in the face:** an insult
    John called me stupid. That's a real *slap in the face.*

20. **elbow room:** space to move around
My kitchen is too small. There is no *elbow room*.

21. **hold one's tongue:** to keep quiet
Please *hold your tongue*—I don't want to hear about it.

22. **wet behind the ears:** having very little experience
He's not ready to be the boss; he's still *wet behind the ears*.

23. **all ears:** willing to listen carefully
Tell me what is bothering you—I'm *all ears*.

24. **cross one's fingers:** to wish for good luck or success
I'll *cross my fingers* that you'll win the race.

25. **on the nose:** exact
Your answer to that question was right *on the nose*.

EXERCISE 1   **Write the letter of the sentence that best shows the meaning of the idiom in italics. (Answers can be found on page 307 of Appendix II.)**

_____ 1. José doesn't *stand on his own two feet*.
   a. He prefers to sit on a chair.
   b. He broke a leg and can't stand up.
   c. He always asks others to help him.

_____ 2. Chocolate *makes my mouth water*.
   a. It makes me hungry.
   b. It makes me thirsty.
   c. It takes away my hunger.

_____ 3. This is getting *out of hand*.
   a. This fell out of my hand.
   b. I burned my hand.
   c. The situation is out of control.

_____ 4. That was a *slap in the face*.
   a. Someone hit me in the face.
   b. Someone insulted me.
   c. Someone complimented me.

_____ 5. Ali is *in over his head*.
   a. He is underwater.
   b. He is very short.
   c. He can't handle the work.

_____ 6. Susanna is *wet behind the ears*.
   a. She didn't dry her ears.
   b. She doesn't have much experience.
   c. She hears well.

_____ 7. Kim doesn't know when to *hold his tongue*.
   a. He always tells important secrets.
   b. He can't roll his tongue up.
   c. He always sticks his tongue out when he is angry.

_____ **8.** They don't *see eye to eye.*

    a. They never look at each other.

    b. They always wear dark sunglasses.

    c. They don't agree with each other.

_____ **9.** That car is *on its last legs.*

    a. It only has one tire.

    b. It needs a paint job.

    c. It is about to break down completely.

_____ **10.** You got it *right on the nose.*

    a. It hit your nose.

    b. It fits your nose perfectly.

    c. You did it perfectly.

EXERCISE 2   **Match each idiom with its meaning. (Answers can be found on page 307 of Appendix II.)**

_____ 1. butterflies in one's stomach	**a.** a nervous feeling
_____ 2. foot the bill	**b.** to deceive someone
_____ 3. by heart	**c.** to be uninterested
_____ 4. pull the wool over someone's eyes	**d.** to pay the costs
_____ 5. not have one's heart in it	**e.** by memory
_____ 6. lose one's head	**f.** to help out
_____ 7. elbow room	**g.** to take a firm stand
_____ 8. cross one's fingers	**h.** to act foolishly
_____ 9. lend a hand	**i.** to wish for good luck
_____ 10. put one's foot down	**j.** space to move

IDIOMS WITH FOODS

The following idioms include names of foods.

1. **as easy as pie:** very easy to do
   A child could do it; it's *as easy as pie.*

2. **a piece of cake:** very easy to do
   I can fix your car in ten minutes. It's *a piece of cake!*

3. **spill the beans:** to tell a secret
   Pierre *spilled the beans* and told me about the surprise party.

4. **like sardines (in a can):** very crowded
   In Tokyo, people pack into the subway *like sardines.*

5. **cry over spilled milk:** to worry about something that has already happened
   You lost your ring a year ago. Don't *cry over spilled milk.*

6. **the cream of the crop:** the best people
   The students who get admitted to that school are really *the cream of the crop.*

7. **lemon:** a product with many defects
   This new car is a *lemon*; nothing works right.

8. **fishy:** seeming wrong or suspicious
   There is something *fishy* about his story; I don't believe it.

9. **as cool as a cucumber:** having much self-confidence and self-control
   The president is *as cool as a cucumber,* even under pressure.

10. **hot potato:** a controversial topic
    The subject of capital punishment is a *hot potato.*

EXERCISE 3 Circle the letter of the phrase that correctly explains the meaning of the idiom. (Answers can be found on page 307 of Appendix II.)

1. spill the beans
   a. to drop vegetables
   b. to tell a secret
   c. to keep a secret

2. a piece of cake
   a. something difficult
   b. a portion of dessert
   c. something very simple

3. fishy
   a. like tuna
   b. right
   c. wrong

4. as easy as pie
   a. easy to bake
   b. easy to do
   c. easy to eat

5. cry over spilled milk
   a. to complain about something in the past
   b. to cry because there's no food
   c. to complain about an unfair situation

6. hot potato
   a. a controversial topic
   b. a person who gets angry easily
   c. a potato that isn't cold

7. like sardines (in a can)
   a. like something sold in supermarkets
   b. very crowded
   c. identical

8. the cream of the crop
   a. something grown on a farm
   b. dairy products
   c. the best people

9. as cool as a cucumber
   a. very self-assured
   b. very cool
   c. lukewarm

10. lemon
    a. a yellow citrus fruit
    b. something that requires a lot of work
    c. a defective product

IDIOMS WITH COLORS

The following idioms include names of colors.

1. **green with envy:** very jealous
   When I won the prize, all my friends were *green with envy*.

2. **blue:** sad
   He is feeling *blue* because his dog died.

3. **in the red:** in debt
   His company's sales are down, and he's *in the red*.

4. **see red:** to be very angry
   My father *saw red* when I broke his new radio.

5. **rosy:** favorable; bright
   Ricardo just inherited a lot of money; his future looks *rosy*.

6. **in black and white:** in a very simple way
   The teacher explained the rules *in black and white*.

7. **golden:** wonderful, priceless
   Lana received a full scholarship to study in France. What a *golden* opportunity!

8. **in the pink:** in good health
   My doctor told me I was *in the pink*.

9. **out of the blue:** unexpectedly
   I hadn't heard from my uncle in fifteen years. Yesterday, he called me *out of the blue*.

10. **white lie:** a lie that is not serious
    The woman told a *white lie*. She said her hair was naturally blonde.

EXERCISE 4

Write the idiom associated with each word. (Answers can be found on page 307 of Appendix II.)

1. jealous _____

2. in debt _____

3. unhappy _____

4. healthy _____

5. wonderful _____

6. good _____

7. unexpectedly _____

8. angry _____

9. clearly stated _____

10. not true _____

MISCELLANEOUS IDIOMS

The following idioms are about a variety of topics.

1. **under the weather:** ill
   Randy isn't going to the party; he's a bit *under the weather*.

2. **throw in the towel:** to give up
   Don't *throw in the towel*; finish your education.

3. **put the cart before the horse:** to reverse the correct order of events
   I *put the cart before the horse* and bought a car before I learned how to drive.

4. **make tracks:** to move fast
   Let's *make tracks* and stop wasting time.

5. **put two and two together:** to guess the meaning of something one has seen or heard
   When we got home and found the front door open, we *put two and two together*: We'd been robbed!

6. **get to the point:** to come to the important part of one's message
   I'm very busy. Please *get to the point*.

7. **beat around the bush:** to speak vaguely or indirectly
   Stop *beating around the bush* and get to the point.

8. **run in the family:** to be characteristic of family members
   All my sisters are tall; height *runs in my family*.

9. **eat one's words:** to take back what one said
   When I learned I was wrong, I had to *eat my words*.

10. **square away:** to finish; to put in order or solve
    The deal is *squared away* now that all the papers have been sent.

11. **pull (some/a few) strings:** to use influence; to manipulate
    You're the boss's son. Can you please *pull some strings* and get me a job?

12. **face the music:** to accept the consequences of one's actions
    The criminal had to *face the music* in the courtroom.

EXERCISE 5 **Substitute one of the following idioms for the italicized words in each sentence. Be sure to use the correct grammatical form of each idiom. (Answers can be found on page 307 of Appendix II.)**

put two and two together	face the music
put the cart before the horse	make tracks
under the weather	square away
get to the point	eat one's words
run in the family	throw in the towel
pull (some/a few) strings	

Example

I used my father's boat without permission. Now I am ready to *be punished*.

Now I am ready to *face the music*.

1. The police collected several clues, which helped them *figure out the mystery*.

2. You don't have much time. *Be direct* and explain yourself clearly.

3. Carl called me a bad cardplayer. He had to *take back what he said* when I won every game.

4. The teacher told the students to *work faster* and finish their assignment.

5. Helga was discouraged and *gave up*. She dropped out of school.

6. Bill caught the flu. He's *not feeling well*.

7. All the problems with my car have finally been *taken care of*.

8. Blond hair *is a common trait in my family*. My mother and three sisters are all blondes.

9. I'd like to be an actress. Do you know any people who could *use their influence* and get me a part in a movie?

10. Elena planned a big party for Linda without first finding out if Linda could come. Elena always *does things backwards*.

Complete each sentence with a phrase that shows an understanding of the idiomatic expression in italics. Be sure to use correct grammar and sentence structure.

Examples

a. The meeting got *out of hand* <u>when everyone started shouting and throwing papers</u>.
b. <u>Good looks and intelligence</u> *run in my family.*
c. We don't always *see eye to eye,* but <u>we are very good friends</u>.

1. I finally *put two and two together* and _____.

2. I feel *blue* when _____.

3. His car is a *lemon* because _____.

4. _____ *like sardines in a can.*

5. He *threw in the towel* when _____.

6. Sue *spilled the beans* by _____.

7. I think *her heart's not in* her work because _____.

8. My friend was *green with envy* when _____.

9. Maria *put the cart before the horse* and _____.

10. _____ *on the nose.*

11. It's time to *put your foot down* and _____.

12. I get *butterflies in my stomach* when _____.

13. The students got *out of hand* when _____.

14. _____ *makes my mouth water.*

15. I'll try to *pull some strings* and _____.

16. My mother *saw red* when _____.

17. I tried to *pull the wool over her eyes* by _____.

18. Julio had to *eat his words* after _____.

19. Elena was feeling *under the weather* because _____.

20. For me, _____ is *as easy as pie.*

21. His story that _____ sounds *fishy.*

22. Please *lend a hand* and _____.

23. Let's *make tracks* and _____.

24. My parents aren't willing to *foot the bill* for _____.

25. I know _____ *by heart.*

26. He *put his foot in his mouth* when _____.

PROGRESSIVE STORY

The progressive story is a fun, informal speaking activity that encourages you to think on your feet and use your imagination. A good progressive story has four main components:

1. a setting (who, what, when, where)
2. an initial event (something happens)
3. an attempt (something is done or an action is taken)
4. a consequence

One person starts a story by providing a setting. He or she then calls on another student to describe what happened next. That person calls on a third student to explain what action was taken; a fourth student concludes the story.

ACTIVITY

CREATE A PROGRESSIVE STORY USING IDIOMS

Work in groups of four to create a progressive story. Use as many idioms from the chapter as possible.

1. Decide on a topic. Below are some ideas. You may also think of others.

an experience	a pet peeve	a fairy tale
an activity	an argument	a dream

2. Create your progressive story.
   a. Speaker A begins a story with a setting and speaks for just under a minute.
   b. Speaker B continues the story for the same amount of time describing an event.
   c. Speaker C describes the action taken, again doing this in under a minute.
   d. Speaker D concludes the story, explaining its consequences.
3. When all the groups have finished creating their stories, each group will share theirs with the entire class.

Example

SPEAKER A (THE SETTING)

My cousin invited me and five friends to go for a drive in his new sports car one Saturday. I was feeling *under the weather*. I said yes, even though *my heart wasn't in it*. We packed ourselves *like sardines in a can* into his small car and drove off. We were really *making tracks* down the highway when, *out of the blue*, something happened. . . .

SPEAKER B (THE EVENT)

What happened was that a policeman stopped my cousin's car. I had *butterflies in my stomach*. The patrol car pulled us over to the side of the road. We tried to *put two and two together* but couldn't figure out what we had done wrong. The policeman told us that one of our taillights was burned out. He then became suspicious of us—probably because we had a sticker from Colombia on the windshield. Things were about to get *out of hand*. . . .

SPEAKER C (THE ACTION TAKEN)

The trooper was *as cool as a cucumber*. He searched our car and found two burlap bags in the small trunk. He thought something was *fishy*. He asked us what the bags contained. He was *all ears* as he waited for our answer. We told him they were bags of Colombian coffee. I had just arrived two days before from a visit with my family in Bogotá, Colombia. My father owned a large coffee exporting company in Colombia. The policeman thought we were *trying to pull the wool over his eyes*. We tried to assure him that we were telling the truth, but . . .

SPEAKER D (THE CONSEQUENCE)

He took us to the police station. We were scared *and held our tongues*. Another policeman took our coffee away. We waited there for three hours. Things were not looking *rosy*. Finally, they tested the coffee and determined it was really coffee. After realizing that we had done nothing wrong, they apologized, gave us back our coffee, and let us go. My cousin made me promise *not to spill the beans* and tell my parents what happened to us.

We sure learned a lesson about living in the United States. Never, never carry your coffee in a burlap bag that says "Colombian" on the side!

PROVERBS

Every language has proverbs or sayings that express advice or wisdom. You may already be familiar with some English proverbs. For example, the proverb *Let sleeping dogs lie* means "Don't bother something or someone if the person or thing is not bothering you."

Improving your ability to understand and to use these expressions will help improve your speech communication skills.

ACTIVITY

LEARN TO USE PROVERBS

Try to find the meaning of each of the following proverbs. Ask anyone who is willing to help you. If possible, write a proverb from your native language that has a similar meaning. Come to class prepared to discuss the expressions. (Possible explanations of these proverbs are provided on pages 307–308 of Appendix II.)

    a. A stitch in time saves nine.

    b. An ounce of prevention is worth a pound of cure.

    c. A watched pot never boils.

    d. The grass is always greener on the other side.

    e. When in Rome, do as the Romans do.

    f. When the cat's away, the mice will play.

    g. People who live in glass houses shouldn't throw stones.

    h. A bird in the hand is worth two in the bush.

    i. Don't put all your eggs in one basket.

    j. Don't count your chickens before they hatch.

    k. Look before you leap.

    l. A rolling stone gathers no moss.

    m. All that glitters is not gold.

    n. It's useless to lock the stable door after the horse has bolted.

    o. Birds of a feather flock together.

    p. Old houses mended cost little less than new before they're ended.

    q. You can't judge a book by its cover.

    r. Cross each bridge as you come to it.

    s. It's easier to catch flies with honey than vinegar.

    t. Half a loaf is better than none.

    u. Strike while the iron is hot.

    v. Give him an inch and he'll take a mile.

    w. That's like borrowing from Peter to pay Paul.

    x. The pot is calling the kettle black.

    y. Too many cooks spoil the broth.

    z. You can't teach an old dog new tricks.

Read the following statements. Figure out which proverb on page 228 is most applicable to each statement. (Check your answers on page 308 in Appendix II.)

Example

My parents are very proud of me. I earned a straight A average this semester. I'd better ask them to buy me the car I want while they are in such a good mood.

Strike while the iron is hot.

1. Sam was sure he was going to win the lottery, so he went out and ordered an expensive car.

2. Jane has a messy house. She often calls her neighbor a sloppy housekeeper.

3. Rudolfo bought a worthless piece of shiny red glass that he thought was an expensive ruby.

4. Tom cheats on his own taxes. He reported Joe to the Internal Revenue Service for tax evasion.

5. Sports teams frequently don't travel on the same plane in case of a plane crash.

6. Jenny hangs around with really smart people. She must be smart too.

7. Andy went to a new club. He saw that everyone was dancing with one shoe off. He also took off one shoe and danced.

8. If you want your little sister to clean up her room, tell her nicely rather than angrily.

9. I told my friend he could borrow my car for an hour. He kept it all day.

10. I don't have enough money to buy a fancy new car. However, I can afford to buy a reliable used car.

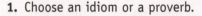

Assignment: Give a speech about an idiom or a proverb.

1. Choose an idiom or a proverb.
2. Prepare notes for a presentation about the idiom or proverb. Include the following components:
   - an attention-getting opener
   - a clear statement of the idiom or expression
   - an explanation of the idiom's or expression's general meaning
   - two examples that illustrate the idiom's or expression's meaning
   - a graceful conclusion
3. Your teacher may use the form on page 259 of Appendix I to evaluate your speech. Look it over so you know exactly how you will be evaluated.
4. Give a 2- to 3-minute speech about the idiom or proverb.

Example

ATTENTION-GETTING OPENER

What would you do if your parents went on vacation and left you home alone? Would you stay out late? Would you throw wild parties and invite all your friends? I'm sure no one here would act so irresponsibly, but there are plenty of people who would!

CLEAR STATEMENT OF IDIOM OR PROVERB

Many of you have heard the expression "When the cat's away, the mice will play."

EXPLANATION

This saying means that animals or people might take advantage of a situation and misbehave if no one is there to supervise.

EXAMPLE A

For example, I left my two dogs at home alone while I went to the store. When I returned, I saw that they had chewed a hole in the carpet. This would not have happened if someone had stayed home to watch them.

EXAMPLE B

Another example happened when my teacher was giving our class a test. He left the classroom for a few minutes. When he came back into the room, everyone was talking and telling each other the answers. If he had stayed in the room, the students could not have cheated.

GRACEFUL CONCLUSION

My brother was complaining that whenever he goes out of town, his employees come in late, leave early, and don't do their work. I told him, "You know what they say, 'When the cat's away, the mice will play!'"

PRONUNCIATION TIP

[i] AND [ɪ]

Some students confuse the vowel sounds [i] (as in *bean*) and [ɪ] (as in *bin*). If they confuse these sounds, **it** sounds like **eat** and **sheep** sounds like **ship**.

The sound [i] is long and stressed. When you pronounce it, tense your lips and spread them into a smile. The sound [ɪ] is short and relaxed. When you pronounce it, don't tense your lips or move your tongue.

EXERCISE 1

Read the following pairs of words and sentences aloud. Be sure to tense your lips and make a long sound when pronouncing words with [i]. Be sure to relax your lips and make a short sound when pronouncing words with [ɪ].

[i]	[ɪ]
1. f**ee**t	fit
2. sh**ee**p	ship
3. t**ea**m	Tim
4. When did he sl**ee**p?	When did he slip?
5. She will l**ea**ve.	She will live.
6. Change the wh**ee**l.	Change the will.

EXERCISE 2

Read the following sentences aloud. Circle the boldfaced words with the vowel sound [i] and underline those with the vowel sound [ɪ].

1. Please **sit** in the **seat**.
2. He **did** a good **deed**.
3. **Tim** made the **team**.
4. Potato **chips** are **cheap**.
5. The shoes don't **fit** my **feet**.

EXERCISE 3

Read the dialog below silently. Circle the words with the vowel sound [i] and underline those with the vowel sound [ɪ]. Then practice reading the dialog aloud with a partner.

JIM: Hi, Tina! Do you have a minute?
TINA: Yes, Jim. What is it?
JIM: My sister is in the city on business. We are going to eat dinner out tonight. Can you recommend a place to eat?
TINA: There is a fine seafood restaurant on Fifth Street. The fish is fresh and the shrimp is great. But it isn't cheap!
JIM: That's OK. It will be "feast today, famine tomorrow"! I'll just have to eat beans for the rest of the week!

CHAPTER 14

Speaking for Special Purposes

By now you have probably given several speeches to your classmates. In the process, you have improved your self-confidence and ability to speak before a group. You have learned how to research, organize, prepare, and deliver a variety of speeches. You have also improved your listening skills, understanding of interpersonal and intercultural communication, and ability to use idioms and other expressions.

In this chapter, you will draw on the skills you have learned in previous chapters. You will find suggestions for making presentations for several special purposes, including introducing a guest speaker, participating in a symposium, participating in a debate, and making a poster presentation.

INTRODUCING A GUEST SPEAKER

This type of speech has several purposes:

- to acquaint the audience with the guest speaker
- to make the speaker comfortable
- to interest the audience in the speaker and his or her topic
- to announce the topic
- to give the speaker's name

A good introductory speech is short—preferably two minutes or less. To create a short, effective introductory speech, use the T.I.S. method, which is based on Dale Carnegie's approach to public speaking: Introduce the *topic*, its *importance*, and the *speaker*.

- **Topic:** Announce the topic to be discussed and the title of the speech.
- **Importance of the topic:** Explain why the topic is important to the audience and why they will be particularly interested in it.
- **Speaker:** Explain why the speaker is qualified to talk about this topic. Relevant background information might include the speaker's education, special honors, special training, professional experience, club memberships, or travel experience. The final words of your introduction should be the speaker's name. Be sure to pronounce it correctly and clearly.

Remember: You owe it to the person you are introducing to be enthusiastic. Follow the T.I.S. method and make your introduction sparkle!

Example A

INTRODUCTION OF A REAL SPEAKER

TOPIC

Our speaker today, Dr. Lam Au, is going to speak about the medical benefits of acupuncture therapy.

IMPORTANCE

As you are all medical professionals, you are committed to providing the most effective treatments to patients who are sick or in pain. Therefore, it is very important for you to learn why acupuncture therapy might be the best course of treatment for your patients. I'm sure you will find Dr. Au's information quite valuable.

SPEAKER

Dr. Lam A. Au received his Ph.D. in toxicology and his M.D. from the University of Illinois. He completed his internal medicine residency at Jackson Memorial Hospital in Miami. He graduated with highest honors from the Acupuncture Research Center in Taiwan. He is a full member of two renowned academies. They are the Academy of Medical Acupuncture and the American Academy of Pain Management.

Dr. Au maintains an active medical practice. He specializes in internal medicine, pain management, and acupuncture. He is currently Chairman of the Department of Medicine at Deering Hospital in Miami and is also an Assistant Professor at the University of Miami School of Medicine. Dr. Au headed a joint study conducted by Harvard University and the University of Miami Medical School on the medical benefits of acupuncture.

It is with great pleasure that I now present one of the foremost acupuncture therapists in the world. *Let us now welcome Dr. Lam A. Au!*

Example B

INTRODUCTION OF AN IMAGINARY SPEAKER

(This speech was created by a student, Katie.)

TOPIC

Dr. Nob Turner is our guest speaker today. He is going to teach you how to effectively and safely turn doorknobs.

IMPORTANCE

As homeowners, it is essential for all of you to know how to turn doorknobs. You will come across many doors and doorknobs in your home. Not knowing how to get out of a room could lead to starvation and death. That is why it is very important for you to know how to turn a doorknob. This information could save your life.

SPEAKER

Dr. Nob Turner has advanced degrees in making and turning doorknobs. He is currently the chief executive writer for a magazine called *Doorknob Safety*. He is the founder and owner of the Dade University's School for Doorknob Safety. He is currently working with his partner to invent a safer and more effective doorknob.

Dr. Turner maintains an active practice of turning doorknobs and has committed his life to teaching children about doorknob safety. He has written many children's books on the subject including *Bear and Owl's Doorknob Adventure*. His books have been translated into thirteen different languages.

Dr. Turner travels to schools all over the United States to promote doorknob safety. Today he comes to you so that you, too, may enjoy a safer tomorrow.

And now, it is a great honor for me to introduce our speaker today. Let's all put our hands together for *Dr. Nob Turner*!!!

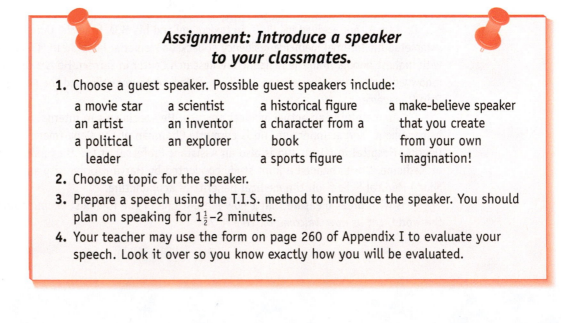

Assignment: Introduce a speaker to your classmates.

1. Choose a guest speaker. Possible guest speakers include:

a movie star	a scientist	a historical figure	a make-believe speaker
an artist	an inventor	a character from a	that you create
a political	an explorer	book	from your own
leader		a sports figure	imagination!

2. Choose a topic for the speaker.

3. Prepare a speech using the T.I.S. method to introduce the speaker. You should plan on speaking for $1\frac{1}{2}$–2 minutes.

4. Your teacher may use the form on page 260 of Appendix I to evaluate your speech. Look it over so you know exactly how you will be evaluated.

SYMPOSIUM

A *symposium* is a group presentation that generally consists of four or five participants. Each participant gives a short speech focusing on a different aspect of the same topic.

For example, let's say your theme is the environmental crisis. Individual members could speak about such related topics as the following, which are all different facets of the environmental crisis:

- Air Pollution
- Acid Rain
- Water Pollution
- Global Warming
- Depletion of the Ozone Layer

Suggested Topics for Group Symposiums

Peace in the Middle East	The Elderly
Censorship	The Homeless
Civil Liberties	Terrorism
Immigration	The AIDS Crisis
Illiteracy	Volunteerism
Biomedical Ethics	Heart Disease
Animal Rights	World Hunger
Inflation	Campus Crime
Students' Rights	Human Rights
Eating Disorders	Automobile Safety

In preparation for the symposium, the participants do the following:

1. Select a group leader.
2. Choose a general topic that is of interest to all.
3. Establish the purpose of the symposium, which could be to inform, to persuade, or to solve a problem.

After brainstorming and evaluating possible subtopics, each participant chooses one and then prepares for their part of the symposium. Finally, they deliver the symposium. (Please refer back to the relevant chapters for detailed guidelines on preparing informative and persuasive speeches—Chapter 4: Speaking to Inform; Chapter 7: Speaking to Persuade. For problem-solving group discussions, see Chapter 9: Participating in Group Discussions.)

CHOOSE A SYMPOSIUM TOPIC

Work in small groups. Imagine that your group is going to give a symposium.

1. Choose a group leader.
2. Decide on a general topic, choosing from the list on page 235 or finding one of your own.
3. Brainstorm possible subtopics that each member of the symposium could research.
4. Write your topics and subtopics on the board and have the group leader present them to the class.

Example A

General Topic: Eating Disorders
Possible Subtopics for an Informative Symposium:

- Anorexia
- Bulimia
- Causes of Eating Disorders
- Treatments for Eating Disorders

Example B

General Topic: Lasik Eye Surgery for Myopia
Possible Subtopics for a Persuasive Symposium:

- Lasik Surgery Is Safe
- Lasik Surgery Is Affordable
- Lasik Surgery Is Painless
- Lasik Surgery Will Simplify Your Life

Group leaders have numerous responsibilities throughout the symposium:

1. At the beginning, they:
   a. introduce the participants
   b. provide an attention-getting opener
   c. preview the subtopics to be covered
2. During the symposium, they provide transitions between each speaker's presentation.
3. At the end, they:
   a. summarize the subtopics discussed
   b. conclude the symposium gracefully
   c. thank the audience and the participants
   d. lead a question-and-answer session

Audience members may direct questions to the entire group or to specific participants.

DEBATE

A *debate* is a speaking situation in which opposite points of view are presented and argued. Each speaker attempts to convince the audience to agree with his or her ideas. A debate thus consists of two opposing persuasive speeches. A debate is between two speakers.

1. Speaker A speaks in favor of the topic or proposition being debated.
2. Speaker B speaks against the topic or proposition.
3. The speakers take turns giving main speeches and rebuttals.
4. In the main speeches, the speakers focus on presenting evidence to convince the audience to agree with them.
5. In the rebuttals, they focus on attacking their opponent's position and trying to disprove his or her evidence.
6. When the speakers have finished, the audience decides which of them has won the debate.

Before the debate:

1. Each pair of opponents decides on the topic to be debated.
2. They form a *proposition,* or a statement that can be argued.
3. They decide who will speak in favor of the proposition and who will argue against it.

Possible debate topics follow:

- Highway speed limits should be lowered.
- Hitchhiking should be legal.
- Students caught cheating should be expelled.
- Uniforms should be required in all public schools.
- Animal experimentation should be illegal.

- The minimum age to receive a driver's license should be eighteen.
- Smoking in public places should be allowed.
- The government should impose rent controls on landlords.
- Required courses in college should be abolished.
- Tuition fees for international students should be lowered.

The remaining steps in preparing for the debate are similar to the steps in preparing for a persuasive speech. Each speaker analyzes the audience, gathers information, and organizes his or her speech. For detailed information about how to prepare for persuasive speeches, review Chapter 7: Speaking to Persuade.

Assignment: Conduct a debate on a topic of your choice.

1. With your opponent, choose a topic.
2. Form a proposition. Decide who will speak in favor of the proposition (Speaker A) and who will speak against the proposition (Speaker B).
3. On your own, prepare for the debate. Analyze the audience, gather information, and organize your speech.
4. Your teacher may use the form on page 261 of Appendix I to evaluate the debate. Look it over so you know exactly how you will be evaluated.
5. Conduct the debate as follows:
   a. Speaker A
      - gives his or her main speech for four minutes.
      - defines or explains, and provides evidence for the proposition.
   b. Speaker B
      - gives a rebuttal for a maximum of four minutes, summarizing his or her disagreement with Speaker A's information.
      - then gives his or her main speech, again for a maxium of four minutes, disagreeing with Speaker A's proposition, providing evidence, and summarizing his or her own view.
   c. Speaker A
      - gives a rebuttal for a maximum of four minutes.
      - restates his or her original points.
      - restates and tries to disprove Speaker B's argument.
      - reemphasizes his or her original argument, providing more evidence.
      - restates his or her original proposition.
6. The audience votes for the better speaker.

Example: Outline for Debate on Topic "Used Car Salespeople Are Dishonest"

SPEAKER A: MAIN SPEECH

I. Introduces the proposition and clearly defines or explains it:
   A. Defines *used car salesperson*
   B. Defines *dishonest*

II. Proves the problem exists: Most used car salespeople will cheat you if they can.
   A. My friend lost $500 when he sold his car last year. The salesperson told him it was worth $1,000 on a trade-in. He could have sold it himself for $1,500.
   B. A used car salesperson didn't tell my friend that the dealership wouldn't service the car after he bought it. This was explained in the contract in very fine print that no one could see.
   C. A used car salesperson never mentions that the car you want has a history of mechanical problems.

III. Summarizes the affirmative view: In summary, most used car salespeople are dishonest.
   A. People lose hundreds or thousands of dollars when they buy or sell cars through used car dealerships.
   B. Used car salespeople are known to tell lies to convince you to buy an old car.

SPEAKER B: REBUTTAL & MAIN SPEECH

I. Summarizes his or her disagreement with the affirmative speaker's information:
   A. Accepts or rejects the other speaker's explanation or definition of the proposition.
   B. Disagrees with the opponent's arguments: I disagree completely with what my opponent just presented:
      1. That used car salespeople want you to lose money
      2. That used car salespeople tell you lies

II. Disagrees with the proposition: Used car salespeople do not purposely try to cheat customers.
   A. I'll admit some people lose money, but it is their own fault, not the salesperson's. Car dealers are in business to make a profit. They will pay you a fair price for your car. If you think it is worth more, you should try to sell it on your own.
   B. A used car salesperson doesn't force anyone to sign a contract without reading it. The first speaker's friend should not have signed anything without reading it. If he had looked at the contract more closely, he would have known the dealership wouldn't service the car.

C. There is no rule that a salesperson must volunteer information about a car's problems.

   1. A salesperson may use "omission." He or she doesn't have to supply information if you don't ask for it. It's the buyer's responsibility to ask specific questions about possible problems.

   2. A buyer must do his or her homework and not rely on a salesperson to supply all the information. A buyer who doesn't do this is like an ostrich with its head buried in the sand!

III. Summarizes the negative view: In summary, used car salespeople are as honest as any group of sales professionals.

   A. A salesperson is in business to make as much money as he/she can.

   B. A businessperson would be crazy to say, "That's too much profit for me, so you should pay less money!"

   C. People must think and argue for themselves. It's our own responsibility to learn to get the best deal we can when we buy or sell a used car. If we don't, it's our own fault.

SPEAKER A: REBUTTAL

I. Restates original points: The facts I presented in my opening speech still hold. I stated that:

   A. Most used car salespeople are dishonest.

   B. They will cheat you if they can.

   C. They will tell lies to convince you to buy an old car.

II. Restates and tries to disprove Speaker B's argument: My opponent tried but could not prove me wrong.

   A. My opponent gave no evidence or examples to prove that used car salespeople do not purposely cheat customers.

   B. My opponent claims it was my friend's responsibility to read the fine print in the contract.

   1. If the contract had been honest, it would have been easy to read.

   2. If the contract had been honest, it would have been in large print.

   C. My opponent claims that a salesperson may use omission.

   1. A deliberate omission is a lie!

   2. The average buyer can't know everything about every car.

III. Reemphasizes original argument and provides more evidence: I know of two other people in this school who have been cheated by used car salespeople.

   A. Humberto's experience

   B. Ulrich's experience

IV. Restates original proposition: In summary, my opponent did not prove me wrong.

   A. Used car salespeople are dishonest.

   B. Please vote for the affirmative side of the proposition.

CAST YOUR VOTE

Use the following Audience Shift of Opinion Ballot to determine the effectiveness of the debaters.

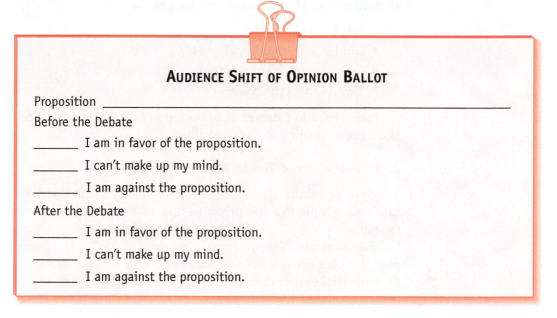

AUDIENCE SHIFT OF OPINION BALLOT

Proposition _____

Before the Debate

_____ I am in favor of the proposition.

_____ I can't make up my mind.

_____ I am against the proposition.

After the Debate

_____ I am in favor of the proposition.

_____ I can't make up my mind.

_____ I am against the proposition.

1. Before the debate, audience members indicate how they feel about the proposition.

2. After the debate, audience members indicate how they feel about the proposition.

3. Your teacher will collect the ballots and tabulate the results. The side that has convinced the most people to change their opinions wins the debate.

INTERACTIVE POSTER SPEAKING

Many professional organizations and conferences schedule "Interactive Poster Display Sessions." Poster exhibitors set up their displays in a ballroom or an exhibition hall. The exhibitors stand by their displays and talk informally with attendees, who learn about new concepts, procedures, and techniques in a relaxed and friendly environment. Visitors have the opportunity to view a variety of exhibits and interact with different presenters.

PREPARING FOR THE INTERACTIVE POSTER SPEAKING EVENT

As with informative and persuasive speeches, you build a poster exhibit display step by step. The guidelines below will help you create a poster display that is visually interesting, informative, and educational for visitors.

The steps for preparing an interactive poster speaking exhibit are:

1. Analyze your audience.

2. Choose your topic area.

3. Create the visual display.

1. Analyze Your Audience

Find out who will attend the interactive poster speaking event. Just as with speaking to inform or persuade, you must know your audience. Who will be attending your class's poster speaking event?

- Your classmates
- Students from other classes
- Teachers from your school
- Guests from the community

Refer back to Chapter 4: Speaking to Inform, pages 62–63, and analyze your audience according to the guidelines.

2. Choose Your Topic Area

Your poster exhibit should focus on any one of the content areas in this textbook. Limit your topic to a few practical tips, techniques, or ideas that would be helpful to visitors.

For example, "Interpersonal Communication" is too general. As the following photograph shows, Giselle limited her poster display to illustrating three aspects of nonverbal communication: mannerisms, appearance and posture, and gestures and movement.

Here are some ideas:

a. How to develop self-confidence when speaking before a group

b. How to use eye contact, posture, gestures, and voice to effectively present information, ideas, and opinions

c. How to organize and outline information clearly

d. How to prepare and present an informative speech

e. How to prepare and present a persuasive speech

f. How to prepare and conduct an interactive poster exhibit session display

g. How to lead a small-group problem-solving discussion

h. How to be an effective participant in a problem-solving group discussion

i. How to listen critically and objectively

j. How to improve your interpersonal communication skills

k. How to improve your intercultural communication skills

l. How to think on your feet and organize ideas quickly

m. How to improve understanding and use of idioms and proverbs

n. How to design and create effective visual aids for an informative or persuasive speech

3. Create the Display

Decide on the concepts you want to get across. Think about how much of this can be communicated by visuals and what needs to be said in writing. (Review Chapter 5: Using Dynamic Visual Aids for ideas.) Base your display as much as possible on visuals. Keep your written material short and easy to read. See Giselle's poster above and Miguel's below for examples of effective displays.

Observe, also, how Miguel narrowed the broad topic of "Intercultural Communication" by focusing on nonverbal aspects of intercultural communication.

Assignment: Create your own interactive poster.

Your teacher may choose to hold the Interactive Poster Speaking Event in a public place on campus such as a lobby reception area, conference center, or lecture hall. You will have a table, an easel, or a bulletin board on which to display your poster.

1. Choose a specific topic based on a content area from this textbook.
2. Work individually or with one other classmate, and create a visual exhibit of this topic area.
3. Your teacher may use the form on page 262 of Appendix I to evaluate your poster display. Look it over so you know exactly how you will be evaluated.
4. Stand by your poster display and talk with visitors about its content. Be prepared to:
   - explain your information with examples and support from the text,
   - discuss how your information can help others become more successful communicators in their daily lives at work, at home, or at school.

PRONUNCIATION TIP

[l] AND [r]

Some students confuse the sounds [l] and [r]. If they confuse these sounds, **rice** sounds like **lice** and **berry** sounds like **belly**.

Pronounce [l] by placing the tip of your tongue against the gum ridge just behind your upper front teeth. Pronounce [r] by curling your tongue upward but not letting it touch the roof of your mouth.

EXERCISE 1 Read the following pairs of words and sentences aloud. Concentrate on pronouncing [l] and [r] correctly.

[l]	[r]
1. late	rate
2. led	red
3. elect	erect
4. Move toward the light.	Move toward the right.
5. It was very long.	It was very wrong.
6. Please collect the papers.	Please correct the papers.

Read the following sentences aloud. Concentrate on pronouncing [l] and [r] correctly.

1. Carry that **load** down the **road**.
2. We saw a **palace** in **Paris**.
3. I left the **rake** near the **lake**.
4. He **lied** about the long **ride**.
5. **Jerry** likes **jelly** doughnuts.

Read the following pairs of words and sentences aloud. Concentrate on pronouncing smoothly the consonant blend at the beginning of each word. Be careful not to insert a vowel between consonants.

Example

	Word Pair:	**bl**oom	**br**oom
Correct Pronunciation:		[blum]	[brum]
Incorrect Pronunciation:		[bəlum]	[bərum]

1. **pl**ay   **pr**ay
2. **cl**ue   **cr**ew
3. **gl**ow   **gr**ow
4. **fl**ock   **fr**ock
5. **cl**ash   **cr**ash
6. We had a **fright** on that **flight**.
7. That **brand** of food is **bland**.
8. Did **Blake break** his leg?
9. The **crew** had no **clue** of the storm.
10. **Fred fled** from the room.

SPEECH 1: Self-Introduction/Picture Story (pages 5 and 8)

Speaker _____   Date _____

DELIVERY	RATING					COMMENTS
Posture	1	2	3	4	5	_____
Eye Contact	1	2	3	4	5	_____
Volume of Voice	1	2	3	4	5	_____
Rate of Speech	1	2	3	4	5	_____
Intelligibility	1	2	3	4	5	_____
Enthusiasm	1	2	3	4	5	_____
Adherence to Time Limit	1	2	3	4	5	_____

CONTENT	RATING					COMMENTS
Background/Early Childhood	1	2	3	4	5	_____
Information About Family	1	2	3	4	5	_____
Present Involvements	1	2	3	4	5	_____
Hobbies/Special Interests	1	2	3	4	5	_____
Future Plans/Dreams	1	2	3	4	5	_____
Supporting Details	1	2	3	4	5	_____
Clear Organization	1	2	3	4	5	_____
Visual Aids	1	2	3	4	5	_____

ADDITIONAL COMMENTS

_____

_____

_____

RATING KEY

1 = Poor   **2** = Fair   **3** = Acceptable   **4** = Good   **5** = Excellent

SPEECH 1: Self-Introduction: The Old Bag Speech (page 7)

Speaker _____ Date _____

DELIVERY	RATING					COMMENTS
Posture	1	2	3	4	5	_____
Eye Contact	1	2	3	4	5	_____
Volume of Voice	1	2	3	4	5	_____
Rate of Speech	1	2	3	4	5	_____
Intelligibility	1	2	3	4	5	_____
Enthusiasm	1	2	3	4	5	_____
Adherence to Time Limit	1	2	3	4	5	_____

CONTENT	RATING					COMMENTS
Item One: (Past)	1	2	3	4	5	_____
Item Two: (Present)	1	2	3	4	5	_____
Item Three: (Future)	1	2	3	4	5	_____
Your Bag Analysis	1	2	3	4	5	_____
Supporting Details	1	2	3	4	5	_____
Clear Organization	1	2	3	4	5	_____

ADDITIONAL COMMENTS

_____

_____

_____

RATING KEY

1 = Poor **2** = Fair **3** = Acceptable **4** = Good **5** = Excellent

SPEECH 2/4: A Personal Experience/Specific Fear (pages 11, 12, and 19)

Speaker _____   Topic _____   Date _____

DELIVERY	RATING					COMMENTS
Posture	1	2	3	4	5	_____
Eye Contact	1	2	3	4	5	_____
Volume of Voice	1	2	3	4	5	_____
Rate of Speech	1	2	3	4	5	_____
Intelligibility	1	2	3	4	5	_____
Enthusiasm	1	2	3	4	5	_____
Adherence to Time Limit	1	2	3	4	5	_____

CONTENT	RATING					COMMENTS
Choice of Topic	1	2	3	4	5	_____
Introduction	1	2	3	4	5	_____
Supporting Details	1	2	3	4	5	_____
Clear Organization	1	2	3	4	5	_____
Visual Aids	1	2	3	4	5	_____
Graceful Conclusion	1	2	3	4	5	_____

ADDITIONAL COMMENTS

_____

_____

_____

RATING KEY

1 = Poor   **2** = Fair   **3** = Acceptable   **4** = Good   **5** = Excellent

SPEECH 3: A Meaningful Object (page 16)

Speaker _____ Object _____ Date _____

DELIVERY	RATING					COMMENTS
Posture	1	2	3	4	5	_____
Eye Contact	1	2	3	4	5	_____
Volume of Voice	1	2	3	4	5	_____
Rate of Speech	1	2	3	4	5	_____
Intelligibility	1	2	3	4	5	_____
Enthusiasm	1	2	3	4	5	_____
Adherence to Time Limit	1	2	3	4	5	_____

CONTENT	RATING					COMMENTS
Choice of Object	1	2	3	4	5	_____
Introduction	1	2	3	4	5	_____
Objective Information	1	2	3	4	5	_____
Subjective Information	1	2	3	4	5	_____
Supporting Details	1	2	3	4	5	_____
Clear Organization	1	2	3	4	5	_____
Visual Aids	1	2	3	4	5	_____
Graceful Conclusion	1	2	3	4	5	_____

ADDITIONAL COMMENTS

_____

_____

RATING KEY

1 = Poor   **2** = Fair   **3** = Acceptable   **4** = Good   **5** = Excellent

SPEECH 5: A Personal Opinion (page 21)

Speaker _____   Opinion _____   Date _____

DELIVERY	RATING					COMMENTS
Posture	1	2	3	4	5	_____
Eye Contact	1	2	3	4	5	_____
Volume of Voice	1	2	3	4	5	_____
Rate of Speech	1	2	3	4	5	_____
Intelligibility	1	2	3	4	5	_____
Enthusiasm	1	2	3	4	5	_____
Adherence to Time Limit	1	2	3	4	5	_____

CONTENT	RATING					COMMENTS
Choice of Topic	1	2	3	4	5	_____
Introduction	1	2	3	4	5	_____
Statement of Opinion	1	2	3	4	5	_____
Supporting Details	1	2	3	4	5	_____
Restatement of Opinion	1	2	3	4	5	_____
Clear Organization	1	2	3	4	5	_____
Visual Aids	1	2	3	4	5	_____
Graceful Conclusion	1	2	3	4	5	_____

ADDITIONAL COMMENTS

_____

_____

RATING KEY

1 = Poor   **2** = Fair   **3** = Acceptable   **4** = Good   **5** = Excellent

Informative Speech (page 85)

Speaker _____   Topic _____   Date _____

DELIVERY	RATING					COMMENTS
Posture	1	2	3	4	5	_____
Eye Contact	1	2	3	4	5	_____
Volume of Voice	1	2	3	4	5	_____
Rate of Speech	1	2	3	4	5	_____
Intelligibility	1	2	3	4	5	_____
Enthusiasm	1	2	3	4	5	_____
Adherence to Time Limit	1	2	3	4	5	_____

CONTENT	RATING					COMMENTS
Choice of Topic	1	2	3	4	5	_____
Attention-Getting Opener	1	2	3	4	5	_____
Preview	1	2	3	4	5	_____
Supporting Materials/ Source Citations	1	2	3	4	5	_____
Transitions	1	2	3	4	5	_____
Supporting Details	1	2	3	4	5	_____
Clear Organization	1	2	3	4	5	_____
Visual Aids	1	2	3	4	5	_____
Summary	1	2	3	4	5	_____
Concluding Remarks	1	2	3	4	5	_____

ADDITIONAL COMMENTS

_____

_____

RATING KEY

1 = Poor   **2** = Fair   **3** = Acceptable   **4** = Good   **5** = Excellent

Persuasive Speech (page 142)

Speaker _____   Topic _____   Date _____

Persuasive Claim _____

DELIVERY	RATING					COMMENTS
Posture	1	2	3	4	5	_____
Eye Contact	1	2	3	4	5	_____
Volume of Voice	1	2	3	4	5	_____
Rate of Speech	1	2	3	4	5	_____
Intelligibility	1	2	3	4	5	_____
Enthusiasm	1	2	3	4	5	_____
Adherence to Time Limit	1	2	3	4	5	_____

CONTENT	RATING					COMMENTS
Choice of Topic	1	2	3	4	5	_____
Building on Areas of Agreement	1	2	3	4	5	_____
Statement of Purpose	1	2	3	4	5	_____
Preview	1	2	3	4	5	_____
Transitions	1	2	3	4	5	_____
Supporting Evidence	1	2	3	4	5	_____
Source Citations	1	2	3	4	5	_____
Clear Organization	1	2	3	4	5	_____
Visual Aids	1	2	3	4	5	_____
Summary	1	2	3	4	5	_____
Concluding Remarks	1	2	3	4	5	_____

ADDITIONAL COMMENTS

_____

_____

RATING KEY

1 = Poor   **2** = Fair   **3** = Acceptable   **4** = Good   **5** = Excellent

GROUP DISCUSSION: Individual Participant (page 177)

Speaker _____   Problem _____   Date _____

PREPARATION	RATING					COMMENTS
Evidence of Planning	1	2	3	4	5	_____
Evidence of Research	1	2	3	4	5	_____

PARTICIPATION	RATING					COMMENTS
Adherence to Organizational Plan	1	2	3	4	5	_____
Respect for Others' Opinions	1	2	3	4	5	_____
Sufficiency of Contributions	1	2	3	4	5	_____

VALUE OF CONTRIBUTION	RATING					COMMENTS
The problem was clearly identified.	1	2	3	4	5	_____
The existence of the problem was proven.	1	2	3	4	5	_____
The causes of the problem were explained.	1	2	3	4	5	_____
Possible future effects of the problem were presented.	1	2	3	4	5	_____
Possible solutions were proposed.	1	2	3	4	5	_____
The best solutions were chosen.	1	2	3	4	5	_____

ADDITIONAL COMMENTS

_____

_____

_____

_____

RATING KEY

1 = Poor   **2** = Fair   **3** = Acceptable   **4** = Good   **5** = Excellent

GROUP DISCUSSION: Group Leader (page 177)

Leader _____   Problem _____   Date _____

EFFECTIVENESS	RATING					COMMENTS
Introduction of Participants	1	2	3	4	5	_____
Introduction of Problem	1	2	3	4	5	_____
Knowledge of Topic	1	2	3	4	5	_____
Ability to Manage Organizational Plan	1	2	3	4	5	_____
Ability to Encourage Participation	1	2	3	4	5	_____
Ability to Handle Conflicts	1	2	3	4	5	_____
Transitions Between Steps	1	2	3	4	5	_____
Graceful Conclusion	1	2	3	4	5	_____
Thanks Conveyed to Participants	1	2	3	4	5	_____

ADDITIONAL COMMENTS

_____

_____

_____

_____

RATING KEY

1 = Poor   **2** = Fair   **3** = Acceptable   **4** = Good   **5** = Excellent

GROUP DISCUSSION: Group as a Whole (page 177)

Participants _____

Problem _____ Date _____

GROUP DYNAMICS	RATING	COMMENTS

GROUP DYNAMICS   **RATING**   **COMMENTS**

Participants freely   1 2 3 4 5   _____
expressed their opinions.

The group stayed on topic.   1 2 3 4 5   _____

All members participated   1 2 3 4 5   _____
equally.

CONTENT   **RATING**   **COMMENTS**

The problem was clearly   1 2 3 4 5   _____
identified.

The existence of the   1 2 3 4 5   _____
problem was proven.

The causes of the problem   1 2 3 4 5   _____
were explained.

Possible future effects of the   1 2 3 4 5   _____
problem were presented.

Possible solutions   1 2 3 4 5   _____
were proposed.

The best solutions   1 2 3 4 5   _____
were chosen.

ADDITIONAL COMMENTS

_____

_____

_____

_____

RATING KEY

1 = Poor   **2** = Fair   **3** = Acceptable   **4** = Good   **5** = Excellent

"Culture Conflict" Speech (page 205)

Speaker _____   Topic _____   Date _____

DELIVERY	RATING	COMMENTS
Posture	1 2 3 4 5	_____
Eye Contact	1 2 3 4 5	_____
Volume of Voice	1 2 3 4 5	_____
Rate of Speech	1 2 3 4 5	_____
Intelligibility	1 2 3 4 5	_____
Enthusiasm	1 2 3 4 5	_____
Adherence to Time Limit	1 2 3 4 5	_____

CONTENT	RATING	COMMENTS
Choice of Topic	1 2 3 4 5	_____
Introduction	1 2 3 4 5	_____
Supporting Details	1 2 3 4 5	_____
Clear Organization	1 2 3 4 5	_____
Visual Aids	1 2 3 4 5	_____
Graceful Conclusion	1 2 3 4 5	_____

ADDITIONAL COMMENTS

_____

_____

RATING KEY

1 = Poor   **2** = Fair   **3** = Acceptable   **4** = Good   **5** = Excellent

Impromptu Speech (page 215)

Speaker _____   Topic _____   Date _____

DELIVERY	RATING					COMMENTS
Posture	1	2	3	4	5	_____
Eye Contact	1	2	3	4	5	_____
Volume of Voice	1	2	3	4	5	_____
Rate of Speech	1	2	3	4	5	_____
Intelligibility	1	2	3	4	5	_____
Enthusiasm	1	2	3	4	5	_____
Adherence to Time Limit	1	2	3	4	5	_____

CONTENT	RATING					COMMENTS
Attention-Getting Opener	1	2	3	4	5	_____
Preview	1	2	3	4	5	_____
Clear Organization	1	2	3	4	5	_____
Supporting Details	1	2	3	4	5	_____
Summary	1	2	3	4	5	_____
Graceful Conclusion	1	2	3	4	5	_____

ADDITIONAL COMMENTS

_____

_____

_____

_____

RATING KEY

1 = Poor   **2** = Fair   **3** = Acceptable   **4** = Good   **5** = Excellent

Idiom/Proverb Speech (page 230)

Speaker _____   Topic _____   Date _____

Idiom/Proverb _____

DELIVERY	RATING					COMMENTS
Posture	1	2	3	4	5	_____
Eye Contact	1	2	3	4	5	_____
Volume of Voice	1	2	3	4	5	_____
Rate of Speech	1	2	3	4	5	_____
Intelligibility	1	2	3	4	5	_____
Enthusiasm	1	2	3	4	5	_____
Adherence to Time Limit	1	2	3	4	5	_____

CONTENT	RATING					COMMENTS
Attention-Getting Opener	1	2	3	4	5	_____
Statement of Idiom/Proverb	1	2	3	4	5	_____
Explanation of Idiom/Proverb	1	2	3	4	5	_____
First Example	1	2	3	4	5	_____
Second Example	1	2	3	4	5	_____
Supporting Details	1	2	3	4	5	_____
Clear Organization	1	2	3	4	5	_____
Visual Aids	1	2	3	4	5	_____
Graceful Conclusion	1	2	3	4	5	_____

ADDITIONAL COMMENTS

_____

_____

RATING KEY

1 = Poor   **2** = Fair   **3** = Acceptable   **4** = Good   **5** = Excellent

Introducing a Guest Speaker (page 234)

Speaker _____   Date _____

DELIVERY	RATING					COMMENTS
Posture	1	2	3	4	5	_____
Eye Contact	1	2	3	4	5	_____
Volume of Voice	1	2	3	4	5	_____
Rate of Speech	1	2	3	4	5	_____
Intelligibility	1	2	3	4	5	_____
Enthusiam	1	2	3	4	5	_____
Adherence to Time Limit	1	2	3	4	5	_____

CONTENT	RATING					COMMENTS
TOPIC						
Guest's Name Clearly Stated	1	2	3	4	5	_____
Guest's Topic Stated	1	2	3	4	5	_____
IMPORTANCE						
Target Audience Acknowledged	1	2	3	4	5	_____
Importance of Topic Established	1	2	3	4	5	_____
SPEAKER						
Guest's Background/ Qualifications Presented	1	2	3	4	5	_____

ADDITIONAL COMMENTS

_____

_____

RATING KEY

1 = Poor   **2** = Fair   **3** = Acceptable   **4** = Good   **5** = Excellent

Debate Assignment (page 238)

Debate Topic _____

Affirmative   Negative

_____   _____
(Speaker A: Name)   (Speaker B: Name)

SPEAKER A					DELIVERY	SPEAKER B				
1	2	3	4	5	Eye Contact	1	2	3	4	5
1	2	3	4	5	Volume of Voice	1	2	3	4	5
1	2	3	4	5	Rate of Speech	1	2	3	4	5
1	2	3	4	5	Pronunciation/Intonation	1	2	3	4	5
1	2	3	4	5	Enthusiasm	1	2	3	4	5
1	2	3	4	5	Posture	1	2	3	4	5
1	2	3	4	5	Adherence to Time Limits	1	2	3	4	5

SPEAKER A					CONTENT	SPEAKER B				
1	2	3	4	5	Definition/Explanation of Proposition	1	2	3	4	5
1	2	3	4	5	Proof that Problem Exists	1	2	3	4	5
1	2	3	4	5	Refutation/Rebuttal	1	2	3	4	5
1	2	3	4	5	Supporting Evidence	1	2	3	4	5
1	2	3	4	5	Effectiveness of Reasoning	1	2	3	4	5

COMMENTS   **COMMENTS**
(Speaker A)   (Speaker B)

_____   _____

☑ I am persuaded to vote for Speaker: ☐ A   (or)   ☐ B

REASONS FOR DECISION: _____

_____

Grade: Speaker A _____   Grade: Speaker B _____

Speaker(s) _____

Topic Area _____

Textbook Reference Pages _____

Other Sources Consulted _____

VISUAL ASPECTS	RATING	COMMENTS
Overall Visual Appeal	1　2　3　4　5	_____
Creativity of Display	1　2　3　4　5	_____

CONTENT	RATING	COMMENTS
Clear Poster Title	1　2　3　4　5	_____
Clearly Written Material	1　2　3　4　5	_____
Effective Presentation of Main Concepts	1　2　3　4　5	_____
Effective Use of Details	1　2　3　4　5	_____

INTERACTION WITH VISITORS	RATING	COMMENTS
Ability to Encourage Visitor Participation	1　2　3　4　5	_____
Ability to Explain Poster Content	1　2　3　4　5	_____
Ability to Stay on Topic	1　2　3　4　5	_____
Ability to Answer Questions	1　2　3　4　5	_____

ADDITIONAL COMMENTS

_____

_____

_____

_____

RATING KEY

1 = Poor　　**2** = Fair　　**3** = Acceptable　　**4** = Good　　**5** = Excellent

APPENDIX II

CHAPTER 1

End-of-Chapter Quiz

For each statement, circle *T* if it is true and *F* if it is false.

1.   T   F   Most people dread the thought of speaking in public.

2.   T   F   It is not normal to be nervous about speaking in front of new people.

3.   T   F   Practicing your speech several times will make you feel more nervous.

4.   T   F   Identifying your specific fears is the first step toward controlling your nervousness.

5.   T   F   It is not important to share autobiographical information with your classmates in a speech class.

6.   T   F   One effective method of preparing and presenting speeches is to use simple hand-drawn pictures or computer clip art as your notes.

7.   T   F   You should use the picture drawing method only if you are an excellent artist.

8.   T   F   Personal experience speeches never need advance preparation.

9.   T   F   "How to Improve Your Study Habits" is a good topic for a specific fear speech.

10.   T   F   A good speaker should never describe personal experiences or share feelings with the audience.

SHARE YOUR STRATEGIES: SUGGESTIONS

REPLACE YOUR FEARS WITH POSITIVE THOUGHTS (PAGE 3)

Possible Fears	Sample Positive Beliefs
1. I'll forget what I want to say.	I practiced and prepared well. I have note cards with key ideas to trigger my memory.
2. No one will be interested in my topic.	I analyzed the audience. My topic should be interesting and relevant to most of my audience.
3. I don't know anyone in the audience.	It doesn't matter if people don't know me personally. They will be interested in my message.
4. I don't speak well in public.	Most people feel the same way. This is a great opportunity to get some practice and improve my skills.
5. I might not be prepared enough.	I planned and practiced. I am as prepared as anyone could be.
6. Listeners won't understand me.	If I speak slowly and clearly, I will do just fine. When I practiced, my listeners understood what I said.
7. My English isn't very good.	No one is expecting me to be perfect. The audience knows I am studying English and learning to improve.
8. The audience won't like me.	The audience wants me to do well. They will respect me for having the courage to speak in public.

*LEARN TO BREATHE DEEPLY AND SLOWLY

1. **How Fast Do You Breathe?**
   Sit in a comfortable chair with your feet flat on the floor. Breathe normally. Use a watch with a second hand and count your breaths for a full minute. How many breaths did you take? Record that number here. _____
   - Your goal is to learn to breathe in a fully relaxed way.
   - Strive for taking between four and ten breaths a minute.

2. **Breathe Correctly**
   a. Place both hands on your stomach. Breathe in and out slowly. Feel your stomach push forward as you inhale and pull in as you exhale. If you feel your stomach pull in as you breathe in, your breathing is incorrect and needs to be changed!
   b. Keep practicing until you feel your stomach push out when you breathe in and pull in when you breathe out.

3. **Breathe Slowly**

Time yourself doing Step 2. Take slow, deep breaths. Remember: Your goal is to take between four and ten breaths in a minute. Now how many breaths did you take? Record that number here. _____

4. **Inhale for Five and Exhale for Ten!**
   a. Repeat Step 2. This time, inhale slowly for five seconds and exhale slowly. Make your exhalation last for ten seconds. If you are out of air before ten seconds, you have exhaled too quickly.
   b. Try it again; slow your exhalation and make it last for ten seconds.

5. **Count for Thirty Seconds While Exhaling**

Keep your hands on your stomach. Inhale slowly. As you begin to exhale, count to yourself. Feel your stomach slowly pulling in as you count. You should be able to count for approximately thirty seconds before you run out of breath.

6. **Don't Hold Your Breath**

Do you ever hold your breath? Many people do this without realizing it, especially when they are stressed. Try to be aware of any tendency to hold your breath. Remind yourself to breathe!

7. **Practice Breathing Before Speaking**

Before you give your next speech, practice slow, deep breathing for a couple of minutes. You will find you are calmer, more relaxed, and more focused.

---

*Adapted from Dr. Jon Eisenson, *Voice and Diction: A Program for Improvement*, (Massachusetts: Allyn & Bacon, 1997)

WRITE LEILA'S NOTES (PAGE 14) Possible Answers

What type of experience was it?	painful, unpleasant, scary
Where were you?	a farm in Kuala Lumpur, Malaysia
When were you there?	when I was in the sixth grade
Who was with you?	a friend from school
What were you doing?	walking home from school
Why were you there?	stopped to see beehive in tree
How were you feeling?	curious, adventurous
Why did you feel that way?	I wanted to show off what I had learned in school about bees.
What was your goal?	to knock the beehive out of the tree and take it with me
How did you react?	surprised, horrified
How did the story end?	my friend ran away up a hill; the bees stung my whole body
Why will you never forget this experience?	Honey always reminds me of the bees.

End-of-Chapter Quiz

For each statement, circle *T* if it is true and *F* if it is false.

1. T F A UCLA professor found that listeners pay more attention to our actual words than to our visual characteristics.

2. T F Facial expressions, gestures, eye contact, and posture make very little difference in the credibility of a speaker.

3. T F Body language can tell your audience how you feel about yourself.

4. T F You will appear more confident if you clasp your hands in front of you during your speech.

5. T F If you are nervous, it's all right to put your hands in your pockets so the audience won't see them shaking.

6. T F The extemporaneous delivery is the least effective form of delivery.

7. T F Good speakers read their speeches from manuscripts.

8. T F An impromptu speech is carefully planned and practiced.

9. T F Manuscript speeches are presented from an outline of main ideas.

10. T F It is a good idea to memorize your speech so you won't need notes.

11. T F It is not necessary to number your note cards.

12. T F Good speakers use short, easy-to-understand sentences.

13. T F "Um," "Uh," and "You know" are called vocal fillers.

14. T F Speakers should always apologize to the audience when they are not prepared for their presentation.

15. T F It is a good idea to begin practicing your presentation several days in advance.

Circle the best answer.

16. Body language includes _____.

   A. posture

   B. gestures

   C. both A and B

17. The "walk of the matador" is _____.

   A. a way of showing respect for your listeners

   B. a way of walking with confidence

   C. pretending to limp so that you look helpless

18. Writing on both sides of your note cards is a good idea because _____.
    A. it will reduce the number of cards you will need
    B. it helps save paper
    C. None of the above.

19. Maintaining eye contact with your listeners _____.
    A. is a bad idea because it makes people feel uncomfortable
    B. indicates familiarity with your material
    C. is the least important aspect of body language

20. The use of disclaimers in a speech _____.
    A. helps the speaker establish rapport with the audience
    B. helps the speaker look confident
    C. weakens the impact of the speaker's words

THINK ABOUT WHAT MAKES AN EFFECTIVE SPEECH (PAGE 33)

Possible Answers

   a. good eye contact

   b. conversational style

   c. clear and logical organization

   d. effective examples

   e. adherence to time limit

   f. ability to keep audience's attention

   g. good voice projection

   h. clear diction

   i. good posture

   j. appearance of confidence

   k. enthusiasm

PRACTICE YOUR EDITING SKILLS (PAGE 38)

Possible Answers

   1. Unfortunately, the college has fewer students this year.

   2. Our travel agent recommended that we also visit Spain on our trip.

   3. Teenagers and their parents often disagree about curfews.

   4. Students and faculty disagree about the final exam schedule.

   5. I fondly remember my first trip to Europe.

CHAPTER 3

End-of-Chapter Quiz

For each statement, circle *T* if it is true and *F* if it is false.

1. T   F   Every speech should have two main parts.

2. T   F   A good speech introduction begins with a preview of main points.

3. T   F   It is not important to begin with an attention-getting opener as long as you have a preview of main points.

4. T   F   One effective way to begin a speech is by asking a question to arouse curiosity.

5. T   F   A speaker should not begin a speech with a brief story because stories are not interesting to most people.

6. T   F   It is better to write a speech out word for word than use an outline.

7. T   F   The preview of a speech alerts the listeners to the main points you will discuss in the body of your speech.

8. T   F   The key to outlining is to identify the subtopics you will include in the body of your speech.

9. T   F   It's not necessary to order your subtopics logically.

10. T   F   Good speakers conclude a presentation by saying "That's it," when they can't think of a more graceful way to end.

Circle the best answer.

11. Which part of a speech should be prepared first?

    A. The introduction
    B. The body
    C. The conclusion

12. Every speech needs _____.

    A. a topic
    B. a purpose
    C. both A and B

13. A good conclusion to a speech has _____.

    A. final remarks that end the speech gracefully
    B. a summary of the main points of the speech
    C. both A and B

14. A "signpost" is _____.

    A. a stand attached to the lectern that supports the speaker's notes
    B. a transition signaling that a part of a speech is about to begin or end
    C. both A and B

15. A good speech has a transition _____.

    A. after the introduction and before the conclusion

    B. between points 2 and 3 of the preview

    C. None of the above

16. Transitions within the body of the speech should _____.

    A. review the subtopic just presented

    B. preview the next section of your speech

    C. both A and B

17. How many transitions should a good speech have?

    A. A minimum of two

    B. A maximum of four

    C. It depends on how many subtopics are contained in the body of the speech.

18. One of the requirements of a good outline is _____.

    A. each outline point contains at least two ideas

    B. each outline point relates to the main point

    C. both A and B

19. Another requirement of a good outline is _____.

    A. outline points may be restated but not repeated

    B. outline points are not restated or repeated

    C. each supporting point contains only one idea

20. Which of the following subtopics might you hear in a good speech about the physical symptoms of stress?

    A. Effects of Stress on the Heart

    B. Psychological Symptoms of Stress

    C. Emotional Symptoms of Stress

    D. both B and C

RECOGNIZE WHAT MAKES A GOOD OUTLINE (PAGE 49)

1. **d** (B is not equal to the other points. "Toasters" is a specific kitchen appliance. It is not a separate category of products as are the other outline points.)

2. **a** (C does not relate to the main point as it is not an *advantage* of freeze-drying.)

3. ✔

4. **b** (B contains more than one idea.)

5. **c** (B restates the main idea in I.)

6. **d** (B is not equal to the other supporting points. "New York" is a specific state. It is not a general region of the country.)

7. **a** (B does not relate to the main point.)

8. **a** (C does not relate to the main point.)

9. ✔

10. **a** (C does not relate to the main point.)

REWRITE SUPPORTING POINTS (PAGE 51)

1. **I.** Polyester is better than silk.
   - **A.** It costs less.
   - **B.** It lasts longer.
     - **1.** It may be washed twice as many times before wearing out.
     - **2.** Its color doesn't fade as quickly.
   - **C.** It's easier to care for.
     - **1.** Dry cleaning is unnecessary.
     - **2.** Ironing is unnecessary.

2. **I.** The United States exports products to countries on several continents.
   - **A.** South America
     - **1.** Brazil
     - **2.** Argentina
     - **3.** Colombia
   - **B.** Asia
     - **1.** Japan
     - **2.** China
   - **C.** Europe
     - **1.** Spain
     - **2.** France
     - **3.** Germany

WRITE AN OUTLINE (PAGE 51)

I. There are many things to do in Mexico City.
   A. Visit interesting places
      1. Chapultepec Park
      2. Aztec pyramids in Teotihuacán
      3. Museum of Anthropology
      4. Palace of Fine Arts
         a. Art exhibitions
         b. Ballet Gran Folklórico de México
   B. Go shopping
      1. Native crafts
         a. Colorful embroidered blouses
         b. Handwoven rugs
         c. Handmade pottery
      2. Onyx items
         a. Ashtrays
         b. Vases
         c. Bookends
      3. Sterling silver pieces
         a. Serving trays
         b. Picture frames
         c. Key chains
         d. Jewelry
            i. bracelets
            ii. necklaces
            iii. rings

COMPLETE THE OUTLINE (PAGE 56)

The complete outline is as follows.

INTRODUCTION

I. Are you wondering what to do for your next vacation? I have the perfect solution for all of you. Why not take a cruise?
II. I'm going to tell you about five highlights you can expect on a fabulous Fantasia Cruise.
   A. Luxurious guest accommodations
   B. Excellent shipboard facilities
   C. Exotic ports of call
   D. Interesting shore-visit activities
   E. Fun shipboard activities

TRANSITION: *First, you'll be pleased to learn about the comfortable cabins that will be your rooms for the week.*

I. Guest accommodations
  A. Fully air-conditioned cabins
  B. Color TV in every cabin
  C. Porthole in every cabin
  D. King-size beds in every cabin

TRANSITION: *Now you can see how comfortable you'll be while in your cabin. However, the ship has many facilities for you to enjoy when you leave your cabin.*

II. Ship's facilities
  A. Casino open twenty-four hours a day
  B. Swinging dance club open all night
  C. Olympic-size swimming pool
  D. Three elegant restaurants

TRANSITION: *As you can see, the ship has many facilities for you to enjoy while onboard. You will need to get off the ship in order to visit the four exciting ports of call.*

III. Visits to four exotic places
  A. Port-au-Prince, Haiti
  B. Georgetown, Grand Cayman
  C. Puerto Plata, Dominican Republic
  D. Cozumel, Mexico

TRANSITION: *You now know which exotic places you'll be visiting. You will have a choice of many fun things to do while on shore.*

IV. Shore-visit activities
  A. Guided tours of each port
  B. Activities for sports lovers
    1. Water sports
      a. Waterskiing
      b. Sailing
      c. Fishing
    2. Land sports
      a. Hiking
      b. Horseback riding
  C. Shopping for native crafts

TRANSITION: *We hope the shore-visit activities won't tire you out too much. You'll need your energy, because once you're back on the ship, many other activities await you!*

V. Shipboard activities
  A. Afternoon and evening bingo in captain's lounge
  B. Costume party
  C. Competitive games
    1. Ping-Pong tournaments
    2. Poolside shuffleboard tournaments
  D. Nightly shows in ship's nightclub
  E. Passenger talent show

TRANSITION: *With all these great onboard activities, you might not even want to leave the ship at all!*

CONCLUSION

I. I'm sure you will now agree that a Fantasia Cruise would be the perfect vacation.
   A. The guest accommodations are second to none.
   B. The ship has wonderful facilities for you to enjoy.
   C. You'll visit four unforgettable places.
   D. There are many shore-visit activities.
   E. There are many things for you to do while aboard the ship.
II. Your dream vacation awaits you. Make your reservation soon and cruise to paradise with Fantasia!

CHAPTER 4

End-of-Chapter Quiz

Circle the correct answer.

1. An important goal of giving an informative speech is _____.
   - **A.** to present information so that it is easily understood
   - **B.** to present information so that it is easily remembered
   - **C.** to convince others to buy a product
   - **D.** both A and B

2. The first step in preparing for an informative speech is to _____.
   - **A.** choose a topic
   - **B.** prepare visual aids
   - **C.** analyze the audience
   - **D.** None of the above

3. The second step in preparing for an informative speech is to _____.
   - **A.** gather your information
   - **B.** prepare visual aids
   - **C.** analyze the audience
   - **D.** None of the above

4. After you choose a general topic for your informative speech, you should _____.
   - **A.** analyze the audience
   - **B.** narrow your topic
   - **C.** gather your information
   - **D.** organize your information

5. In choosing a topic for your informative speech, you might consider _____.
   - **A.** hobbies or special interests you have
   - **B.** work experience you have had
   - **C.** a subject that you already know something about
   - **D.** All of the above

6. Audience analysis consists of learning about your audience's _____.
   - **A.** general background
   - **B.** economic level
   - **C.** age range
   - **D.** All of the above

7. A good informative speech topic _____.
   - **A.** is general
   - **B.** contains only one idea
   - **C.** is specific
   - **D.** both B and C

8. An example of an informative speech topic that is achievable is _____.

   A. How to Weave an Oriental Rug
   B. How to Fly an Airplane
   C. Basic Techniques of CPR
   D. Guaranteed Ways to Win the Lottery

9. Good outside sources to consult when researching information for an informative speech include _____.

   A. books
   B. magazines
   C. newspapers
   D. All of the above

10. The topic "Ways to Fight Inflation" is _____.

    A. not achievable
    B. not specific
    C. not relevant to most audiences
    D. a good topic

11. The topic "Cosmetics Testing on Animals Should Be Banned" _____.

    A. is a good informative speech topic
    B. contains more than one idea
    C. is not achievable
    D. is more of a persuasive topic than an informative one

12. An example of a good open-ended interview question is _____.
    A. "What is your opinion of the new president?"
    B. "Have you ever been scuba diving?"
    C. "Do you know anyone on a diet?"
    D. both A and B

13. Which of the following topics uses a "time" organizational pattern?

    A. Advantages of Stem-Cell Research
    B. Effects of Air Pollution
    C. Steps to Take When Applying for a Car Loan
    D. Causes of Global Warming

14. Which organizational pattern divides a topic into different geographical areas?

    A. Past-Present-Future
    B. Location
    C. Related Subtopics
    D. None of the above

15. Which organizational pattern is not effective when speaking to inform?

    A. Related Subtopics
    B. Personal Opinion
    C. Advantage-Disadvantage
    D. Cause-Effect

1. b   **2.** a   **3.** a   **4.** ✓   **5.** a   **6.** c   **7.** ✓   **8.** a   **9.** a   **10.** a   **11.** b
12. ✓   **13.** ✓   **14.** b   **15.** ✓   **16.** ✓   **17.** ✓   **18.** ✓   **19.** b   **20.** c

RECOGNIZE ORGANIZATIONAL PATTERNS (PAGE 76)

1. b or c   **2.** d   **3.** a   **4.** c   **5.** b   **6.** g   **7.** h   **8.** c   **9.** f   **10.** g

CHAPTER 5

End-of-Chapter Quiz

For each statement, circle *T* if it is true and *F* if it is false.

1.   T   F   Visual aids help listeners understand and remember information.

2.   T   F   If your picture is small, it is a good idea to pass it around so each listener can view it carefully.

3.   T   F   When using visual aids, a speaker should look at the visual aid rather than at the audience.

4.   T   F   Keep visual aids covered or hidden until you are ready to display them at an appropriate point in your speech.

5.   T   F   Once you display a visual aid, keep it in sight for the rest of the speech so listeners can study it while you are speaking.

6.   T   F   Charts and graphs are especially helpful in a speech presenting numerical data and other statistics.

7.   T   F   All capital letters are the easiest to read on a PowerPoint slide.

8.   T   F   Audio aids are rarely as effective as visual aids in a presentation.

9.   T   F   You can black out the continuous display of a PowerPoint slide by pressing the "B" on your keyboard.

10.   T   F   Images you find on the Internet are never as good as visual aids that you create yourself.

CHAPTER 6

End-of-Chapter Quiz

Circle all the correct answers.

1. In gathering materials on the Internet, a speaker tests evidence by asking all of the following questions EXCEPT _____.

   A. Are the Internet sources of evidence reliable and trustworthy?
   B. Is the author of the information a credible authority?
   C. Could this material be the result of identity theft?
   D. Do other researchers cite information from this author or organization?

2. Which of the following about "phrase searches" is true?

   A. Key words are used to ask questions.
   B. Information is found by searching through broad categories of information.
   C. Double quotes are used to tell a search engine to only find documents in which those exact words appear together
   D. They are the least effective method of searching for information on the Web.

3. A good way of evaluating Internet sources is to _____.

   A. find out who wrote the information
   B. ask other students in your class
   C. look for professional-looking sites with lots of sophisticated graphics
   D. look for a site that provides no links to other sites

4. Quoting information found on an Internet site without giving credit is _____.

   A. called "general content researching"
   B. permissible if you find the same general information on at least three sites
   C. paraphrasing
   D. plagiarism

5. Credible Internet sites generally _____.

   A. try to sell something
   B. contain spelling and grammatical errors
   C. provide links to other sites
   D. use dark backgrounds with light-colored fonts for contrast

6. A good way to find information on the Internet is to use _____.

   A. search engines
   B. government agency websites
   C. educational institution websites
   D. All of the above

7. The URL extension stands for _____.

   A. Uniform Resource Locater
   B. United Real-World Learning
   C. Uniform Regulation Learning
   D. Unrealistic Resource Locater

8. If you are giving an informative speech, you should _____.

    A. cite only government website sources in your speech

    B. cite your print media and Internet sources in your speech

    C. cite only your Internet sources in your speech

    D. avoid information from nonprofit group sites

9. The World Wide Web is often called _____.

    A. the great miscommunication information agency

    B. the world's greatest source of useless information

    C. the least credible place to find information

    D. the world's largest library

10. Which of the following statements is not true?

    A. Memorable and trustworthy information is rarely found on the Internet.

    B. Looking for information on the Internet can be frustrating.

    C. Information found on the Internet is not always accurate or credible.

    D. All of the above

CHAPTER 7

End-of-Chapter Quiz

For each statement, circle *T* if it is true and *F* if it is false.

1. T F You should choose a topic that you personally feel strongly about.

2. T F It's easier to persuade listeners to change their behaviors if you suggest a large change.

3. T F You should never choose a controversial topic for a persuasive speech.

4. T F If you determine that your audience disagrees completely with your persuasive speech topic, you should choose another topic.

5. T F The general goal of persuasive speaking is to teach your listeners new information about an unfamiliar subject.

6. T F Research is unnecessary when preparing a persuasive speech.

7. T F A good persuasive speech begins with a statement of purpose.

8. T F Good persuasive speakers cite a variety of credible sources that support their persuasive claims.

9. T F If members of the audience are undecided about your persuasive purpose, you should choose another topic.

10. T F If all the members of the audience already agree with your persuasive claim, you should choose another topic.

Circle the best answer.

11. Before you begin gathering information for your persuasive speech, you should _____.

   A. organize the speech
   B. prepare visual aids
   C. analyze the audience
   D. both A and C

12. The general goal of persuasive speaking in to convince listeners to change _____.

   A. a belief
   B. a behavior
   C. an opinion
   D. All of the above

13. A goal of a persuasive speech designed to change audience behavior is to convince listeners _____.

   A. to do something they are not currently doing
   B. that an event was represented accurately
   C. that a policy is fair or unfair
   D. both B and C

14. A good persuasive speech _____.

    A. avoids all controversy
    B. teaches listeners how something works, runs, or operates
    C. convinces listeners to change a behavior, belief, or opinion
    D. None of the above

15. Building on common areas of agreement in a persuasive speech _____.

    A. is not important
    B. is a good technique to use in your concluding remarks
    C. is not always effective as it distracts listeners from your specific purpose
    D. helps your audience to trust you and view you as a sensible person

16. Hostile listeners are audience members who _____.

    A. agree completely with your claim
    B. are indifferent to your claim
    C. strongly disagree with your claim
    D. both B and C

17. In order to persuade listeners who are indifferent to your topic, you must _____.

    A. interest them in your topic
    B. convince them that it is important
    C. convince them that their reasons for disagreeing with you are not valid
    D. both A and B

18. "Everyone should do at least fifty hours of community service a year" is _____.

    A. not a good persuasive speech topic
    B. a good persuasive topic to change audience behavior
    C. a good persuasive topic to change audience beliefs
    D. both B and C

19. The purpose of analyzing your audience before preparing a persuasive speech is to _____.

    A. make certain that your audience strongly agrees with your views
    B. find out how your audience feels and why they feel as they do
    C. determine their hobbies and special interests
    D. learn their occupations and socioeconomic levels

20. Which of the following statements could be the topic of a persuasive speech?

    A. Product testing on animals should be banned.
    B. Catholic priests should be allowed to marry.
    C. Eliminate all beef, pork, and poultry from your diet.
    D. All of the above

1. c **2.** a **3.** b **4.** b **5.** a **6.** b **7.** b **8.** c **9.** b **10.** b

OUTLINE FENG'S SPEECH (PAGE 139)

INTRODUCTION

I. We all know someone who has been sick or in pain at some point in their lives. Maybe you, a friend, or a family member has had painful surgery, or suffers from depression. Often, the medicines the doctors prescribe have side effects and make the patient feel even worse. No one likes to suffer. When we don't feel well, we would all like to recover and feel better as quickly as possible. Acupuncture might be the solution for what is ailing you.

STATEMENT OF SPECIFIC PURPOSE

II. Consider acupuncture when you are sick or in pain.

PREVIEW OF MAIN POINTS

III. There are many reasons to consider acupuncture instead of traditional Western medicine.
    A. Acupuncture is a proven medical treatment.
    B. Acupuncture is safe and painless.
    C. Acupuncture effectively treats many conditions.

TRANSITION: *Many of you might be skeptical about acupuncture because you believe it is a new and unproven treatment. You will be amazed to learn that acupuncture has been used effectively for thousands of years and is medically respected in the United States.*

BODY

I. Acupuncture is a proven medical treatment.
    A. Acupuncture is an ancient Chinese technique.
        1. Relieves pain
        2. Cures disease
        3. Used in China for 2,500 years
    B. Acupuncture is respected by known national and international health organizations.
        1. National Institutes of Health (NIH)
            a. Acupuncture has been clinically proven to be effective against a variety of medical problems.
            b. "The data in support of acupuncture are as strong as those for many accepted Western medical therapies."

    2. Food and Drug Administration (FDA)
        a. <u>Endorses acupuncture as a medically proven treatment.</u>
        b. <u>Classified acupuncture needles as medical instruments.</u>
        c. (Show visual aid—picture of acupuncture needles)
    3. <u>World Health Organization (WHO)</u>
        a. <u>Endorses acupuncture as a medically proven treatment.</u>
        b. WHO has endorsed acupuncture use for over fifteen years.

TRANSITION: *Many of you might be worried that acupuncture is not safe. You will be very pleased to learn that acupuncture is extremely safe and painless.*

  II. <u>Acupuncture is safe and painless.</u>
    A. There are no side effects.
    B. Acupuncture is nonaddictive.
    C. <u>There is no risk of contracting a disease.</u>
      1. <u>Needles are sterilized</u>
      2. <u>Needles are disposable</u>
    D. Acupuncture is painless.
      1. <u>Slight tingling sensation</u>
      2. <u>Massage therapy effect</u>
      3. (Show visual aid of patient receiving acupuncture treatment.)

TRANSITION: *Some of you might think that acupuncture is helpful for only a few minor problems. I will now prove to you that acupuncture treats a wide variety of problems and diseases.*

  III. <u>Acupuncture treats a variety of conditions.</u>
    A. <u>Chronic pain</u>
      1. <u>headaches</u>
      2. <u>arthritis</u>
      3. <u>back pain</u>
      4. <u>menstrual cramps</u>
      5. <u>postoperative pain</u>
      6. <u>musculoskeletal pains</u>
    B. Physical problems and diseases
      1. <u>allergies</u>
      2. <u>asthma</u>
      3. <u>heart problems</u>
      4. <u>infertility</u>
      5. <u>insomnia</u>
      6. <u>reduces nausea</u>
        a. <u>surgery</u>
        b. chemotherapy

C. Emotional and psychological problems

    1. Addictions

        a. <u>smoking</u>

        b. <u>drugs</u>

        c. <u>alcohol</u>

    2. Eating disorders

    3. <u>Obsessive behaviors</u>

    4. Anxiety disorders

    5. <u>Stress</u>

    6. Low self-esteem

    7. <u>Depression</u>

D. Helps the immune system function better

    1. <u>Helps avoid respiratory infections</u>

    2. <u>Effective form of preventative medicine</u>

CONCLUSION

SUMMARY

I. I hope I have convinced you to consider acupuncture as a medical treatment.

  A. Acupuncture is a clinically proven and respected medical treatment.

  B. Acupuncture is perfectly safe and painless.

  C. Acupuncture treats a wide variety of physical and emotional problems.

MEMORABLE CONCLUDING REMARKS

II. Throw away those medicines that bother your stomach or make you sleepy. Remember: There is an alternative. The next time you aren't feeling well, acupuncture may be the way to go.

End-of-Chapter Quiz

For each statement, circle *T* if it is true and *F* if it is false.

1.   T   F   Listening is the least frequent form of human behavior.

2.   T   F   College students spend close to ninety percent of their time listening.

3.   T   F   A good way to improve your listening skills is to concentrate on people's speech patterns rather than their words.

4.   T   F   Good listeners fake attention when they are bored with what a speaker is saying.

5.   T   F   Looking for distractions does not hinder your ability to listen.

6.   T   F   It is more important to concentrate on the details of a speech than to listen for the main ideas.

7.   T   F   Listening is improved when you allow yourself to react to trigger words.

8.   T   F   Deciding in advance that a topic is boring is a bad listening habit.

9.   T   F   Bad listening habits prevent you from fully understanding what you hear.

10.   T   F   There are several "cures" to help you improve your listening skills.

1. a **2.** c **3.** f **4.** d **5.** f **6.** b **7.** a **8.** e **9.** a **10.** e

COMPREHEND MAIN IDEAS AND DETAILS

EXERCISE 1 (PAGE 154)

Passage to be read aloud by the teacher:

"Lying well is a special talent which is not easily acquired," says a University of California psychologist who has studied lying for twenty years. Good liars must be natural actors, have charming manners, and be able to manage their expressions. Experts report that even with standard polygraph tests, it can be very difficult to detect particularly good liars. Polygraph, or lie-detector, tests are used about one million times a year by private companies, police departments, and federal agencies, including the military and the CIA.

There is much controversy over the accuracy of polygraph tests. Over four thousand articles and books have been published which insist that polygraph tests are reliable. However, many experts are convinced that the lie detectors can be fooled by biting one's tongue, or using drugs, hypnosis, and biofeedback.

Throughout history, people have tried to detect lies. In ancient India, a favorite method was the "donkey tail" system. People suspected of lying were sent into a dark hut to pull the tail of a donkey inside. They were told the donkey would bray if the person pulling the tail were guilty. The suspected liars didn't know that the donkey's tail had been covered with soot. The guilty parties would be the ones without soot on their hands.

Answers

Step 1		Step 2	
1. T	**4.** F	**1.** c	**4.** a
2. F	**5.** F	**2.** a	**5.** b, c
3. T		**3.** a, b, c	

EXERCISE 2 (PAGES 155–156)

Passage to be read aloud by the teacher:

Almost all people daydream during a normal day. They tend to daydream the most during those quiet times when they are alone in their cars, sitting in waiting rooms, or preparing for bed. Daydreaming or fantasizing is not abnormal; it is a basic human characteristic. Most people report that they enjoy their daydreams. Some people have very probable and realistic daydreams, while others have unrealistic fantasies such as inheriting a million dollars.

Psychologists report that men daydream as much as women, but the subject of their daydreams or fantasies is different. Men daydream more about being heroes and good athletes, while women tend to daydream about fashion and beauty. As people grow older, they tend to fantasize less, although it is still evident in old age. Older people tend to daydream a lot about the past.

Daydreaming or fantasizing enters into the games of children. Psychologists believe that it is very important for children to participate in fantasy play. It is a normal part of their development that helps them develop their imaginations.

Daydreaming has advantages and disadvantages. In some situations, it can reduce people's fear or anxiety. It can also keep them entertained or awake under dull or boring conditions. Unfortunately, to engage in a daydream or fantasy, people must divert part of their attention from their environment. When it is important for people to remain alert and pay attention to what is going on around them, daydreaming can cause problems.

Answers

Step 1

  1. T   **3.** F

  2. T   **4.** T

Step 2

  1. F (Men daydream <u>as much as</u> women.)

  2. T

  3. F (Daydreaming helps children develop their <u>imaginations</u>.)

  4. F (Daydreaming keeps people <u>awake</u> when they are bored.)

  5. T

  6. F (Most daydreaming occurs when people are <u>alone</u>.)

EXERCISE 3 (PAGES 156–157)

Passage to be read aloud by the teacher:

The heart is a powerful organ. It is located in the chest directly under the breastbone. The human heart, and that of other mammals such as bears, monkeys, and horses, is divided into four chambers. A bird's heart is also divided into the same four chambers. These chambers are the left and right auricles and the left and right ventricles. The functions of the auricles are to receive blood from the veins and to push it into the ventricles. The functions of the ventricles are to pump the blood out of the heart and then to pump it around the body.

Answers

  I. Two General Facts About the Heart

    A. <u>It's a powerful organ.</u>

    B. <u>It's located in the chest under the breastbone.</u>

  II. Living Beings with Four-Chambered Hearts

    A. <u>Human beings</u>

    B. <u>Other mammals</u>

      1. Bears

      2. <u>Monkeys</u>

      3. <u>Horses</u>

    C. <u>Birds</u>

III. Four Chambers of the Heart
   A. <u>Left auricle</u>
   B. <u>Right auricle</u>
   C. <u>Left ventricle</u>
   D. <u>Right ventricle</u>
IV. Heart Functions
   A. Functions of auricles
      1. <u>receive blood from veins</u>
      2. <u>push blood into ventricles</u>
   B. Functions of ventricles
      1. <u>pump blood out of heart</u>
      2. <u>pump blood around body</u>

EXERCISE 4 (PAGE 157)

Passage to be read aloud by the teacher:

Umbrella is a Latin word. It comes from *umbra,* which means "shade."

    The first person to use an umbrella was the cave dweller, who tied several palm leaves together to provide shade from the hot sun.

    In the early 1900s, umbrellas were very large and heavy. They had forty ribs that were made of whalebone and covered with a heavy canvas. Today, umbrellas are lightweight and compact. The ribs are made of aluminum and covered with plastic or other waterproof material. But they still haven't made an umbrella you won't leave behind! Bus, train, and cab companies say they find more umbrellas than anything else.

Answers

   I. <u>Umbrella</u>
      A. Latin word
      B. Comes from *umbra*
      C. Means "shade"
  II. <u>Cave dweller</u>
      A. First person to use an umbrella
      B. Tied palm leaves together for shade
 III. <u>Umbrellas of the past</u>
      A. Large
      B. Heavy
      C. Ribs made of whalebone
      D. Canvas-covered ribs
  IV. <u>Today's umbrellas</u>
      A. Lightweight
      B. Compact
      C. Ribs made of aluminum
      D. Waterproof material covers ribs

V. Companies that find umbrellas
  A. Bus
  B. Train
  C. Cab

EXERCISE 5 (PAGE 158)

Passage to be read aloud by the teacher:

People who work at night between 10:00 P.M. and 6:00 A.M. are often affected by lack of sleep. This is a very serious disorder that causes 50 percent of all accidents at work.

There are several symptoms of sleep deprivation. These include extreme drowsiness and difficulty concentrating. People who don't get enough sleep often complain of headaches. They also suffer from insomnia when they do try to sleep during the day.

Night-shift workers have a greater risk for developing health problems associated with a lack of sleep. They often develop gastrointestinal disorders, digestive problems, as well as heart attacks.

Night-shift workers avoid sleeping during the day for many reasons. They use the day as an opportunity to do other things like take a second job. They often run errands such as grocery shopping and driving their children to school. They also set appointments with doctors and auto or home repair people. They even use the day to visit with friends.

Experts offer some tips for helping night-shift workers sleep more easily during the day. They stress the importance of making sleep a priority and state the body needs 8 hours of sleep daily. They suggest that night workers split daytime sleeping periods in two and sleep from 7:00 to 11:00 A.M. and again from 4:00 to 8:00 P.M.

The experts also offer suggestions for overcoming insomnia when night-shift workers try to sleep during the day. They recommend creating a quiet and dark environment to sleep in. Further, avoid doing household activities in bed, like balancing your checkbook or making grocery lists. Dr. Gary Richardson, a researcher at the Sleep Disorders Center of Henry Ford Hospital in Detroit, says to stop drinking caffeinated drinks or alcohol several hours before bedtime. He also states that daily exercise will have an effect on your quality of sleep.

Answers

Step 2
  I. Symptoms of sleep deprivation
    A. Extreme drowsiness
    B. Difficulty concentrating
    C. Headaches
    D. Insomnia

  II. Effects of sleep deprivation
    A. Gastrointestinal disorders
    B. Digestive disorders
    C. Heart attacks

III. Causes of sleep deprivation
- **A.** <u>Take a second job</u>
- **B.** Run errands
  - **1.** <u>grocery shop</u>
  - **2.** <u>drive children around</u>
- **C.** Set appointments
  - **1.** <u>doctors</u>
  - **2.** auto repair
  - **3.** home repair
- **D.** <u>Visit with friends</u>

IV. <u>Solutions</u>
- **A.** Make sleeping a priority
  - **1.** <u>Get eight hours of sleep daily</u>
  - **2.** <u>Split sleeping periods in two</u>
    - **a.** 7:00–11:00 A.M.
    - **b.** <u>4:00–8:00 P.M.</u>
- **B.** <u>Overcome insomnia</u>
  - **1.** Create an environment conducive to sleeping
    - **a.** <u>quiet</u>
    - **b.** <u>dark</u>
  - **2.** <u>Avoid household chores in bed</u>
    - **a.** <u>balancing checkbook</u>
    - **b.** making grocery lists
  - **3.** <u>Avoid caffeine</u>
  - **4.** Avoid alcohol
  - **5.** <u>Get daily exercise</u>

EXERCISE 6 (PAGES 160–161)

Short passages to be read aloud by the teacher:

1. Mr. Hemmi plays poker every single night of the week. He hasn't missed a game in five years. Last week he won two thousand dollars.

   a. Mr. Hemmi plays poker seven times a week.
   b. Mr. Hemmi plays poker too often.
   c. Mr. Hemmi is a great poker player.

2. The man spoke for one hour and fifty-five minutes. He talked about the use of computers in education. More than half the people left before he finished.

   a. The man's speech was too long.
   b. Many people left because the speech was boring.
   c. Computers in education is a boring topic for a speech.

3. Amir was in a car accident yesterday. It was his fourth automobile accident in a year. Fortunately, no one was hurt.

    a. Amir is a bad driver.
    b. The accident was probably Amir's fault.
    c. Amir has been in previous accidents.

4. There is no freedom of speech or press in communist countries. The United States is a democratic country. The Bill of Rights guarantees freedom of speech in the United States.

    a. Democracy is better than communism.
    b. There is freedom of speech in the United States.
    c. Citizens of democratic countries are happier than those living in communist countries.

5. Soccer is played all over the world. It is especially popular in Central America, South America, Australia, and Europe. Outside the U.S., it is called "football," although it is not the same as "American football."

    a. Soccer is more exciting than American football.
    b. Soccer is a popular sport throughout the world.
    c. Central and South Americans find soccer to be more exciting than American football.

6. According to the United States Immigration and Naturalization Service, over nineteen million tourists visit the United States each year. The largest number, approximately four million, comes from Japan. Three million come from the United Kingdom, two million come from Germany, and one million come from Mexico.

    a. The United States allows too many tourists to visit each year.
    b. More Japanese tourists than German tourists visit the United States.
    c. Millions of tourists visit the United States each year.

7. Lorna is a college freshman. She plays tennis, ice hockey, water polo, and softball. Last term she got Ds in two classes and failed chemistry.

    a. Lorna participates in too many sports.
    b. Lorna should play fewer sports and study more.
    c. Lorna plays various sports.

8. Sergio works only ten hours a week. He drives an expensive car and takes several vacations a year. He couldn't pay his rent last month, so his cousin loaned him the money.

   a. Sergio should rent a less expensive apartment.
   b. Sergio should get a full-time job.
   c. Sergio borrowed money from a relative.

9. Professor Evans gave his geography students a final exam. Twenty-eight out of thirty students failed the test.

   a. Geography is a difficult subject.
   b. The majority of students failed the test.
   c. The final exam was unfair.

10. According to the U.S. State Department, Americans adopt thousands of orphans from many countries each year. China is the most popular country for Americans to adopt children. The second-largest number of orphans come from Russia, and the third-largest number come from Guatemala.

    a. Americans adopt children from different continents.
    b. Americans prefer adopting children from countries other than the United States.
    c. Most orphans adopted by Americans come from China.

Answers

1. **a.** Fact (This is clearly stated in the passage.)
   b. Opinion (Mr. Hemmi's wife might feel that seven days a week is too much. Mr. Hemmi might feel it's too little and would like to play fourteen times a week if he could!)
   c. Inference (This is an inference based on the information that he won two thousand dollars last week. Maybe he lost two thousand dollars the week before and he just got lucky last week. We don't know from the passage whether or not he's a good player.)

2. **a.** Opinion (Who is to say what is too long? Some listeners might have wanted the speech to be longer.)
   b. Inference (We don't know why people left. We are assuming it is because they were bored. Maybe they had other appointments. The passage states that more than half the people left; it doesn't state why.)
   c. Opinion (Some people might find the topic fascinating. This is an individual judgment.)

3. **a.** Inference (The passage does not say Amir was driving. The passage has insufficient information for the reader to draw the conclusion that Amir is a bad driver.)
   b. Inference (Again, the passage does not say Amir was driving. There is insufficient information for the reader to conclude that Amir was at fault.)
   c. Fact (The passage specifically states that Amir has been in four automobile accidents in a year.)

4. a. Opinion (This is a matter of personal opinion. Communist leaders might feel that communism is better; citizens of the free world would disagree.)

   b. Fact (This is clearly stated in the passage.)

   c. Inference (The passage doesn't say this. Without interviewing citizens of communist countries, we can't know for sure who is happy and who isn't.)

5. a. Opinion (This is a matter of personal opinion. Many might agree or disagree with this statement.)

   b. Fact (The passage clearly states that soccer is popular on several continents.)

   c. Inference (The passage doesn't state this directly. We can only assume this to be true based on the popularity of soccer in Central and South America.)

6. a. Opinion (Who is to say how many is too many? This is a matter of personal opinion.)

   b. Fact (This is clearly stated in the passage.)

   c. Fact (This is clearly stated in the passage.)

7. a. Opinion (Who is to say how many is too many?)

   b. Inference (This is an assumption we might make because Lorna received such poor grades. We don't know the reason for her poor performance.)

   c. Fact (The story specifically states the names of four sports that Lorna plays.)

8. a. Inference (This statement assumes Sergio's rent is more than he can afford. We don't know this for sure from the passage.)

   b. Opinion (This is an opinion. Maybe Sergio just needs to spend less money on entertainment, clothes, etc.)

   c. Fact (The passage clearly states he borrowed money from his cousin.)

9. a. Opinion (Some people might find geography to be easy. This statement cannot be proven either way.)

   b. Fact (This is clearly stated in the story.)

   c. Inference (This statement assumes the test was unfair because so many students failed it. Maybe the students didn't study enough. We can't know from the passage.)

10. a. Fact (This is clearly stated in the passage.)

   b. Inference (This statement assumes that foreign adoptions are the preference due to the large number of foreign adoptions. Maybe adoption laws simply make it easier to adopt foreign babies.)

   c. Fact (This is clearly stated in the passage.)

EXERCISE 7 (PAGE 162)

Passage to be read aloud by the teacher:

A young man of 21 sat down next to an elderly woman on a bench at a bus stop. The woman started up a conversation with the young man. "I feel like I'm 75 years old today," said the elderly woman.

"I'm so sorry; that's too bad," answered the young man.

"No, it isn't; it's wonderful," said the woman. "You see, today is my eighty-fifth birthday!"

EXERCISE 8 (PAGE 162)

Passage to be read aloud by the teacher:

A businessman went into a coffee shop one afternoon for lunch. He had a very bad cold and kept sneezing. The waiter, who had known the businessman for twelve years, told him, "You look and sound awful."

"Yes, I have a very bad cold," the businessman said.

The waiter shook his head sadly and replied, "It's too bad that you don't have pneumonia. They know what to do for that!"

EXERCISE 9 (PAGE 162)

Questions to be read aloud by the teacher:

1. If Mrs. King's rooster lays an egg in Mrs. Smith's yard, who should keep the egg?

2. If you take three marbles from eight marbles, how many will you have?

3. Do they have the Fourth of July in France?

4. A plane full of English tourists crashes on the border between Spain and Portugal. Where should the survivors be buried?

5. If you drive a bus with fifty people on board from New York City to Miami, Florida, and drop off five people in Washington, D.C., five people in North Carolina, and five people in Georgia, when you arrive in Miami thirty-six hours later, what is the driver's name?

6. How many times can you take two from twelve?

7. What do you sleep in, sit on, and drink from?

8. If you had a match and entered a dark room with a fireplace, a candle, and an oil lamp, what would you light first?

9. Which statement is correct: Seven plus five **IS** eleven, or Seven plus five **ARE** eleven?

10. A rancher had twenty-seven horses. All but seven died. How many did he have left?

Answers

1. Neither. Roosters do not lay eggs.
2. Three
3. Yes. It's a date there but not a holiday.
4. Nowhere. The survivors are alive.
5. (Student's name)
6. Only once. After that, you take it from ten.
7. A bed, a chair, and a glass
8. The match
9. Neither. Seven plus five equals twelve.
10. Seven

EXERCISE 10 (PAGE 163)

Directions to be read aloud by the teacher:

1. Put a checkmark to the right of all the odd numbers and circle all the even numbers.
2. Underline the names of colors and cross out the names of furniture.
3. Draw circles around the letters that are in the first half of the alphabet and underline the others.
4. Draw three circles. Write the first letter of your first name in the center circle.
5. Put the number 7 in the square and the letter R in the triangle.
6. Circle the names of fruits and underline the names of vegetables.
7. A boy had a dozen eggs. He broke six and gave one away. Write the number of eggs he had left.
8. Draw a circle in a square and draw a circle around a triangle.
9. Put the number 1 in the middle section, the number 2 in the smallest section, and the number 3 in the first section.
10. Write the names of seven different parts of the body. Three should be parts of the face.

Answers

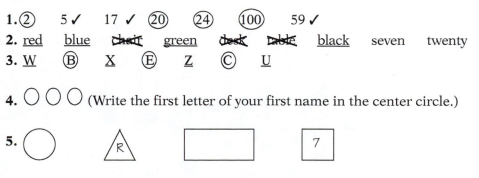

1. ②   5 ✓   17 ✓   ⑳   ㉔   ⑩⓪   59 ✓
2. <u>red</u>   <u>blue</u>   ~~chair~~   <u>green</u>   ~~desk~~   ~~table~~   <u>black</u>   seven   twenty
3. <u>W</u>   ⑧   <u>X</u>   ⑥   <u>Z</u>   ⓒ   <u>U</u>

4. ○ ○ ○ (Write the first letter of your first name in the center circle.)

5.

Copyright © 2006 by Pearson Education, Inc. Permission granted to reproduce for classroom use.

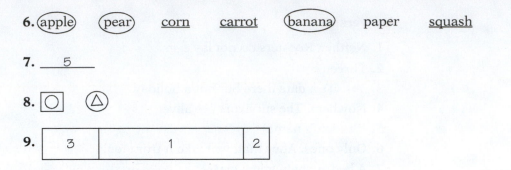

6. (apple) (pear) <u>corn</u> <u>carrot</u> (banana) paper <u>squash</u>

7. ___5___

8. ▢ △

9. | 3 | 1 | 2 |

10. **Possible Answers**

Parts of face: cheek, chin, eyes, lips, mouth, nose

Other parts of body: ankle, arm, back, calf, finger, foot, hand, heel, knee, leg, stomach, toe, ears (part of head rather than face)

End-of-Chapter Quiz

For each statement, circle *T* if it is true and *F* if it is false.

1.   T   F   Group discussion participants should not disagree with one another during the discussion.

2.   T   F   Evidence is not important in a group discussion.

3.   T   F   When several people exchange and evaluate information, they are having a group discussion.

4.   T   F   It is not important to prepare for a group discussion because all participants should feel free to talk about anything.

5.   T   F   Brainstorming is time consuming and not always worthwhile.

6.   T   F   Brainstorming can help you produce many ideas for the group to consider.

7.   T   F   While brainstorming, it is important to evaluate ideas as they are presented.

8.   T   F   Since brainstorming can get out of hand, it is important to limit the number of ideas each group member may contribute.

9.   T   F   A group discussion should follow a specific organizational plan.

10.   T   F   Shy group members who don't contribute to the discussion should be ignored.

11.   T   F   It is not necessary to designate a group leader if all participants contribute to the discussion.

12.   T   F   An effective group leader monopolizes the discussion because someone needs to be in charge.

13.   T   F   A group member with lots of ideas to share doesn't need to listen to the other participants' contributions.

14.   T   F   An effective group leader makes sure that all participants stay on track.

15.   T   F   An effective group leader allows outspoken participants to monopolize the discussion.

Circle the best answer.

16. The purpose of a group discussion is to _____.

     A. share information with others

     B. solve a common problem

     C. present a variety of viewpoints to an audience

     D. All of the above

17. Many group discussions are not effective because _____.

    A. participants are not prepared with ideas and evidence

    B. participants go off on tangents and say whatever pops into their heads

    C. participants are open-minded and respectful of others' opinions

    D. both A and B

18. Before discussing the future effects of the problem if it is not solved, a group should _____.

    A. brainstorm possible solutions to the problem

    B. discuss the causes of the problem

    C. brainstorm advantages and disadvantages to various solutions

    D. both A and C

19. Which of the following questions should group members ask about each proposed solution to determine if it is a good one?

    A. Will this solution eliminate one or more of the causes of the problem?

    B. Will this solution create more problems?

    C. Will this solution make the politicians happy?

    D. both A and B

20. Transitions between each of the steps in a group discussion should _____.

    A. always state at least one specific solution

    B. always refer back to the causes of the problem

    C. summarize the step discussed before moving to the next step

    D. both A and B

End-of-Chapter Quiz

For each statement, circle _T_ if it is true and _F_ if it is false.

1. T F Misunderstandings occur much less frequently when people take the time to clarify a speaker's message.

2. T F Misunderstandings often occur because listeners assume they understand what a speaker meant.

3. T F Misunderstandings happen to everyone.

4. T F The tendency to jump to conclusions is a barrier to good interpersonal communication.

5. T F Most people realize when they make assumptions based on insufficient information.

6. T F It's important to draw conclusions based on what you actually know to be true.

7. T F People who use an aggressive style of communication are generally respected and well liked.

8. T F People who are assertive communicators tend to be passive and rarely get what they want.

9. T F People who use an indirect communication style tend to be very clear, effective communicators.

10. T F The "assertive style" of communication has been called the "golden mean."

11. T F Direct communicators tend to be misunderstood much of the time.

12. T F People who use an assertive style of communication appear confident and sure of themselves.

13. T F Phrasing your requests as questions leads to clear, direct interpersonal communication.

14. T F "You are rude and inconsiderate! Go to the end of the line." is an example of aggressive communication.

15. T F "Excuse me. I ordered tea, not coffee. Please bring me some tea." is an example of assertive communication.

TEST YOUR ABILITY TO EVALUATE EVIDENCE (PAGES 186–187)

1. T (This is definitely true because it is directly verified by the story.)
2. ? (This might or might not be true. We don't know that there was a murder. The killing could have been an accident.)
3. ? (This might or might not be true. Maybe some of the others have also been cleared of guilt. We just know that Slinky Sam has been cleared for sure.)
4. T (This is definitely true because it is directly verified by the story.)
5. ? (This might or might not be true. The story doesn't tell us what the police know or not.)
6. ? (This might or might not be true. We don't know if there was a foul deed. The killing could have been an accident.)
7. ? (This might or might not be true. We don't know that Smith has been murdered. He could have been killed in an accident.)
8. F (This is definitely false because the story clearly contradicts it.)
9. ? (This may or may not be true. The killing could have been an accident, not an assassination.)

DISCOVER YOUR COMMUNICATION STYLE (PAGE 189)

1. **a.** A   2. **a.** B   3. **a.** C
   b. C   **b.** A   **b.** A
   c. B   **c.** C   **c.** B

PRACTICE DIFFERENT COMMUNICATION STYLES (PAGES 190–191)

Possible Answers

1. **a.** "What kind of low-class outfit is this? This is an outrage. I want my car cleaned now!"
   b. "You're welcome." (Accept the car as is and drive away feeling disappointed.)
   c. "Excuse me. I'm sure it was an oversight, but this car is filthy. Please bring me my car when it has been carefully washed."

2. **a.** "Why can't you get a simple order straight? Give me my money back."
   b. "I don't want to be a bother. This pizza will be fine." (Accept the pizza and pick the anchovies, mushrooms, and sausage off before you eat it.)
   c. "I ordered a double cheese pizza. Please exchange this for the kind I ordered."

3. **a.** "Would you shut up? We can't hear the movie with you yapping like that."
   b. (Say nothing. Suffer in silence, unable to concentrate on the movie.)
   c. "Excuse me. I'd appreciate it if you would keep your voices down. I can't hear the movie."

4. **a.** "You know I don't want to move off campus. You have no sense of loyalty."

   b. (Against your better judgment, move into an apartment with your friends. You are so upset for the rest of the semester that your grades suffer.)

   c. "Thanks for inviting me to join you, but I prefer living here. I'll miss you both if you decide to move."

5. **a.** "Hey, you have some nerve cutting in on me. Who do you think you are? Go to the end of the line and wait your turn like everyone else."

   b. (Say nothing and feel annoyed and angry that someone has taken advantage of you.)

   c. "Excuse me. This is the front [middle] of the line. You probably didn't realize it, but the end of the line is over there." (You point to where the end of the line is.)

PRACTICE BEING DIRECT (PAGE 192)

Possible Answers

1. We would really prefer that table by the window, please.
2. I'm really tired. I'd like to go home soon.
3. Please close the windows. I feel cold with them open.
4. Please keep your voices down. I really need to concentrate on my work.
5. Please don't smoke in my car. The smoke bothers me.

CHAPTER 11

End-of-Chapter Quiz

For each statement, circle _T_ if it is true and _F_ if it is false.

1. T   F   Intercultural communication occurs when people from different cultures exchange information with each other.
2. T   F   "Ethnocentricity" refers to the attitude that one's culture is inferior to others.
3. T   F   "All women love to shop" is an example of a stereotype.
4. T   F   Most stereotypes are accurate.
5. T   F   People from the same culture all behave exactly the same way.
6. T   F   Although individuals within a culture differ, there are similarities in communication styles within each culture.
7. T   F   Nonverbal communication styles rarely differ between cultures.
8. T   F   Intercultural communication is really interpersonal communication between people from different cultures.
9. T   F   People from cultures with a direct communication style tend to avoid stating a specific point of view.
10. T   F   People from cultures with an indirect communication style tend to express their opinions openly.

DISCUSS THE IMPACT OF STEREOTYPES (PAGE 200)

Sample Response

Step 1:

I'm Mexican, and I've heard many Europeans and North Americans from the United States say that Mexicans are not ambitious.

Step 2:

1. This stereotype is not accurate. We are very hardworking and do what is necessary to do well in school and live well.

2. I think people feel this way because we are very relaxed and easygoing. We don't worry so much about deadlines and getting things done immediately.

3. I don't like this stereotype that some people have about Mexicans. We get our projects and work done well. What's the difference if we do it in the morning or in the afternoon?

4. Sometimes this stereotype does interfere with effective interpersonal communication. When I feel that another person thinks I don't work hard, I don't want to be their friend or try to get to know them better. So I don't ask them questions and don't want to tell them how I feel about things because they might not respect my opinions.

THINK ABOUT HOW WE INTERPRET BEHAVIOR (PAGE 200)

Sample Interpretations

Student's Behavior	Interpretation
sits at the back of the classroom and does not participate in class discussions	*finds class boring*
acts extremely embarrassed when called on by the teacher	*is not prepared*
constantly apologizes	*lacks confidence*
asks lots of questions	*likes to be the center of attention*
offers opinions frequently without being asked	*is aggressive*
never offers opinions, even when asked	*is not interested in topic; is uninformed*
doesn't look at other people when speaking	*is shy; is dishonest; dislikes person*
shrugs shoulders when asked questions	*is not interested in topic*
says "yes" to everything	*has no respect for himself or herself*

Analysis

Tomiko, the Japanese student, was raised in a culture that uses an indirect communication style. Professor Johnson was raised in a culture in which people communicate in a very direct way. While Tomiko was standing there wordlessly, the professor was expecting her to make a specific point or ask a specific question. Tomiko did neither. The teacher was frustrated because she knew Tomiko wanted to say or ask something specific, but didn't know what. She became impatient because she felt Tomiko was wasting her time.

If Professor Johnson had realized that the situation was simply an example of an intercultural communication misunderstanding, she might have responded differently.

Tomiko's way of communicating reflected the norms of her background—that of a culture with an indirect communication style. Instead of directly asking for a schedule of future workshops, Tomiko was hoping that Professor Johnson would figure out what she wanted and offer the information. Professor Johnson was frustrated and annoyed because Tomiko didn't get to the point and make a specific direct request for information.

End-of-Chapter Quiz

For each statement, circle *T* if it is true and *F* if it is false.

1. T F "Thinking on your feet" means being able to deliver a perfectly prepared speech.

2. T F A "thinking on your feet speech" is the same as an "impromptu speech."

3. T F People rarely make short impromptu speeches in their everyday lives.

4. T F Good impromptu speakers are well informed about current events.

5. T F A good way to prepare for an impromptu speech is to become familiar with different organizational patterns.

6. T F A mental outline is written on paper or note cards.

7. T F A good way to begin an impromptu speech is to state, "I'm going to talk about ____."

8. T F A good way to conclude an impromptu speech is by saying, "I can't think of anything else. That's it."

9. T F An attention-getting opener is not necessary when making an impromptu speech.

10. T F If you forget what to say while giving an impromptu speech, you should apologize to the audience.

End-of-Chapter Quiz

For each statement, circle *T* if it is true and *F* if it is false.

1.   T   F   Idioms are popular expressions that don't always mean what one would expect.

2.   T   F   Idioms are found only in English.

3.   T   F   An idiom generally does not translate literally.

4.   T   F   Improving your understanding of idioms will not help you to be a better communicator.

5.   T   F   Proverbs are expressions that express advice or wisdom.

6.   T   F   "Birds of a feather flock together" means that it is easy for people of different cultures to communicate with one another.

7.   T   F   To be feeling "under the weather" means that the weather outside is terrible.

8.   T   F   "Spill the beans" means to keep a secret.

9.   T   F   To "beat around the bush" means to communicate clearly and directly.

10.   T   F   "Out of the blue" refers to an unexpected occurrence.

Answers

EXERCISE 1 (PAGES 219–220)

1. c **2.** a **3.** c **4.** b **5.** c **6.** b **7.** a **8.** c **9.** c **10.** c

EXERCISE 2 (PAGE 220)

1. a **2.** d **3.** e **4.** b **5.** c **6.** h **7.** j **8.** i **9.** f **10.** g

EXERCISE 3 (PAGE 221)

1. b **2.** c **3.** c **4.** b **5.** a **6.** a **7.** b **8.** c **9.** a **10.** c

EXERCISE 4 (PAGE 222)

1. green with envy
2. in the red
3. blue
4. in the pink
5. golden
6. rosy
7. out of the blue
8. see red
9. in black and white
10. white lie

EXERCISE 5 (PAGES 223–224)

1. put two and two together
2. Get to the point
3. eat his words
4. make tracks
5. threw in the towel
6. under the weather
7. squared away
8. runs in the family
9. pull some strings
10. puts the cart before the horse

LEARN TO USE PROVERBS (PAGE 228)

Possible Answers

a. Taking care of a small problem when it firsts occurs prevents a bigger problem from developing.

b. Taking minor steps to prevent a problem from occurring helps prevent having to take major steps to rectify the problem later.

c. When you impatiently wait for something to happen, it seems to take forever.

d. People think that others always have better lives than they do.

e. In a given situation, behave as you see others around you behaving.

f. People (or animals) misbehave if an authority figure is not present to supervise.

g. People who have done something improper shouldn't accuse others of improper behavior because they leave themselves open to attack.

h. It's better to have a sure thing than the promise of something better.

i. Exercise more than one option at a time. If one is not successful, you haven't lost everything.

j. Don't assume that something will happen until it has happened.

k. Analyze a situation carefully before you become involved.

l. A person who moves around a lot usually has few responsibilities or possessions.

m. Something that looks great doesn't always have value.

n. Don't wait until a problem or an emergency occurs before taking steps to prevent it.

o. People choose friends with similar interests and characteristics.

p. It's often cheaper to buy something new than to fix something broken.

q. The way something looks on the surface is not always an indication of its true value.

r. Take care of each problem when it happens. Don't worry about it beforehand.

s. It's easier to be successful by being nice than by being nasty.

t. Something is better than nothing.

u. Act quickly to take advantage of an opportunity while it is still available.

v. If you make a small concession to a person, he or she will take advantage of you.

w. That's like incurring one debt or obligation in order to meet another one.

x. One person is criticizing another for having the same faults as he or she has.

y. Too many people involved in a project can cause disorganization or delays.

z. People who have done things a certain way for a long time will not change their habits.

EXERCISE 7 (PAGE 229)

1. Don't put the cart before the horse.

2. The pot is calling the kettle black. *or*
People in glass houses shouldn't throw stones.

3. All that glitters is not gold.

4. People who live in glass houses shouldn't throw stones. *or*
The pot is calling the kettle black.

5. Don't put all of your eggs in one basket.

6. Birds of a feather flock together.

7. When in Rome, do as the Romans do.

8. It's easier to catch flies with honey than vinegar.

9. Give him an inch and he'll take a mile.

10. Half a loaf is better than none.

End-of-Chapter Quiz

For each statement, circle *T* if it is true and *F* if it is false.

1.	T	F	A well-organized symposium needs a group leader.
2.	T	F	In a debate, opposing points of view are presented and argued.
3.	T	F	A debate consists of two informative speeches.
4.	T	F	A good debate focuses on personal opinions rather than on persuasive evidence.
5.	T	F	A good introductory speech is brief, preferably two minutes or less.
6.	T	F	A good introductory speech does not include the speaker's topic.
7.	T	F	A good introductory speech includes an explanation of why the speaker is qualified to speak about his or her topic.
8.	T	F	*T.I.S.* stands for *Topic, Introduction, and Speaker*.
9.	T	F	In a symposium, speakers should feel free to talk about anything.
10.	T	F	Symposiums can be informative or persuasive.

ANSWERS TO END-OF-CHAPTER QUIZZES

Chapter 1

1. T   2. F   3. F   4. T   5. F   6. T   7. F   8. F   9. F   10. F

Chapter 2

1. F   2. F   3. T   4. F   5. F   6. F   7. F   8. F   9. F   10. F
11. F   12. T   13. T   14. F   15. T   16. C   17. B   18. C   19. B   20. C

Chapter 3

1. F   2. F   3. F   4. T   5. F   6. F   7. T   8. T   9. F   10. F
11. B   12. C   13. C   14. B   15. A   16. C   17. C   18. B   19. C   20. A

Chapter 4

1. D   2. C   3. D   4. B   5. D   6. D   7. D   8. C   9. D   10. D
11. D   12. A   13. C   14. B   15. B

Chapter 5

1. T   2. F   3. F   4. T   5. F   6. T   7. F   8. F   9. T   10. F

Chapter 6

1. C   2. C   3. A   4. D   5. C   6. D   7. A   8. B   9. D   10. A

Chapter 7

1. T   2. F   3. F   4. F   5. F   6. F   7. F   8. T   9. F   10. T
11. C   12. D   13. A   14. C   15. D   16. C   17. D   18. B   19. B   20. D

Chapter 8

1. F   2. T   3. F   4. F   5. F   6. F   7. F   8. T   9. T   10. T

Chapter 9

1. F   2. F   3. T   4. F   5. F   6. T   7. F   8. F   9. T   10. F
11. F   12. F.   13. F   14. T   15. F   16. D   17. D   18. B   19. D   20. C

Chapter 10

1. T   2. T   3. T   4. T   5. F   6. T   7. F   8. F   9. F   10. T
11. F   12. T   13. F   14. T   15. T

Chapter 11

1. T   2. F   3. T   4. F   5. F   6. T   7. F   8. T   9. F   10. F

Chapter 12

1. F   2. T   3. F   4. T   5. T   6. F   7. F   8. F   9. F   10. F

Chapter 13

1. T   2. F   3. T   4. F   5. T   6. F   7. F   8. F   9. F   10. T

Chapter 14

1. T   2. T   3. F   4. F   5. T   6. F   7. T   8. F   9. F   10. T